Economics and power

Economics and power

An inquiry into human relations and markets

RANDALL BARTLETT
Smith College

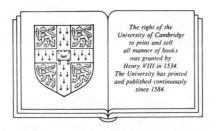

The right of the
University of Cambridge
to print and sell
all manner of books
was granted by
Henry VIII in 1534.
The University has printed
and published continuously
since 1584.

CAMBRIDGE UNIVERSITY PRESS
Cambridge
New York   Port Chester   Melbourne   Sydney

Published by the Press Syndicate of the University of Cambridge
The Pitt Building, Trumpington Street, Cambridge CB2 1RP
32 East 57th Street, New York, NY 10022, USA
10 Stamford Road, Oakleigh, Melbourne 3166, Australia

© Cambridge University Press 1989

First published 1989

Printed in Canada

Library of Congress Cataloging-in-Publication Data
Bartlett, Randall, 1945–
Economics and power : an inquiry into human relations and markets /
Randall Bartlett.
p.   cm.
ISBN 0–521–35562–1
1. Economics.   2. Power (Social Sciences)   I. Title.
  HB71.B3137   1989   88–31571
  330.1 — dc19   CIP

British Library Cataloguing-in-Publication Data
Bartlett, Randall
Economics and power: an inquiry into human relations and markets
1. Economics. Social aspects
I. Title
330

ISBN 0–521–35562–1 hard covers

For Catherine and the kids,
Randall, Ellika, and David,
who have the unknowing power
to make my life complete

Contents

Preface

Throughout my professional life I have been bothered by the narrow economic vision of "society" as a "place" where persons transact, but do not otherwise interact, or at least where transactions and interactions are somehow wholly independent and separable. Economists examine markets and exchange without clear reference to the actions and interactions that come before and after. The institutional structures of the real world, and of its markets, are far richer and more complex than the mythical ones of that abstract model. This book is an attempt to consider, explicitly and rigorously, the implications for human relationships of interacting in that broader environment. In writing it I have set myself two goals. The first is common in economics. I wish to make a serious contribution to the way in which economists think about the world. The second goal is much less common. I have tried to make that contribution intelligible. There is really no need for the writing in economics to be as horrid as it is. Meaningful analysis does not have to be so painful to read. There is a tendency in economics to equate turgid prose or elegant mathematics with careful thought. They are not inconsistent, of course, but neither are they identical. It is possible to care about both substance and style without sacrificing either.

I come from a long line of preachers. I have seen the power of a simple illustration to illuminate a complex abstraction. I have seen the force that careful phrasing can have in implanting ideas in others' minds. I have tried to apply those lessons in this book. Sometimes I have succeeded; other times I have failed. I only hope that an occasional digression into literature or philosophy or history will not detract from the real economic core. I hope that my occasional attempts at humor will not obscure the seriousness of the content.

As I worried about both substance and style, I struggled with the problem of "inclusive" language. The formal rules of grammar dictate that masculine pronouns be applied generally. A female reader is supposed to know that I also mean her when I say "him." Many, however, may not. The other solution is always to include both mas-

culine and feminine pronouns. Each reader will have a different reaction to that approach. He or she should decide whether his or her
personal sensitivities are better served by saying "his or hers" every-
time I address him or her. I am fully committed to the principle of
inclusive language, but that seems to butcher the prose. I have thus
tried to preserve the rhythm of the language, but also to be inclusive,
by adopting a policy of equal time. Sometimes I use "she" as a general
pronoun; sometimes I use "he." I have tried to give each approximately equal time. That will have to do.

I have not written this alone. Other people have played important
roles. I should mention the most significant. Jill Constantine worked
diligently and effectively as a research assistant during the initial draft-
ing of the book. She had a difficult task. Other research assistants in
economics are asked to review articles in the *American Economic Review*
or to gather statistics on unemployment in the nineteenth century.
Jill never knew what I would ask next. One week I would want references on feral children, the next, legal cases on "unjust termination,"
and the next, data on the health hazards of asbestos. She never com-
plained. She always came through. I never dared ask what she was
thinking.

Several of my colleagues at Smith College have helped bring the
book to completion. Deborah Haas-Wilson, Charles Staelin, and Roger
Kaufman read various drafts of various pieces. They made a number
of valuable suggestions, which have been incorporated. It is customary
to say that. It is also true. They also made a couple of mediocre ones,
which I ignored. It is not customary to say that. It is also always true.
I appreciate their willingness to do both. It is a great asset to have
such talented colleagues with whom I can discuss freely. They also
acted as unpaid research assistants and as an informal seminar, as did
my other Pierce Hall neighbors, Stuart Brown and Mahnaz Mahdavi.
My office is cluttered with piles of material, one belonging to each.
They have endured many a lunch reacting graciously to my unor-
thodox questions and unusual assertions. I appreciate all that they
have contributed.

Colin Day of Cambridge University Press was most supportive of
this project and deserves substantial credit for its finally seeing the
light of day. Timur Kuran of the University of Southern California
first read a draft of the entire manuscript as an anonymous reviewer
for Cambridge. He willingly dropped that veil and shared openly his
good judgment, his insight, and his knowledge of sources previously
unknown to me. Much of the improvement in the manuscript is due

to his careful reading and helpful comments. I only regret that I have been unable to develop fully all of the suggestions he has made. Perhaps I will face those issues more effectively another time.

Finally, it is also customary to acknowledge the debt due to family. I have often read of homage paid to a spouse who should "in all honesty be listed as a coauthor." I have equally often read of a partner who "graciously removed the burdens of everyday life so that I could concentrate on this book." I would very much like to acknowledge those contributions from my own family. I cannot. It is a new age. My wife is a practicing physician. We have three young children. She has not read the book. She has not offered valuable insights at each stage. She has no time for economics or academics. We are lucky to have the time to discuss who will pick up which child, let alone the significance of a new wrinkle in economic theory. In fact, I almost dedicated the book "to my family, without whom this would have been written long ago." The contribution of my family to the completion of this book has been unambiguously negative.

Their contribution to things of true value has, however, been immense and wholly positive. I have, on occasion, gone home troubled about some aspect of theory, grumbling about my day. Catherine meanwhile has been dealing with a family whose child's leukemia has just been diagnosed. It is an appropriate lesson in humility, perspective, and relative value for an academic. She gives so much and takes so little. She brings meaning, stability, and caring to all our lives. She is my foundation, my inspiration, my joy. That's better than a coauthor any day.

The hours spent each day with my children did nothing for this book. They never played quietly in the other room so I could write. They regularly assaulted me so that I could not, but I am thankful for it, for they thus share with me their contagious and seemingly boundless enthusiasm for life. They thus share their un-self-conscious delight in learning. They give themselves. They "light up my life." That is far better than a longer vita.

And now the months of effort are at an end. I cannot help but remember, and say "amen" to, Huckleberry Finn:

So there ain't nothing more to write about, and I am rotten glad of it, because if I'd a knowed what a trouble it was to make a book I wouldn't a tackled it and ain't agoing to no more.

PART I

The need for new theory

CHAPTER 1

Power in economics

> That some people have more power than others is one of the most palpable facts of human existence. Because of this, the concept of power is as ancient and ubiquitous as any that social theory can boast. ...one could set up an endless parade of great names from Plato and Aristotle through Machiavelli and Hobbes to Pareto and Weber to demonstrate that a large number of seminal social theorists have devoted a good deal of attention to power and the phenomena associated with it.
>
> Robert A. Dahl, "The Concept of Power"

Economics is about the quality of human lives. It is about what humans have, what they do, and how they interact with each other. It is a *social* science, indeed self-coronated as the "queen of the social sciences." The measure of success in economic activity is the welfare experienced by human beings, in the broadest sense of the term. It is not just material things that affect persons, but the qualities of their relationships with each other. One characteristic of a relationship might be the presence of some form of "power." One locus of a relationship might be an economic market. I have for several years been trying to understand what role power might play in market-based social interactions. I have searched widely, seeking a well-defined vision of power that is truly amenable to serious analysis of that question. I have been disappointed in what I have found.

One might expect, in the light of Robert Dahl's claim that power is both ubiquitous and ancient, to find analyses of power everywhere within economics. Power certainly has been a central topic of concern for sociology and political science. However, it has been only a peripheral interest for mainstream economists or a central interest of (mainstream-defined) peripheral economists. There is, as yet, no well-structured theory of power in economic relationships that can be used to look for power. There are many assertions about the role of power but precious few carefully derived conclusions. Nor is there a coherent vision of power in other social sciences that can be readily transplanted to an examination of markets and human relations.

In Thomas Kuhn's now classic analysis of the progression of scientific knowledge, he defines a period of "prescience" in which each analyst must define and defend key concepts, in which the questions to be asked must be raised and justified by each new author.[1] There are, of course, well-defined paradigms in economics. There are carefully structured texts that set forth a shared vision constituting a Kuhnian "paradigm." When the issue is the qualitative element in relations among persons, there is no such shared vision. It is not possible to speak of *the* vision of power in economics. It is not even possible to speak of a consistent vision of power in an individual school of economics. Certainly there are large differences among traditions. There are equally large ones within traditions. Power is a term and concept without shared content. In economics, the study of power is clearly in a "prescientific" state.

Any attempt at a quick survey of the literature on power in economics would thus fail. It could not simply recount extensions, refinements, and applications of a shared vision. It would have to present scores of conflicting concepts and critically evaluate each. That would be a volume or two in itself and would only support a definitive conclusion that "it is an interesting topic and lots of people have thought about it, some more than others."

Economic theories of power

Neoclassical economics, the dominant school in contemporary Western academia, has had the very least to say about power. Several years ago I was teaching at Williams College, a truly exceptional liberal arts college. Its economics department compares favorably with many of the best university departments in terms of its size and the research records of its members. It was a custom at that time to aid a library search by posting a request for any references or sources related to a topic by the mail boxes that were visited daily by all members of the department. Having discovered a number of important sources via that method in the past, I confidently posted a note asking for help in locating neoclassical analyses of power in economics. My seventeen highly trained colleagues seemed to give it serious thought, but after two weeks the page remained blank. Not a single reference was cited. Neoclassical reference to power, when it exists at all, is so far on the fringe that it has not penetrated the consciousness of the profession.

---

[1] Thomas Kuhn, *The Structure of Scientific Revolutions*, 2nd ed., University of Chicago Press, Chicago, 1970.

I have since learned that the set of such analyses is not quite empty, but it is certainly not overly full. What work there is, is undeveloped. The best uncovers phenomena that could be seen as power in some form but seldom recognizes it as such. The worst does not analyze at all but merely asserts ideological positions.

Certainly very little power indeed is to be found in the pages of formal microtheory textbooks. The word is used in only two contexts, and in both the form of power is exceedingly benign. The archvillain of the textbook world, the monopolist, is said to possess one form of power − monopoly power − but it is not power to harm anyone. A monopolist, via her ability to control the level of output, is able to restrict production and force the price higher than it would be in a competitive market. But no one is forced to trade with the monopolist at the higher price! Each person who does so, does it freely and hence must be considered to be made better off by the trade, *relative to a no-trade position*. The harm done by a monopolist is a refusal to offer still better terms.

The second mention of textbook power involves sharing the mutual benefits from trade. Given initial endowments, the set of Pareto-optimal outcomes defines a "contract curve," but the position attained on that curve is indeterminate. The final outcome will depend upon the ill-defined bargaining power of the two parties.

Other covered phenomena could be characterized as forms of power, but the term is seldom, if ever, applied. Externalities allow an actor to inflict harm on another human being without compelling compensation for the act. The ability to harm is recognized, but it arises in the theory solely because the interaction is taking place outside of the market.[2] It is analysis of power when markets are absent, not of power when they exist. Indeed, it is used as further evidence that power is absent from, even antithetical to, markets.

Some forms of game theory, of course, speak of strategies that somehow impose losses on other players, but they seem not to speak of this as "power" nor to see it as a possibility in a market trade. Moreover, the structure of the game, the source of this power, is often taken as given rather than explained. The participants are more likely to be analogous to competitors than to traders. The concepts are developing, but they have been applied little to the question of power and markets.

Power has been examined as an item that is traded. Herbert Simon

---

[2] The classic article expounding this argument is Ronald Coase, "The Problem of Social Cost," *Journal of Law and Economics*, October 1960, pp. 1–44. His position will be explained in more detail in Chapter 8.

has argued that power, or at least authority, is the key element of the labor relation and that it is a submission to authority that is being purchased in that market.[3] Yet Alchian and Demsetz wholly reject that view and deny any possibility of power in markets as either part of the process or part of the things exchanged.[4] Power is not part of their model. It cannot, therefore, be part of the market. Resolution of this conflict is simply not possible without some consistent and well-defined understanding of power. Absent that, we simply throw words at each other without sharing much meaning.

In other areas when power is uncovered it is not always recognized as such. Oliver Williamson's "new institutional economics" devotes explicit attention to the nature of human relationships and highlights possible exercises of power.[5] He focuses, however, on issues of resource allocation rather than qualitative aspects of human relations. Having uncovered a potential for power he reburies it under a language of "information impactedness coupled with opportunistic behavior."

It is when neoclassical economists enter political debate that they are most likely explicitly to consider power, not because they have truly studied power, but because they believe that they have studied its absence. Milton Friedman makes no mention of power in his formal theoretical writings but mentions it often in his political works. In *Capitalism and Freedom* he presents a persuasive, though largely tautologic, analysis that power is coercion, where "coercion" is defined as the absence of a bilateral, voluntary trade.[6] Markets are *defined* as collections of bilateral, voluntary trades and hence power and markets are mutually exclusive. Government does not use bilateral, voluntary trades and hence exercises power. Markets equal freedom. Government equals coercion. That is an explicit discussion of power, but it is more assertion than conclusion.

Neoclassical economists have only occasionally digressed to a consideration of power and human relations. Institutionalist, or as now sometimes entitled "evolutionary," economists have the opposite problem. Power is a central element in the economic relationships of the

---

[3] Herbert Simon, *Models of Man*, Wiley, New York, 1957, and *Administrative Behavior*, 2nd ed., Macmillan, New York, 1961, are two of the important sources making this argument.

[4] Armen Alchian and Harold Demsetz, "Production, Information Costs, and Economic Organization," *American Economic Review*, Vol. 62, December 1972, pp. 777–795.

[5] See Oliver Williamson, *Markets and Hierarchies: Analysis and Antitrust Implications*, Free Press, New York, 1975.

[6] Milton Friedman, *Capitalism and Freedom*, University of Chicago Press, Chicago, 1962, esp. Chapter 1.

institutionalist world. That is apparently so obvious that it needs no demonstration. It is self-evident. Institutional economists can gather collections of readings on *The Economy as a System of Power*.[7] They can devote special issues of their most important journal to "The Economics of Power."[8] They can write books about power in economic relations. Yet they do so with no commonly accepted definition or understanding. Each analysis must begin by presenting its own definition and defending its own vision. The same author may even change the definition over time to fit the argument of the day.

For John Kenneth Galbraith, *American Capitalism* has been a system of countervailing power, as organized interests struggle, ultimately canceling each other out.[9] In *The New Industrial State*, power can be unequally held, for it arises from the control of the scarcest factor of production in each stage of history.[10] In dissecting society to display *The Anatomy of Power*, it becomes "the submission of some to the will of others."[11] Each is an interesting analysis, though each suffers from internal contradictions as well as inconsistencies with the concept of power offered in the other books. None of them is a well-articulated, general concept of power that can be broadly applied.

Refereed articles in journals demonstrate little more consensus or consistency. Most preach to the converted rather than attempt a conversion of agnostics. For example, William Dugger, in one of the better articles in the *Journal of Economic Issues'* special edition on power, begins by offering his definition and a forewarning of his presumptions regarding power's importance:

Power shall refer to the ability to tell other people what to do with some degree of certainty that they will do it. When power wielders must coerce others, power is tenuous and obvious. When coercion is unnecessary, power is secure and unnoticed. (Emphasis in original)[12]

This is an interesting concept. It may even be an accurate one, but it is one asserted at the beginning rather than derived at the end. It is one that varies from the visions of others in the same issue. It is also one that brings us full circle. For Friedman, the absence of overt

---

[7] Warren Samuels, ed., *The Economy as a System of Power*, Transaction Books, New Brunswick, N.J., 1979.

[8] *Journal of Economic Issues*, Vol. 14, December 1980, devoted the entire issue to articles on power in economics.

[9] John Kenneth Galbraith, *American Capitalism: The Concept of Countervailing Power*, Houghton Mifflin, Boston, 1952.

[10] John Kenneth Galbraith, *The New Industrial State*, Houghton Mifflin, Boston, 1967.

[11] John Kenneth Galbraith, *The Anatomy of Power*, Houghton Mifflin, Boston, 1983.

[12] William Dugger, "Power: An Institutional Framework of Analysis," *Journal of Economic Issues*, Vol. 14, December 1980, pp. 897–907, quote from pp. 897–98.

coercion is proof of the failure of power. For Dugger, the presence of coercion is proof of the failure of power; its absence is evidence of power's strength. How is one to unravel this conflict without some systematically developed concept of power in markets? They are using the same words but are not speaking the same language.

To turn to another institutional economist is to discover another concept of power. For A. Allan Schmid, property itself is best understood as power:

Power is inevitable if interests conflict. If everyone cannot have what they want simultaneously, the choice is not power or no power, but who has the power. Power is the ability to implement one's interests when they conflict with those of others. With respect to a single issue or resource, equal power is impossible.[13]

A person without property is therefore a person without power.

In Marxism power is a central concept in understanding economic relationships among persons. Power can reside in persons or, even more significantly, in "classes" − a concept wholly incomprehensible to neoclassical economics. Capitalists as a class have the power to force workers into a relationship of "wage slavery." They can expropriate a surplus from labor via the exercise of power, though it may not be apparent as the overt coercion for which Friedman is looking.[14]

There is a further power that supports the dominance of capitalists in the distribution of income. Capitalists have the power, through seen and unseen ways, to determine the nature of the superstructure. They (and the logic of the system) can determine the nature of the culture, the government, the law, religion, and social values so that each supports the system of class dominance, that is, the system of power.[15]

There is, however, no proof of the presence of this power independent of the assumptions made. It is part of the model Marxism uses as an entry into real-world data. It will be found by all who look through that lens, just as it will be invisible to those who view the world with neoclassical eyes. In each case vision depends more upon the refraction of the theoretical lens than the character of the object under study.

[13] A. Allan Schmid, *Property, Power, and Public Choice: An Inquiry into Law and Economics*, Praeger, New York, 1978, p. 9.
[14] For a more complete description of Marx's method see, Paul Sweezy, *The Theory of Capitalist Development*, Monthly Review Press, New York, 1942, or Ben Fine, *Marx's Capital*, Macmillan Press, London, 1975, or Karl Marx, Preface to *A Contribution to the Critique of Political Economy*, reprinted in Robert C. Tucker, ed., *The Marx–Engels Reader*, 2nd ed., Norton, New York, 1978, pp. 3–6.
[15] Marx, Preface, p. 4.

Sociological and political visions of power

One might hope that the failure of economists to develop a consistent theory of power applicable to markets might be remedied by that endless parade noted by Dahl at the beginning of this chapter. Alas, that hope will not be fulfilled by sociologists or political scientists despite their endless efforts. They too are in Kuhn's prescientific stage, where each theorist must start at the very beginning, defining concepts, defending perceptions, including and excluding variables, and drawing limits around the boundaries of analysis. The result is a multiplicity of concepts seemingly impossible to unravel.

James T. Duke has attempted to distill much of that thinking about power into a book suitable for college courses.[16] It is significant that, unlike a microeconomic theory book that says, "Here is *the* theory," Duke's book is a sequence of chapters each of which says, "Here is *one* theory." Early on he feels compelled to warn readers of the unmapped jungle into which he is about to lead them:

First, power has sometimes been treated as a *potential* for social action, at other times as an indicator only of *actual* behavior. Second, power has sometimes been distinguished from force, coercion, persuasion, and influence, and sometimes has been used as inclusive of all of these. Third, power has sometimes been viewed as asymmetrical – involving a single direction of influence (leader to follower); at other times it has been treated as symmetrical or involving reciprocal influences between two parties, as for example between a leader and his follower. Fourth, power has sometimes been associated with the illegitimate use of force, at other times only with legitimate use by established leaders. Fifth, power has sometimes been viewed as a zero-sum possession in which the holding of power by one precludes possession by another; at other times it has been treated as a sharable commodity such that possession by one does not forestall possession by another. Relatedly (sixth), power has sometimes been treated as a possession or commodity, other times as an available resource. Seventh, power has sometimes been viewed as a generalized capability available in all situations; by others it has been treated as situationally-specific.[17]

That is certainly not an encouraging beginning. Others have tried to sort through this endless terrain and to give it some coherent shape. Steven Lukes, for example, has provided one useful scheme.[18] He

---

[16] James T. Duke, *Conflict and Power in Social Life*, Brigham Young University Press, Provo, Utah, 1975.

[17] Ibid., pp. 41–42.

[18] Steven Lukes, *Power: A Radical View*, Macmillan Press, London, 1974. Lukes provides a good summary bibliography of power research in his book. It would be superfluous to recreate it here. The reader is refered to his volume.

categorizes visions of power into three groups. The first he calls "one-dimensional power." This power is to be seen in the context of group decisions. It is a characteristic of conflict situations. It involves explicit winners and losers. These analyses start with a definition like that offered by Max Weber: "Power is the probability that one actor within a social relationship will be in a position to carry out his own will despite resistance."[19]

Power arises when a decision must be made within a social structure and some actor(s) are able to impose their preferences on others. Power is exercised in the context of decisions. In some variations it is power only if negative sanctions can be imposed. In others it is also power if concessions can be bought.

Lukes's second category involves control over the issues to be considered rather than the decisions reached. Any social organization has an agenda defining the issues to be dealt with at any given time. There are also a large number of potential issues that will not be dealt with. Control of the agenda is "two-dimensional power."

But some of the concepts Lukes finds go further yet. What if the values people are pursuing are themselves the product of human processes? What if what people actually want is subject to forms of influence and control? Then there is a power far more extensive than simple control over appointments to the local school board. For Lukes, that power is "three dimensional." Behavior alone is much too narrow a focus. Three-dimensional power parallels Dugger's vision. Overt behavior power is exercised only when the more subtle social controls over values are weakened.

The need for a new theory

There is no consistent, widely accepted concept of power within either economics or its sister social sciences. What concepts there are seem applicable primarily to situations of group decision making. But my concern in this book is not the selection of policy via the processes of public choice. It is the nature of the relationship between identifiable human beings when their interactions include market exchanges. I seek here to approach the issue of power in markets via a path that allows me to find it if it is there, to see its absence if it is not, and to distinguish between cases when it is absent and those when it is present.

[19] Max Weber, *The Theory of Social and Economic Organization*, Oxford University Press, New York, 1947, p. 152.

I find myself now at the juncture so often met by Oliver Hardy in his adventures with Stan Laurel. When Laurel failed time and again to meet the standards of performance as defined by Hardy, Hardy would proclaim with disgust, "I'll do it myself." If I wish such an exploration of power, it seems that I, too, shall have to do it myself. I can only hope the results will not be as comically absurd as those that inevitably derived from Hardy's efforts.

The chapters that follow present my efforts in that task. Part II defines and develops a concept of power that is explicitly suited to economic analysis. Part III applies this concept to a series of inter-related aspects of economic society. It explores where, if ever, power might be found in market relations. Part IV tackles the most important, and most often ignored, question in economic theorizing – so what? What difference does it make if ever there is power? How likely is it that it is a significant factor?

The argument builds, progressing from one topic to the next. Issues once covered develop new shadings as further elements are introduced. It is, therefore, not an argument that can be followed partially. It is not one whose pieces should be finally judged upon first exposure. The organism should be seen in its entirety before it is evaluated. I thus urge readers to take it as an owl does a mouse. Swallow it whole. Digest all that you can. There will be ample opportunity later to discard any parts that simply will not go down.

This is a book that makes real demands upon its readers. The only justice is that it made even greater ones upon its author. Those demands are twofold. The first is one of scope. I have been mercilessly teased by my colleagues in the writing of this book. They have argued that its category number in the *Journal of Economic Literature* should be 000–999. To say that modern economic research is an exercise in saying more and more about less and less has become a timeworn cliché. It is certainly not a tendency to which I succumb in this book. I hope, however, that I have not merely said less and less about more and more. It is my intention to force a more comprehensive look at the whole.

Before I am done, I will have dealt with law and economics, the economics of information, medical economics, labor market theory and institutions, the economics of organizations, welfare economics, the nature of humans, the meaning of "probability," and the intricacies of decision theory. I will have dabbled in English history, the psychology of feral children, classical poetry, sociobiology, timeless fables, American literature, and moral philosophy. Specialists in any of those areas will find ample evidence that I have treated none in the full richness and sophistication common among those who live their professional lives in but one neighborhood or the other. To those charges I plead unmitigated guilt. I should therefore offer ample opportunity for attack and criticism from virtually every quarter.

I am not here attempting, however, to refine further our vision of the various pieces of the economic puzzle. I am here concerned with the less examined, interconnected whole rather than the molecular structure of the pieces themselves. If one of our purposes is to understand how the quality of life is affected by particular sets of human institutions, especially markets, then the whole needs to be seen as well as the parts. Doctors are often accused of reducing patients to parts. "There is an interesting gall bladder up in 406." Economists may often fall victim to the same tendency. By broadening our vision we may, on occasion, know somewhat less about the gall bladder (or the utility of rats under conditions of risk),[20] but it is not really the gall bladder we wish to cure. It is the person. It is not the small piece of a society I wish to understand. It is the whole.

The second demand made by this book involves a willingness to bring a freshness of vision. Much of what follows takes the most basic, axiomatic beginning of economic analyses, the "boilerplate" of modeling, and asks for a full and explicit examination of its implications. The essay may also ask readers to reconsider the validity of occasional standard techniques and propositions. As trained economists we sometimes become so accustomed to a tool well suited to one particular task that we unthinkingly apply it to other tasks without examining its fitness. Readers should be willing to reexamine the real utility (in the mundane sense) of tools that have become comfortable standards.

In considering the analysis of power in economic relations, I am reminded of the following two lines from Shelley's "Hymn to Intellectual Beauty":

> The awful shadow of some unseen Power
> Floats, tho' unseen, amongst us

The lines are, of course, taken out of context, and so lose his meaning and take on mine, expressing a position for economics I cannot accept. Whatever it is that "floats . . . amongst us" as we interact in markets I am no longer content to have "unseen." Nor am I content to judge it only on the basis of its shadow. I seek to turn a harsh spotlight on

---

[20] One of the leading journals in economics recently published, as its lead article, R. C. Battalio, J. H. Kagel, and D. N. McDonald, "Animals' Choices over Uncertain Outcomes," *American Economic Review*, Vol. 75, September 1985, pp. 597–613. The profession, at times, seem to give more attention to small questions than large ones.

market interactions. If power is ever there in any form, I wish to see it clearly. If it is not, I wish to observe its absence directly.

I am confident that the argument about to begin will prove enlightening to some, infuriating to others, but I hope stimulating to all. I will be gratified if the answers ultimately derived prove valid. I will be even more gratified if the questions raised are accepted as significant. It is time now to begin the development of a systematic economic theory of power.

PART II

An economic theory of power

CHAPTER 2

An economic concept of power

How then to build a tightly reasoned theory of power that can be usefully applied in an economic context and can be called economic? The question is the more difficult because there are nearly as many definitions of "economic" as there are of power. To use Marxist or institutional economics is to keep the consideration of power on the periphery of the discipline, no matter how well constructed the theory. To use neoclassical economics is to risk confrontation with, and perhaps confirmation of, a basic ideological precept dominant among its practitioners. In the former case, power could be more easily found, but it might be too easily accepted, for evidence of its presence is there desired. It would be easily discarded, or simply ignored, by others, for in their terms the analysis is not truly "economic."

Analysis that arises directly from the restrictive foundations of neoclassical economics will be challenged, criticized, and perhaps distrusted by all – by neoclassicists because it violates ideology and by others because of its suspect methodology. If it stands after that, it will be hard to deny. Neoclassicists would have to accept the potential for power or admit to the charge of ideological, rather than purely logical, analysis. Those from other traditions would have to admit to some value in a methodology they have largely scorned, though perhaps taking some perverse pleasure in seeing one of their central concepts invading a theoretical world heretofore held pristine and inviolate.

I choose, therefore, to build this analysis of power upon the most hostile of foundations. I seek to work within the least charitable environment to create and apply concepts of power in economic activity that can survive the harsh scrutiny of those most reluctant to recognize it. What then are the essential tenets of such a method? Gary Becker is one of the most faithful adherents to the precepts of neoclassicism. Indeed, it is not even neoclassical analysis, but "true" economic analysis for Becker when these conditions are fulfilled. What makes an analysis economic is not, for Becker, the character of the activity studied but the tools applied, that is, "the assumptions of maximizing behavior,

17

market equilibrium and stable preferences, used relentlessly and unflinchingly."[1]

In general I am less willing than Becker to define economics and economists in such narrow terms, yet I will accept his restrictions in the rest of this book, if only for the sake of argument. From now on, "economics" will mean neoclassical economics, "economists," neoclassical economists. If there is to be a recognition of any potential role for power in economics, there must be developed a serious, careful framework within the context of such analysis. Economists are an inbred race and seem to recognize things only when they come from within the tribe, expressed in the local dialect, paying homage to the special deities. I shall attempt to do that here. I shall try not to flinch.

The core of this method is to start with a consideration of individuals

- making choices,
- attempting to maximize something, and
- being subject to constraints.

It assumes scarcity, that is, that wants exceed possibilities. It works from a presumption that the solution to the dilemma is to do the very best you can, subject to that constraint, by making trade-offs at the margin until no further trade-offs yield net gains. If Mick Jagger is correct that "you can't always get what you want," you can at least get what you prefer.

The basic definition of the model

Starting from its beginnings in individual choice, one of the central functions of economic theory is to give explanatory and predictive order to the seeming chaos of human behavior. Why, specifically, do people do what they do? Why do different people do such different things? Why does the same person do different things at different times? How are all of these individual choices reconciled in social contexts? These are ancient puzzles.

Nearly 2,500 years ago, Herodotus, the father of history in the Western world, wrote of Darius, king of ancient Persia. Having expanded his empire from the Mediterranean into India, Darius was surrounded in court by representatives of vastly different cultures and became aware of the extraordinary differences in values around the world:

[1] Gary Becker, *The Economic Approach to Human Behavior*, University of Chicago Press, Chicago, 1976, p. 5.

When he [Darius] was king of Persia, he summoned the Greeks who happened to be present at his court and asked them what they would take to eat the dead bodies of their fathers. They replied that they would not do it for any money in the world. Later in the presence of the Greeks, and through an interpreter, so they could understand what was said, he asked some Indians, of the tribe called Callatiae, who do in fact eat their parents' dead bodies, what they would take to burn them. They uttered a cry of horror and forbade him to mention such a dreadful thing.[2]

More mundane variations in behavior are also puzzles seeking solution via this methodology. As a child I would readily spend much of my very limited income on sour-apple bubble gum. Even though wealthier now, I no longer buy it. It seems less a delicacy. The morning cup of coffee now essential to life itself would have been unthinkable in years past. Peoples' willingness to pay huge sums for totally unnecessary gems and nothing for a glass of life-giving water seems insane. The premiums paid for "Cabbage Patch" dolls one year, and the unsold inventory, even at a discounted price the next, seems strange indeed. Why do people do what they do?

For economists, the answers lie in that method stressed by Becker, the application of a theory of constrained maximization. The answer cannot be fully defined, however, until there is some specification of the "thing" that is to be maximized. Becker calls it "stable preferences," but it needs further consideration. Not all economists accept his specific meaning of the term. Economic theory has come to accept "utility" as the ultimate goal. Utility refers to the psychic satisfaction that results from the acquisition and use of goods, from exposure to processes, and from relationships with persons. For want of a better term, it is "good feelings" *subjectively generated from objective reality.* Each of the individual actors of the model is attempting to get to the highest level of utility, or "good feelings," possible. The utility function describes the transformation of "Stuff" into utility within an individual's psyche. Things for which I have a higher preference yield more good feelings.

The problem of constrained maximization thus has two very real elements. The first is the constraints, that is, how much of the objective Stuff is attainable. The second is how the objective Stuff is transformed into psychic satisfaction, that is, how much utility is obtainable from a given amount of Stuff. The final level of utility could thus be changed either by altering the constraints (the amount of Stuff) or by altering the way it is transformed into utility. With few exceptions, economists have considered only the first possibility, assuming that

---

[2] Herodotus, *The Histories*, translated by Aubre de Selincourt. Penguin, Harmondsworth, 1972, pp. 219–220.

preferences precede economic behavior (that the utility function is given). The power of the method then lies in predicting and explaining changes in behavior based only on changes in constraints (primarily in prices or income). With all preferences "given" and all individuals thus free of social influences on values, all potential for power such as Lukes's three-dimensional variety has been excluded by assumption. If the question is one of the nature of human relationships, then that limitation is less obviously reasonable. It should result from analytical conclusions rather than analytical convenience. It is worth, therefore, some time and effort to clarify the nature of the utility to be maximized in this model.

What is to be maximized?

To be an economic model, individual choice must be based on this process of constrained maximization. Any such model must make some explicit or implicit assumptions about the nature of preferences. There are three different questions each such set of presumptions must resolve. What is the initial source of these preferences? How do they differ over time within any individual? How do they differ among individuals? Mo   ls tend to take one of three approaches in answering these questions.

Preferen   given, fixed over time, but variable among persons

The standard te..book vision of preferences is that each person enters this world with some "given" utility function. Given by whom or what is never made clear. Preferences just precede all economic and social activity so that an individual's utility function never varies. All variations in the behavior of an individual then reflect changes in constraints. These actors, embarking on human interaction with fully formed preferences, are the creatures whose indifference maps shape market behavior. Every standard textbook begins constructing its elegant models upon a foundation of these given functions.

But of course different people do different things, even when they face seemingly equal constraints. Why? Because they must have been given different utility functions. Why the functions differ, what causes them to differ, is unspecified. They are simply given. Why did Greeks have a preference for cremation and Callatiae for cannablism? Why did not the preferences and practices overlap, some Greeks preferring each method? Why did not some Greeks adopt cannibalism when Darius offered virtually unlimited payoffs for doing so? Why were the Callatiae willing to maintain the practice for nothing? Such questions are not answered. Indeed, they are not asked. These issues simply precede analysis.

In his early years, even Gary Becker felt compelled to adopt this vision of individually differing preference functions to explain otherwise paradoxical results. In *The Economics of Discrimination* he attempted to explain both the causes and consequences of discriminatory behavior.[3] The basis for such feelings were beyond economic analysis; hence they must come from some form of given preference functions.

If the degree of discriminatory feeling differed among individuals or subgroups of the population, there could be no further explanation than a difference in preferences. Discussing measures of overt expressions of racial hostility in the United States, in the 1940s, Becker is initially puzzled by systematic regional differences. He tries to find some explanation in measurable differences in situations, but finally gives up. It must simply be because they were given different preferences:

In 1940 tastes for discrimination in the South appear to have been, on the average, about twice those in the North. Although relatively more Negroes live in the South this does not seem to explain much of the regional difference in discrimination, nor do other variables explain this difference, and at present *it must be accepted as reflecting a regional difference in tastes.*[4] (Emphasis added)

This approach is useful in very short term models. It has historically been most common in formal mathematical models in which "givens" are a normal part of model specification. For the models to be determinate, there must be a limit to the endogenous variables. They require abstraction. They cannot be holistic. They are models most often concerned with choices far less grand than value conflicts between ancient cultures. They tend to focus on income allocation questions between beer and pizza purchases. When the primary concern is with limited variations in the composition of Stuff, such a vision of utility can be a valuable abstraction.

But even within these narrow limits, paradoxes develop that seem irresolvable if the utility function is always constant and only constraints vary. There is empirical evidence of individuals changing their behavior in ways in which the constraints say they should not. Gary Becker, no longer content with given differences and changes in pref-

---

[3] Gary Becker, *The Economics of Discrimination*, University of Chicago Press, Chicago, 1957.
[4] Ibid., p. 156.

erences, is bothered by evidence that purchases of heating oil invariably rise in the winter even though the price per gallon also rises. With incomes constant and preferences unchanged, the rising price should result in reduced purchases. He is bothered by evidence that the purchase of sporting equipment is highest among the young. Given that incomes increase with age, and if preferences are fixed, then with higher incomes the purchases should increase, not decrease.[5] These are seemingly inexplicable results.

Preferences given but variable over time and among persons

The easy way out is simply to assume that preferences change. In the winter I prefer heating oil. In the summer I prefer trips to the beach. When I am young I prefer skiing. When I am older I prefer reading. Preferences can still be fixed for the short period surrounding a given purchase, but over longer periods of time they may vary. That is the easy way out, but it is an exit that smashes directly through the foundation wall of microeconomics. The remaining structure is of much less use. The initial forces that shape market behavior become variable and wholly unexplained. The model itself is not then so powerful. If given preference functions can be given new form at any time, then knowledge of that process and its controls becomes essential to recapture the explanatory power of the view discussed in the last section. Now *both* differences among individuals and temporal changes in behavior are explained via the *deus ex machina* of an unexplained change in preferences. If the theory is to be powerful in predicting and explaining human behavior, it ought not to have as the ultimate cause a completely exogenous force such as given but changeable preferences.

Preferences given, immutable and identical

Assuming invariant preferences makes it difficult to explain many observed changes in behavior. Assuming variable ones implies that the fundamental forces behind many important changes in behavior are outside the economic model. If only some way could be found to resolve the observed paradoxes and to preserve the assumption of immutable preferences, the power of economic analysis could be restored. There is an approach that, at one level at least, seems to do that. It was in presenting that approach that Gary Becker initially

---

[5] Becker, *Human Behavior*, p. 133.

asked his questions about heating oil and sporting goods. Not surprisingly, he raised those questions publicly only when he was ready to supply the answer via a route now sometimes known as the "new home economics." He cannot accept the answer that changes in behavior result from changes in preferences. The model then would be incomplete without a theory of causality in preference changes. He is not comfortable working with such an incomplete model so he closes it by the following assumption:

Since economists generally have had little to contribute, especially in recent times, to the understanding of how preferences are formed, preferences are assumed not to change substantially over time, nor to be very different between wealthy and poor persons, or even between persons in different societies and cultures.[6]

The Greeks and Callatiae, to say nothing of Americans and Zulu, rich and poor, ancient and modern, must all have the same basic, immutable, human preference function. Our behaviors differ, then, only because of differences in the costs and constraints we face. Paradoxical behavior can be explained if households are viewed not as consuming actors, but as producing actors, combining market-acquired goods and services with owned resources including time and human capital to produce more basic commodities, which in turn affect this fixed utility function. Production functions for these base commodities may change, but the relation among these commodities and the immutable preference function are always fixed. I always feel the same about a certain level of physical comfort. At different times that level is easier, or more difficult, to attain. Thus the increase in the purchases of heating oil is explained because the production function for comfort changes seasonally, and it takes more oil to generate the optimal level of comfort. The purchases of sporting goods decline because physiological differences result in lower productivity for those inputs in generating good feelings or some other undefined Becker commodity.

Without some such adjustment in approach, the economic theory of behavior is only a "second-level" theory of behavior. If you tell me what given preferences are or what variable preferences have become, then and only then can I begin to predict what behavior will follow. Without it economics itself diminishes. Economists facing this dilemma are much akin to physicists in the 1920s and 1930s. Having built a vision based on detailed determinancy of every physical phe-

---

[6] Ibid., p. 5. See also G. Stigler and G. Becker, "De Gustibus non Est Disputandum," *American Economic Review*, Vol. 67, No. 2, March 1977, pp. 76–90.

nomenon, they were shaken to the core when subatomic processes seemed to be random events. To be sure, subatomic events seemed to be "controlled" by fixed probability distributions, but the determination of which individual nucleus of a radioactive element would give up a proton at any moment, for example, was strictly random.[7] Albert Einstein was unwilling to accept the mounting evidence of randomness at the most basic core of the physical universe. Hence his famous statement that "I cannot for a moment believe that He [God] plays dice."[8] Despite the fact that there is now general consensus among subatomic physicists that "God does indeed play dice," the new home economics offers an anchor of determinacy to economists who choose to cling to it.

Utility in an economic theory of power

The model being constructed here is to be used in an economic exploration of the potential for power. The issue is not simply the internal consistency of the model. It is its suitability for considering power. If I am to postulate a world of utility-maximizing individuals subject to sets of binding constraints, then any concept of power will have to involve the ability of one individual to affect the choices and the outcomes of other individuals. Conceptually, either element of a constrained-maximization problem could be involved. The exerciser could affect the quantity or quality of Stuff that is transformed into utility. It is also possible that the exerciser of power could affect the transformation itself. The person subject to power could have the same Stuff but be made to feel differently about it. Adopting a vision of immutable preferences automatically excludes any possibility of power in the latter form. There thus ought to be a stronger reason for such a presumption than simple analytical convenience.

Becker is quite explicit about the reason he adopts that view. It is because "economists generally have had little to contribute . . . to the understanding of how preferences are formed." I am less concerned with simple cleanliness and more with clarification. Is such a presumption clearly justifiable on grounds stronger than convenience?

There is, of course, the peculiar epistemological assertion that the current absence of a satisfactory answer negates the validity of the question. There is no well-regarded theory to explain why human

---

[7] For a discussion of the development of modern quantum physics see Heinz R. Pagels, *The Cosmic Code: Quantum Physics as the Language of Nature*, Simon & Schuster, New York, 1982.

[8] Quoted in Pagels, *Cosmic Code*, p. 160.

beings age. It would be folly to decide, therefore, to assume and act as if they did not. Moreover, assuming no change virtually ensures that little contribution will ever be made to answer such a question.

Setting epistemology aside, there is still reason to challenge the assumption of permanent preferences on grounds of simple implausibility. To assume totally fixed utility functions is not to escape the need to explain preference formation. It is to assume, implicitly, an explanation that would be difficult to defend if stated explicitly. If human preferences are wholly independent of social and physical environmental influences, then there remains only one possible root cause. Somewhere in the complex DNA chains that define human life there must exist genetic material that determines for all time what preferences will be. Both the standard textbook case and the new home economics are, in fact, postulating just such causation. Just as gender, predisposition to certain diseases, and hair color are determined at the time of conception, so also are all lifelong preferences for basic commodities.

The two models of fixed preferences differ, however, in their compatibility with normal perceptions of genetic processes. The standard textbook case is, in fact, more consistent with those processes than is Becker's. At least there, individuals may have different (genetically determined) preferences. There may be a distribution of genotypes and variation within a species, as well as selective adaptation over time. The Becker view is really consistent only with an assumption that, of all genetically determined human characteristics, the fixed preference function is the only one that never varies. Not only is the genetic composition of an individual invariant; so is the genetic composition of the species. Given the vast range of genotypes for all other genetic characteristics, it is perhaps strange that this one alone is invariant. People vary dramatically in height, intelligence, physical coordination, capacity for musical performance, all forms of sensory perception, and susceptibility to various diseases, but never in basic commodity preferences.

This is an intellectual trap difficult to escape. The basis of preferences implicit in the standard textbook approach is consistent with our understanding of genetic processes but leaves unresolved Becker's paradoxes. The new home economics preserves fixity of preferences and resolves the paradoxes, but only by postulating wholly absurd visions of genetic processes.

There is, of course, a principle that holds that the plausibility of the assumptions is irrelevant to the validity of the model. A theory should be judged by the quality of its predictions, not of its assumptions.[9] Even if that argument were accepted as valid, it would hold only if the purpose of the model were solely to predict. If it is also to explain and perhaps evaluate what did happen, the nature of the assumptions becomes more crucial, for then the analyst goes backward into the model. It would never be valid to begin by postulating that preferences never change, to make some verified predictions on the basis of that assumption, and then to assert that fixity of preferences had been proven. That, however, is the nature of the problem here. I am not setting out to predict changes in the composition of Stuff. I am setting out to explain possible forms of human relations and thus basing the analysis on an absurd assumption, which incidently precludes many conceivable forms of social interaction and would seem to be a dangerous beginning.

Assuming fixed and invariant species or individual utility functions that are independent of all social influence would be an unpromising start. Yet to adopt the position of the second approach, that preferences are variable, but that the casuation is wholly beyond the realm of economic analysis, is unappealing as well. This is a problem that needs to be resolved if any useful general economic theory of power is to be developed.

The general utility function

The only way out of this dilemma is to meet it head on. Utility functions should be specified in the most extensive form possible. The complex nature of utility should not be obscured by a mere simplifying assumption. It should be illuminated by the analysis itself. The utility that drives the actors in this model is thus initially specified in the most general terms possible. It can be restricted in various ways within the analysis to see what difference various forms of utility make. The specific form can be revised in response to empirical data. It is a form of utility that will permit the widest possible exploration of power.

Each actor, i, has a given (perhaps genetically determined) utility function of the following general form:

$$U_i = U(X_i; E_i; S_i) \tag{2.1}$$

where X_i refers to the goods consumed by individual i, E_i refers to the physical environmental conditions experienced by i, and S_i refers to the human-created social conditions experienced by i. It is assumed

[9] Cf. Milton Friedman, *Essays in Positive Economics*, University of Chicago Press, Chicago, 1953, pp. 3–43.

that any of the partial derivatives may assume any value. If it turns out that $\partial U_i/\partial S_i = 0$ at all times and for all sets of social conditions and that $\partial U_i/\partial E_i = 0$ at all times and for all sets of conditions, then the function simply collapses to the form commonly assumed in the standard textbook case. If only the $\partial U_i/\partial S_i$ are equal to 0, then I have a respecification of the new-home-economics approach. However, the unconstrained specification leaves open the possibility of finding that some human-created conditions do in fact alter the utility derivable from a given package of Stuff. I can explore the widest possible range of human relations.

Becker, or course, admitted to the potential for external influence in his household production functions, which then ultimately led to changes in experienced utility. Indeed, it was only the introduction of those influences that permited the resolution of his heating-oil and sporting-goods paradoxes. Celestial bodies move. Human bodies age. Household production functions are thus altered. The utility derivable from fixed packages of goods is changed. It is interesting that, in his examples, the external forces are all natural. They are not products of the behavior of other humans. If power is a relationship between people, Becker admitted only to nonhuman external influences, but not to power.

The use of this very general utility function (2.1) allows changes in the physical environment to act directly on the utility derivable from heating oil and sporting goods. It also allows the social environment to affect the utility experienced by Greeks and Callatiae from eating the bodies of their dead parents. (Those populations probably differed more in cultural exposure than genetic material.) It does this without having to rely upon a presumption of both individual and species-wide invariant genes.

The specification also permits some resolution of the differences between the standard textbook case and the presumption of variable preferences. It assumes a given total utility function but permits the utility derivable from any package of goods to vary for *systematic reasons*, that is changes in environmental or social conditions. What matters is not that relative preferences for specific goods never vary but that any such variations be systematically caused. The explanatory problems only develop from random variations in behavior.

Finally, this general form of a utility function provides analytic flexibility. It is now possible, first, to assume all social influences to be zero and to explore the forms of power that result. It is possible, then, to relax the assumption and to compare the power implications under the two sets of conditions. It is possible to undertake empirical analyses to determine if, in fact, social factors ever do alter the amount of utility derivable from a fixed package of goods. I can meet Becker's demand for an unflinching devotion to individual maximization of a stable set of preferences but can proceed in a fashion open to an unbiased search for power.

The world of this economic model is populated, then, with self-interested, maximizing individuals. Each starts with a utility function of the most general form and interacts with others via market institutions, and perhaps in other contexts as well. What I wish to know is whether, within these relationships, there ever arises something that could be called "power." To complete preparations for exploring that question, it is necessary to spend some time defining what it is I am seeking. What, specifically, is "power"?

Elements of the power concept

If the theory is to maintain its economic orientation, there are certain elements of the concept of power that ought to hold.

Power is part of a human relationship

Friedman's distinction between limits on behavior imposed by nature and those imposed by other persons is a useful one.[10] I am here concerned with the interactions of individuals making interdependent choices. My concept of power needs to be restricted to impacts that humans have on each other as they pursue this process of constrained maximization.

Power is infinitely variable

Any analysis that assumes only discrete endpoints, that assumes either total presence or total absence, should ring false to the economic ear. Economic analysis has largely proceeded in the last century by focusing on sequences of small adjustments in continuously variable elements. Certainly such marginal analysis is the accepted key to solving problems of constrained maximization. In modern economics the significant questions have never been concerned with the simple presence or absence of things such as capital, utility, skill, or wheat; they have centered on issues of more or less. The same should hold true

---

[10] Milton Friedman, *Capitalism and Freedom*, University of Chicago Press, Chicago, 1962, Chapter 1.

for any economic analysis of phenomena such as freedom or power. Those too are seldom absolutes. Power needs to be defined so that it can be less than everything, but still more than nothing. The concept must be shaped to allow questions of more or less.

Power is situational

Any useful economic concept of power must be situational. Just as there is no given relationship between a buyer and a seller without the defining context of a market, there can be no power relationships between individuals without a defining context. Power is not genetically established. The nature of the power relationship between a judge and a mugger depends upon whether they are meeting in criminal court or a dark alley.

Power is social

Charles Lindblom has argued that authority "exists whenever one, several, or many people explicitly or tacitly *permit* someone else to make decisions for them for some category of acts."[11] Those subject to authority must in some sense accept it. Those exercising authority must in some sense earn obedience. He also argues that power comes, not from an individual, but from a constructed base of support.[12] One of the simple, but powerful conclusions of economic analysis is that for every single sale there is a purchase. The terms of the purchase depend partly on the decisions of the traders and partly on the decisions of others who are not party to the particular trade but who, nevertheless, are part of the surrounding market.

Lindblom's vision of authority parallels that wisdom. Any time power is exercised there is a person exerting power and another feeling it. The scope of that power is not defined exclusively by these two parties but is part of a larger set of social interactions. His definition of authority is narrower than the concept of power I will propose shortly, but it illustrates important aspects of any concept of power.

The definition of "power"

In elementary school I had a teacher intent upon improving our vocabularies. Each week we were given lists of words with short definitions to memorize. She was fond of telling us, however, that this was not sufficient for real learning. We had to "use the words several

---

[11] Charles Lindblom, *Politics and Markets*, Basic, New York, 1977, pp. 17–18.
[12] Ibid., pp. 120–122.

times to make them really ours." It is good advice to recall at this time. Any usable definition of "power" will of necessity be somewhat vague. It must be short enough to qualify as a definition rather than a dissertation. It must be broad enough to cover a multitude of situations and must do so without becoming a "tax code" filled with exemptions and variations. I begin, then, with such a definition, which can be "learned" at this stage but which will not really be "ours" until after it is used in Part III. The definition is very broad in scope. It is intended to cover a variety of situations and behaviors. It defines forms of human interaction that are neither obviously good nor obviously bad. Its purpose is neither to condemn nor condone power if and when it exists in human relationships. It is simply for the purpose of permitting recognition.

Power: *The ability of one actor to alter the decisions made and/or welfare experienced by another actor relative to the choices that would have been made and/or welfare that would have been experienced had the first actor not existed or acted.*

This definition implies at least three essential elements of a power-based interaction: the "exerciser," who is able to use the power to affect an outcome, the "subject," whose behavior or welfare is being changed, and the specific set of choices or events that are affected. Thus the definition focuses on a relationship between persons who in turn are making maximizing choices, but it is a relationship restricted to particular situational subsets of individual choices and social interactions.

Obviously this is a very broad definition. Under its terms, my threat of mayhem upon your body may be considered power. So also may my offering to sell you a car at a very attractive price. It encompasses the broadest range of human influences. It covers interactions varying in both quality and degree. It defines any form of impact by one human on another as a form of power. To be useful at all, the definition must be developed to permit distinctions between different categories of interaction and different levels of power. In the next chapter I will distinguish among different forms of power, but I cannot do so until the tools of formal decision analysis have been presented. Before turning to that, it is necessary to develop standards for evaluating the scope of power.

Evaluating power

The sixteenth-century French philosopher and essayist Michel de Montaigne was reluctant to judge the happiness of any living human. He thus wrote an essay insisting "That Our Happiness Must Not Be

Judged Until After Our Death" opening with the following three lines
from Ovid:[13]

> No man should be called happy till his death;
> Always we must await his final day,
> Reserving judgment till he's laid away.

In short, Montaigne's position was that seeming happiness in one
moment may soon give way to unhappiness as the full consequences
of a life unfold. It is folly to judge a life, or presumably an action,
until it is fully developed.

Economists seldom set forth to judge lives. They are more commonly concerned with describing and prescribing momentary choices
that will ultimately affect resource allocations. They thus treat time
and happiness differently, usually looking from the present toward
the future rather than from the life's end toward the past. I, however,
am setting forth seeking power, and power is now defined as a force
that alters the quality of human lives. I must therefore be prepared
to answer the philosopher's question "What is the good life?" as well
as the economist's query "What is the efficient choice?"

The definition of power used here ultimately involves changes in
the welfare of the individual subject to power. A change in welfare
here means a change in "lifetime utility," defined as the simple sum
of the utility experienced at each moment *as contemporaneously measured*. A lifetime is made up of a sequence of moments. In each of
those moments, choices are made and utility realized. Of that currently
felt utility, some may result from anticipation of future events, some
from memory of past events, but actual utility is contemporaneously
experienced at each moment. If I wish not to describe a single choice
or to evaluate a single moment, but instead to judge an entire lifetime,
I must add all of those current moments together to get a measure
of total utility experienced. But for the exercise of power, the subject
of that power would conceptually experience some baseline level of
such lifetime utility. Any exercise of power that increases the lifetime
utility of the subject may then be termed "positive." Any exercise that
decreases it will be termed "negative." And any that leaves total utility
unaffected will be termed "neutral."[14]

---

[13] Michel de Montaigne, "That Our Happiness Must Not Be Judged Until After Our
Death," reprinted in *Michel de Montaigne: Twenty Nine Essays*, Franklin Library edition,
Franklin Center, Pa. 1982, pp. 34–36.

[14] This can all be done in more formal terms. Let

$$W_i = \int_{t=0}^{t} U_i \, dt$$

where U_i is the current utility specified by equation (2.1) and W_i is the sum total of

Present versus contemporaneous values

This definition of "lifetime utility" will ring false to the trained economist's ear. All noncurrent events, it is usually argued, must be reduced to present values. One of the key principles of economics is a presumption of "positive time preference." That is a postulate about the nature of utility functions that specifies that people prefer good things to happen now and bad things to happen some other time. That is, of course, the basis of the common marketing pitch to take delivery now but pay later. Indeed, Henry Ford, who was unquestionably a manufacturing genius, was seemingly a marketing moron in that he did not understand that principle. His idea for selling Model Ts was to contract with a buyer to "start paying now but delay delivery for several years until the final car payment is made."[15] Needless to say, that did not catch on as a sales incentive.

Analysts such as Jon Elster have occasionally considered how time preferences may vary over the future.[16] They have not turned backward, however, to consider the past, yet the principle should imply that the *current* significance of an event diminishes as the event recedes in time *in either direction, past or future.*[17] The entire universe will ul-

---

utility experienced over a lifetime, that is, the integral over time, from birth to death, of the utility function. Let W_1 be the lifetime utility if the exerciser of power either does not act or does not exist. Let W_1 be the level of welfare that exists. If the exerciser of power does cause the decider to shift from path 1 to another, and if the welfare of the new path is W_j, then power may be said to be

$$
\begin{array}{ll}
\text{"positive"} & \text{if } W_j > W_1 \\
\text{"negative"} & \text{if } W_j < W_1 \\
\text{"neutral"} & \text{if } W_j = W_1
\end{array}
$$

[15] Daniel Boorstin, *The Americans: The Democratic Experience*, Random House, New York, 1973, p. 422–423. The program was called the Ford Weekly Purchase Plan. In its first year over 400,000 signed up, but barely a third completed their total payments and took delivery. Those who dropped out were able to reclaim their money.

[16] Cf. Jon Elster, *Sour Grapes: Studies in the Subversion of Rationality*, Cambridge University Press, 1983; *Ulysses and the Sirens*, Cambridge University Press, rev. ed. 1984.

[17] Economists never consider the problem of discounting from the past forward. The theory of positive time preference is almost always stated as a relationship between the present and the future. I want good things to happen sooner. Because the past is unchangeable, because there are no more choices to be made about it, economists simply ignore it. But the past does matter. How can it be included? There are but a few options. It could be that all past events have zero present value, that is, there is a different, infinite discount rate to be applied to the past. Thus I do not care at all now whether I fought in a jungle war, or whether I did it last decade or last week. There would seem to be at least anecdotal evidence to indicate that people do care.

It could be that the discount rate is zero, that is, that the position in time of any timately collapse into a lifeless black hole. The current significance of that fact would be substantially affected if it were expected to happen in a few days rather than a few billion years. The event will occur. It matters when. A plague has killed much of the population of the known world. The current significance changes if the event occurred hours rather than centuries ago. The same event occurred. It matters when.

The same holds true of events within a single life. To have been rich in years past does not much diminish my current hunger, nor does the prospect of wealth in future years. I will unquestionably enjoy it when it comes, but it does little for me now. If that were not well recognized, mystery writers would be unable to call so often on impatient heirs as suspects in their novels.

Economists, concerned with guiding decisions to affect resource allocations, require that judgments be drawn about choices on the basis of the currently valued, future implications of a choice. But that standard process ceases to be valid when the issue makes the subtle shift from prediction to evaluation. Present value analysis yields good predictions. It offers no unambiguous guide to wise choices.

Aesop, Ovid, and economics

Consider for a moment Aesop's classic fable of the ant and the grass-hopper. The ant, industrious and hardworking, spent the summer laying away food for the harsh winter ahead. The grasshopper, un-schooled in deferred gratification, played all summer heedless of the cold winds to come. Each made choices. Each experienced conse-quences. Each could have its behavior evaluated by Montaigne and by an economist, but the conclusions would differ.

As summer began, each faced two possible paths, with two possible sets of consequences. Figure 2.1 displays those options. The vertical

---

past event is irrelevant. I do care now about my experiences in that war, and just as intensely as I did when I was there. It never fades in significance. Each moment is a composite reliving of all past events. There is little to recommend that either.

It could be that past events increase in value as they recede in time. Certainly the value of a sum invested in the past is higher the longer ago it was invested. But that would mean that I am much happier that my wife who has left me loved me in that past than if she loved me now, or that the pain of her departure only increases with time. That approach works with capital because it may be stored and earns interest. Psychic utility can do neither.

All that is left, then, is the symmetrical presumption that events diminish in im-portance as they recede from the present in either direction. Time does heal all wounds. It does dim all triumphs. Any of the other options leads, simply, to absurd results.

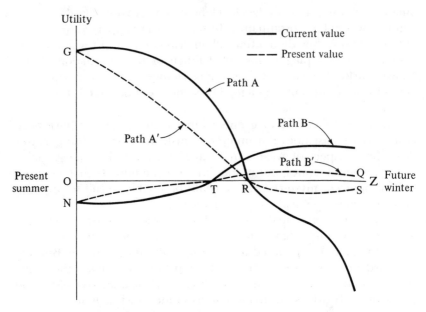

Figure 2.1. The economist's view: future discounted to present.

axis measures utility; the horizontal axis measures time. Path *A* displays the current utility from playing in the summer and paying the
consequences later. Path *B* displays the current utility from working
first and receiving the delayed payoffs later.

The economist begins by claiming a concern only with explanation
and prediction. Which path will be chosen? That depends upon the
rate of time preference of the two insects. Assume that the grasshopper has a very high rate of time preference and the ant a very low
one. Paths *A'* and *B'*, shown as dashed lines, display the discounted
present value of the utility to be experienced from each choice as
evaluated by the grasshopper. He cares primarily about now. Future
events are highly discounted and thus diminish greatly in value *as
viewed from the present*. The total present value of each choice – the
sum of the momentary, discounted utilities – is the net area between
the horizontal axis and *A'* and *B'* respectively. The present value of
playing all summer and facing the consequences later is, for the grasshopper, *OGR* (large and positive) plus *RSZ* (small and negative). The
present value of working, evaluated in early summer, is *ONT* (large
and negative) plus *TQZ* (small and positive). The net present value
of playing is greater.

Armed with this information, the economist can now predict the

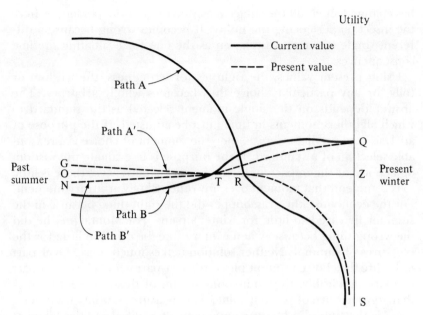

Figure 2.2. Ovid's view: past discounted to present.

choice to be made by the grasshopper. She can also explain the choice made, after the fact, by reference to the revealed high rate of positive time preference. It is a very short, but very drastic step, however, to say that it was the "right" choice because it maximized the present value of expected utility from the action and was thus "efficient." That step has now selected at random a single moment to be used as the basis of evaluating a lifetime of consequences. It is undoubtedly the relevant moment to use to *predict* a choice. It is simply an arbitrary one to use as the basis of evaluating one.

Indeed, Montaigne and Ovid explicitly rejected that moment as appropriate. Their relevant picture for moral evaluation would be Figure 2.2. Paths A and B are the same. Paths A' and B' are also present value measures, but in relation to the *end* of the time period rather than the beginning. When all of the consequences have worked themselves out and the hungry grasshopper is on his deathbed, his own subjective evaluation of his prior decision is that it was wrong. The total discounted present value payoff of playing all summer is now the new OGR plus RSZ. The payoff from working has become ONT plus TQZ, which is now clearly superior. The choice made, while explainable by a high rate of time preference, has nevertheless become the "wrong" choice. It has become wrong not because the standard has changed. It is still the subjective evaluation of the person, or here the insect, experiencing the utility. It becomes wrong because a different single moment was chosen as the one for evaluating lifetime consequences.

Using present values, the rightness or wrongness, the wisdom or folly, or any particular choice thus becomes wholly arbitrary. The answer depends on the single moment selected as the standard to which all other moments in time must be adjusted. If the purpose of analysis is to predict a choice, then the moment of choice is a reasonable selection of a standard. If the purpose is to evaluate the wisdom of a choice or the impact on lifetime utility experienced, there is little to recommend that moment over any other wholly arbitrary moment. For the economist, the grasshopper did the right thing because in the summer he cared so little for winter's pains. For Montaigne, he did the wrong thing because, when winter came, he cared so little for the pleasures of summer. Neither solution makes much sense. Over part of his life the choice brought pleasure, over part pain. The net impact is, more defensibly, the undiscounted sum of those current utilities than *any* measure of present value. The measure of utility used here, then, is the sum of a lifetime's moments of realized utilities taken at their current values. If it mattered much to me at the time it occurred, that is its lifetime contribution. Humanly caused changes in the total of utility experienced are thus, by this definition, exercises of power.

This is certainly not a perfect measure. It certainly does not eliminate all ambiguity. It permits impacts that at first seem negative to the subject to become positive as time progresses. Parents have always assumed that to be possible; so now does this model. It permits impacts that at first seem positive to the subject to become negative as time progresses. Faust ultimately discovered that to be possible; so now does the model. Lives cannot be evaluated from the perspective of any single moment. They must be taken whole.

CHAPTER 3

Decision theory and power

Power now involves external human intervention into the constrained maximizing behavior of individuals. If I can affect the final utility experienced from that behavior, I have some form of power. Maximizing subject to constraints is, in turn, a process of making choices. Therefore, a careful examination of the potential for power requires a systematic look at decision processes. In recent years a formal theory of decisions has been developed. Though originally structured as a tool for improving the quality of decisions reached, it is equally useful for isolating the elements of a choice and for identifying possible locations for the exercise of power. This chapter begins by presenting the tools of formal decision theory and then proceeds to use them for that purpose.

Decision trees

The central tool of decision theory is the schematic diagram known as a "decision tree." Choices are separated into distinct elements that are systematically related to each other in a strict sequence of time.[1] Decision theory postulates four elements in such a choice: "decision nodes," "chance nodes," "probabilities," and "payoffs." It places them in explicit sequence under a strong assumption of linear time. Each moment comes but once, following all previous ones, preceding all later ones. Decisions are part of a flow of time. The various elements of a decision process must be placed carefully along this linear time scale, running diagrammatically from left to right, creating a map of the possible paths through life. Paths traveled in the past define current possibilities. Choices made now determine future possibilities.

---

[1] For a detailed discussion of decision theory see Howard Raiffa, *Decision Analysis*, Addison-Wesley, Reading, Mass., 1968. For a look at decision analysis as a policy-making tool, see Edith Stokey and Richard Zeckhauser, *A Primer for a Policy Analysis*, Norton, New York, 1978, Chapter 12, and as a general management tool, see Paul Vatter, Stephen Bradley, Sherwood Frey, and Barbara Jackson, *Quantitative Methods in Management: Text and Cases*, Irwin, Homewood, Ill., 1978.

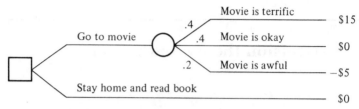

Figure 3.1. The Big Night Out problem.

Figure 3.1 displays a simple decision tree for a "Big Night Out" problem. It is Saturday night, and I must decide how best to use the time. Should I go to see the movie at the local theater or stay home and read a book? The tree in Figure 3.1 is really, of course, only part of a much larger mapping.

Decision nodes

Affected by the past, impacting the future, there is a juncture where I must choose my path. The film starts at 7:30, and if I am to attend, I must explicitly decide to go. Decisions that must be made are denoted with a square. The branches leading to the right (the future) are the potential paths that may be chosen. The formal theory requires that at each decision node the entire list of options be specified, that is, that the map of branches be "mutually exclusive and collectively exhaustive." In short, it expects global rationality. All conceivable options should be considered. In practice, however, such maps almost always are structured in more limited terms. Only a subset of the possible options is presented. I could probably also spend my Big Night Out visiting friends, collecting night crawlers, exploring cemetaries, scrubbing the kitchen floor, or any number of other options. For convenience, I have restricted the choices to two.

Chance nodes

Is the movie any good? Will the book be boring? Will the theater catch fire? I do not choose a certain future. I can choose only the chance I will take. There are in life and in choices variable outcomes that I do not control. These "chance" events occur in time after the choice. I can ultimately find out if the movie is pleasing only after deciding to go. On many of the branches of decision trees there will occur events in time that are outside my control when I must take what fate, or often someone else, offers. Chance nodes are denoted by circles.

The branches radiating from them are paths that will be selected, not by my choice, but by the outcome of what is to me an uncertain event.

This example is oversimplified in that, if the movie is boring, I can always leave. Each branch emanating from the chance node should have a decision node about whether to go home and read or stay and watch. But the page is small. My time is limited. There are thus only three possible outcomes noted. The movie may be awful, okay, or terrific. No matter which, I will stay until the bitter end.

Probabilities

Even if the potential outcomes are virtually infinite, they are not all equally likely. Attempting to make the best choice, I will want to know the probabilities of each outcome emanating from a chance node. What are the odds that the movie will turn out to be terrific (or awful)? If the tree is to be a truly useful guide, the probabilities used must be accurate reflections of true chances. In many cases, including this one, there is no such thing as a true probability.[2] There is only an intuitive feel, sometimes termed a "subjective probability." In the example, I have assumed subjective probabilities for the three outcomes, terrific ($p = .4$), okay ($p = .4$), and awful ($p = .2$).

Payoffs

Only after the choice has been made and the outcome of chance events has been determined will I know what I have done. Each final path through the tree yields an ultimate payoff. If I do go and it is a terrific movie, just how good is it? Is it as good as a week in Tahiti, a steak dinner, or a trip to the Super Bowl? All of the outcomes must be translated into directly comparable terms. In practice, money is used as the common measure. Conceptually, utility would be the more appropriate quality.

For the Big Night Out the values of the paths are given in dollars at the right edge of Figure 3.1. There must always be some situation taken as the standard for comparison, and in this case the "base" is staying home and reading the book. Hence its payoff is listed as $0, whereas attending a boring movie is $5 worse than staying home,

[2] The problems associated with calling unknown outcomes of nonrepeatable events "probabilities" is discussed in some detail in Chapter 4, especially pp. 57–8. Placing that uncertainty under the name of "subjective probability" can actually serve to obscure power in that it takes something under the control of another human and makes it sound like some random process.

attending a terrific one is $15 better, and attending an okay one is the same as staying home.

The process, laid out in this fashion, was designed to aid good decision making. Simply breaking the choice into its elements of decisions, chance events, probabilities, and payoffs, all structured in strict time sequence, helps one to understand the dimensions of a decision. It is also possible then to manipulate the structured data for more explicit guidance in making the right choice. It is possible to work backward in time and calculate the expected value just prior to each chance node. In this case the movie branch has an expected value of $1, as calculated by multiplying each payoff times its probability and adding the outcome for each branch ($.4(-\$5) + .4(0) + .2(\$15)$). The stay-at-home branch has an expected value of $0. At the decision node, then, I can select either an expected outcome of $1 by going to the movie or an expected value of $0 by staying home. The movie is the best choice available in this tree.

There is an important element of the treatment of time that should be emphasized here. Next Saturday night I will again have to decide which thrills to seek. But I cannot simply return to the decision node of Figure 3.1 and make the same choice over again. Water does not flow uphill. A path through a decision map never moves to the left. Once I have left my decision node I can never return to exactly the same point. Next Saturday night, having gone to a movie last week that turned out to be terrific, I can choose a movie or a book. Time is always linear. No two choices, made at different times, are ever exactly the same. They may not be much different, but they are never the same.

Though developed to permit better decisions to be made, I propose to abandon the normative content of the theory and use the mapping process in a descriptive mode, simply defining the decision process of my constrained, maximizing individuals. Life for each, then, is a one-way journey, left to right, through an infinitely complex tree with choice and chance branches radiating through time. There are intermittent payoff fruits to be harvested, but then the tree continues on. Individual decisions are part of a much larger structure.

This complex individual tree does not stand alone. If the concern is social processes and human interactions, the tree for each individual is part of a larger forest in which branches of one overlap parts of another. In an exploration of power, it is in the interaction of two or more decision trees that this social phenomenon would be found. In Chapter 2, I promised a clarification of the various forms of power

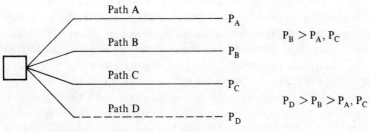

Figure 3.2. Simple economic power.

possible under the broad definition provided. It is now possible to fulfill that promise.

Forms of power

Decision power

If life is a vast decision tree, "behavior" is the decision nodes. There the individual has some control: making choices, selecting paths, deciding what to do in response to, and anticipation of, external events and conditions. Clearly, there is a conceptual possibility that power could be exercised over choices, that is, at decision nodes. If another person can alter the path taken from such a node relative to the one that would have been taken without any exercise, that is, by my definition, a form of power. Decision power could itself come in at least two forms, one well recognized by economists, the other largely ignored.

Simple economic power. Economics most often considers moments of choice, when individuals select consumption packages, production methods, or investment paths. It recognizes one form of external influence on choices as the very foundation of market behavior. Someone may change the decision by making a better offer. In Figure 3.2 there is an isolated decision node with three possible paths (marked A, B, and C). Assume that B is the option with the highest expected payoff as evaluated by the decider. Another individual enters and adds a fourth path (marked D). If it is superior to the other three in terms of the expected payoffs, the choice is changed. Power has been exercised, but it is positive power welcomed by its subject.

This power is well recognized in formal microeconomic theory. It is the ability to change a decision by making a better offer than anyone else. It is power in a positive-sum game, such that both the exerciser and the subject of such power benefit. Such power is the very foundation of neoclassical theory. All of the coordination of human activity in a world of pure, theoretical markets results from the pervasive, decentralized exercise of this seemingly weak form of power.

Even monopoly power, though roundly criticized in the literature, is simple economic power. It is an ability to make an offer that, while still better than any other, is not as good as the one a competitive firm would have made. The decider is still free to accept or reject as he wishes.

Decision control power. Is there any other conceivable way one person might affect the choices of another? Could anyone ever exercise power over choices except as simple economic power? Certainly Friedman recognizes the ability of government to make decisions for other people. Indeed, his basic argument, translated into my terms, is that markets involve only simple economic power, only governments exercise *negative* decision control power, and hence markets are the answer to negative power.[3]

Is it possible to conceive of any actor, other than a government, having decision control power? Consider a single example, later developed in detail in Part III. Rational maximizing persons can and do turn over control of their decisions to other persons in "agency" relationships. In effect, the ultimate "decider" (the principal) abandons the decision node to the agent, who evaluates options and makes choices for him. The doctor decides the course of treatment the patient will pursue. The lawyer decides the strategy the plaintiff will adopt. The employee decides on the source of materials the employer will use. Rational principals must expect the power to be positive, or they would not accept the relationship. There is a growing literature demonstrating that that expectation need not always be met.

Decision control power could conceivably take other forms as well. It might involve control over information. It might involve threats of bodily harm or the destruction of property and wealth. It might involve some form of psychological authority to dictate decisions, for example, a parent who can tell an adult child what career path to follow. I do not here argue that such forms of power are pervasive in markets, only that they are conceptually possible. Such decision control power could be positive, negative, or neutral.

---

[3] Milton Friedman, *Capitalism and Freedom*, University of Chicago Press, Chicago, 1962.

Event power

In a complete tree, decision nodes are preceded and followed by what are, from the perspective of the map, chance events. Many of those, however, are not truly chance events. They are merely decisions that will be reached by someone else. Those events, often separated in time from decision nodes, may not truly be separable in an analysis of power. Suppose I dig a deep pit, fill it with poisonous snakes, and throw you in. I then stand on the edge of the pit and offer to sell you a ladder. To buy or not to buy is not the only question. What prior events made you need to buy, and my influence over them, are also relevant. Power entered, not at a moment of choice, but at a linked chance node. Event power could be willingly granted by the subject. It need not be.

Ungranted event power. In *The Reivers* William Faulkner presents an example of ungranted event power.[4] The narrator, a small boy of eleven, and two adult accomplices "borrow" a car for a trip to Memphis. Along the way they come to a patch of dirt road that has been plowed and watered by the local farmer, who sits beside the road with a team of mules waiting for unsuspecting travelers. He then graciously offers to tow them out of the mud for a "reasonable" fee. In the book the farmer admits that he earns more from "farming his mud hole" than from any other activity on his farm. He is exercising event power prior to the moment of choice by the reivers. To be sure, they are made better off by the tow, *after they are stuck*, but if the farmer had neither existed nor acted, they would never have become stuck. That seems to be negative, ungranted event power. The reivers and the mud farmer clearly recognized it as such.

If a new competitor decides to move into a limited market, there is an impact on the existing firms. If a state, under pressure from farmers, opts not to enforce school attendance and child labor laws, those events will later affect the options open to, and decisions made by, the next generation of migrant laborers.

Timur Kuran notes the praise or opprobrium that interested parties can confer on persons who express public positions on political issues. It is an event, and probably a negative one, to be publicly branded a racist. It is an event under the control of other persons.[5]

Externalities are ungranted event power. External costs are reduc-

---

[4] William Faulkner, *The Reivers*, Random House, New York, 1962, Chapter 4.
[5] Timur Kuran, "Cameleon Voters and Public Choice," *Public Choice*, No. 53, pp. 53–78, 1987.

tions in welfare that can be generated by an external actor at his will. External benefits are nothing but examples of positive event power. Economists have long looked at externalities as problems because of their implications for resource allocation. They have seldom considered them as a form of power.

The *process* of defining and assigning property rights, as opposed to merely transfering them, is another form of event power appearing at an individual's chance, rather than decision, nodes. If any party can act to influence the definition of rights but not necessarily the exchange later made, it is potentially as significant as digging a snake-pit or farming a mud hole. The altered structure of rights may be positive for some, neutral for others, and negative for others still.

In each of these examples the power to affect the welfare of the subject was not something willfully granted by the subject. Other forces and factors in the social structure have determined who has this event power and its scope. In other cases control over events may have been explicitly granted to the potential exerciser of power by the potential subject.

Granted event power. In any trade between parties in which the time of performance differs, the one who goes first grants to the other control over a significant future event. On the decision map of the first person the response of the other appears as a chance event. On the map of the second it is a decision node. We have now, not a single decision tree, but overlapping trees whose structure varies with perspective. Consider a simple contract as an example. A is now a farmer deciding at T_1 which crops to plant. B is a tomato canner who asks A to plant tomatoes and agrees to buy those tomatoes at harvest. Farmer A also has an offer from C to buy corn if A agrees to plant that instead. The overlapping pieces of the decision trees of A and B are shown in Figure 3.3.

If A decides to plant tomatoes, he then faces a chance node at T_2 when the crop matures. Canner B could live up to the bargain or B could back down. From A's perspective, this is a chance node, but of course on B's decision tree it is a decision point. For A the outcome appears probabilistic; for B it is controllable. Whenever there is a difference in the time of performance for the two parties to even a bilateral, voluntary exchange, there is a granting of real power to the later performing party. Farmer A, having started down the path of planting tomatoes, has given to B a power to make A worse off. As time progresses, power shifts from one party to another, but A has willingly granted to B that power.

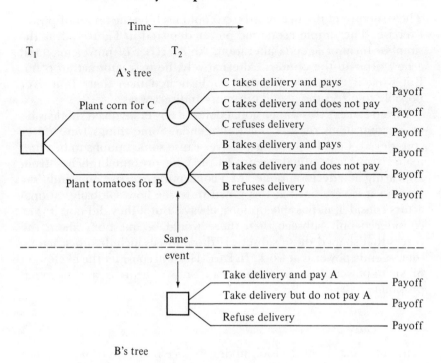

Figure 3.3. Overlapping decision maps.

Of course, assuming A to be a rational maximizer, he will dislike having control over important events pass to B and will seek either compensation for the risk or protection against the exercise of that power. It is just such shifts of power and fear that the power will be exercised that gives rise to contract law. In the presence of external authority that will force B to live up to the agreement or to compensate A for failing to do so, the potential for negative event power is reduced. Contract law, while affecting allocations of resources, is also restructuring patterns of power. Who may do what to whom, when. It establishes limits to the exercise of event power but does not wholly eliminate it. Moreover, it reduces the scope of general event power only by substituting government power. One form of power is used to control another.

Agenda power

Changes in the behavior of an actor facing a decision tree need not be restricted to actions in given sets of decision and chance nodes.

The structure of the perceived tree could itself be the target of power exercise. The simple economic power depicted in Figure 3.2 is the simplest form of agenda alteration. An exerciser of power may add a new offer to the options. Alternatively, he may subtract an offer. But what if the power is more sophisticated than that? Is it ever possible to affect the agenda in more indirect ways?

Steven Lukes's two-dimensional political power involved subtle ways of keeping items off the political agenda. Some things were never considered. Could another actor ever cause some options to be eliminated from a personal agenda? Could he prevent branches from appearing at a decision node? As a conceptual exercise one could say yes, but it is very hard at this juncture to see how. Globally rational actors consider all possible options, always. But if they did not, if they considered only subsets, then there would be questions about the forces that shaped those subsets. If those forces include other actors, then agenda power is at work. In Part III, I will consider the likelihood of such power, though here I can only note it as a conceptual possibility.

Value power

The full structure of decision nodes, chance nodes, and probabilities determines what a decider may ultimately get. Until outcomes are translated into payoffs, it is impossible to answer "so what?" Payoffs reflect subjective valuations of events. Event power may alter the objective outcomes; value power would alter the subjective valuations placed upon given events. It implies, therefore, some ability to alter, not just behavior, but the utility experienced from given goods and actions. It implies that some of the $\partial U_i/\partial S_i$ in (2.1) are, in fact, not equal to zero. It is conceptually possible, in a model with utility functions like (2.1), that changes in preferences result from strategic behavior on the part of other actors. If I can actually "make you like" an item that you previously did not, I have exercised power of an extraordinary kind.

Any of the other forms of power could be spoken of as unambiguously positive, negative, or neutral. They altered outcomes in a way that changed the lifetime welfare of the subject as defined by the subject's own utility function. When the relationship between economic commodities and utility is itself subject to endogenous change, such terms become ambiguous. Indeed, all of welfare economics becomes ambiguous. I shall return to this topic in the concluding chapter.

Conclusions

Decision power, whether the simple economic or decision control type, coincides with actions taken at decision nodes. Event power would be manifested at chance nodes. Agenda power would appear in a restructuring of the shape of the branches in a segment of the tree. Value power would change neither the chance events nor the objective outcomes but would be manifested in changes in the subjective valuations of those events in defining payoffs. These forms of power do not necessarily have clearly defined boundaries. Any particular exercise of power might have elements of several different forms. Power is potentially a complex phenomenon, but these conceptual categories will provide a framework for seeking and comprehending it.

The basic elements for a theory of power have now been specified. I have postulated a world of individuals who maximize subject to constraints. They are driven by a desire to maximize a utility function of the most general sort. They proceed through life in decision maps whose paths overlap in intricate patterns with life mappings of others. They chart their routes rationally. There is now a definition of power, a method of evaluating the impact of power, and a clarification of the conceptually possible forms of power. Only one set of questions remains. Would the exercise of power ever be in the strategic interest of some of those postulated individuals? Would it ever make sense for some of them to "spend" precious time and resources doing it? Would it ever make economic sense for some of those individuals to succumb to the exercise of power? To complete the economic theory of power, it is necessary to answer these questions. That is the topic of the next chapter.

CHAPTER 4

The exercise of power as economic behavior

> Human behavior is not compartmentalized, sometimes based on maximizing, sometimes not, sometimes motivated by stable preferences, sometimes by volatile ones, sometimes resulting in an optimal accumulation of information, sometimes not. Rather all human behavior can be viewed as involving participants who maximize their utility from a stable set of preferences and accumulate an optimal amount of information and other inputs in a variety of markets.
>
> Gary Becker, *The Economic Approach to Human Behavior*

Becker's maximizers could be assumed to live quietly offstage in isolated, soundproof booths. They could emerge solely to consumate a market exchange, retreating quickly and avoiding all other forms of human interaction. They could. But if the model is to be consistent, they would do so only when maximizing behavior itself so dictates. If and when the payoffs justify it, such persons must place the moment of exchange into a larger context of social interaction. In short, maximizing behavior may *require* the exercise of many forms of power.

Simple economic power is undoubtedly common. It will, however, be the exclusive form of human interaction relevant to markets if and only if, at *all* times and in *all* situations, *all* other forms of power are *always* clearly inferior as measured by net gains to potential exercisers. If any other form of power is ever more *productive*, the theory requires that form to be chosen. This is a proposition so central to the argument of this book that it needs careful statement and elaboration. Why and in what forms would one rational actor choose to exercise power over another?

The formal model

Consider two actors, A, who is faced with a choice that will affect another actor, B. Actor A is somewhere along a lifetime decision tree, having already made a number of unalterable decisions. He is pre-

48

paring to move farther to the right along some possible branch, contemplating

- decision nodes listing the options of which A is aware,
- potential outcomes emanating from the chance nodes located along each choice path,
- the estimated probabilities associated with each outcome, and
- estimations of the values of the outcomes at the end of each tree branch.

Free of all power and using the information contained in such a conceptual tree, A would make a selection designated as path A_0. Actor B, however, will be affected by that choice. His general utility function of type (2.1) can be made explicitly interdependent by recognizing that his utility will depend on the choice by A. Holding all other things constant, his utility will then become a function of the path followed by A, A_j. The utility function for B may then be rewritten as

$$U_B = U_B(A_j) \tag{4.1}$$

If B does nothing at all, A will select path A_0 and B will experience utility $U_B(A_0)$. As a rational maximizer, B must ask, however,

1. whether there are other paths that A could take that would be better from his perspective,
2. how much better those alternatives are,
3. whether there are actions B could take that would cause A to shift paths, and
4. how costly the various options for action are.

In short, the choice about whether to exercise power and the best form in which to exercise it must be economic decisions. This is a standard problem in production theory: the evaluation and selection of techniques of production. Here, however, the "product" is the change in B's utility resulting from a caused change in A's behavior. "Production" is the exercise of power. The value of the product is the impact of the change in A's path.

Define G_j as the gain to B of having A select A_j over A_0,

$$G_j = U_B(A_j) - U_B(A_0) \tag{4.2}$$

where of course G_j may be positive, zero, or negative. In most cases it will be zero; A's choice will not affect B's utility. Occasionally, however, it will; that is, $G_j \neq 0$.

Of course, producing a change in A's path is not costless for B. He

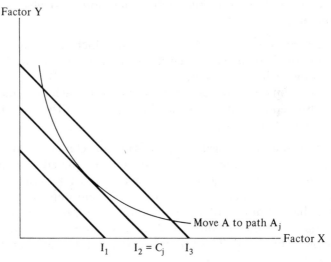

Figure 4.1. Power as produced change.

must consider whether power ever pays and, if so, which technique pays best. If all of the forms of power previously outlined are conceptually possible, then they must be within the collection of strategies considered by a rational B. Rejection of power options must be on economic, rather than moral, grounds if the maximizing assumption is to hold.

Infinitely variable forms of power

Figure 4.1 contains an isoquant with factors of production on the axes and the traditionally convex curve as the locus of all combinations of factors that generate a shift from path A_0 to path A_j. The origin represents the situation if A remains on path A_0. No resources are expended by B; A's path remains unchanged. This picture differs from normal isoquant maps in one significant aspect. In traditional production problems the level of output is continuously variable. Hence there are, in each such mapping, an infinite number of isoquants, each associated with a given level of output. There would be, for example, a curve displaying the inputs necessary to produce 100 tons of steel and another for producing 105.

Here, however, there is only a single isoquant in each possible map, but there are a number of separate, one-isoquant figures. What each such map reflects is a discrete movement from path A_0 to another path A_j. Because all such paths are, by definition, mutually exclusive, the movement is explicitly discrete. It is not possible to be a little more or less pregnant. It is not possible to be a little more or less on path A_j. A is either wholly on it or wholly off it. There is thus but one isoquant associated with causing movement onto each path A_j. There are as many one-isoquant graphs as there are options A_j.

Does it ever pay B to undertake the process of causing some shift in path? If so, what is the optimal technique to employ; what is the best form of power to exercise? That, of course, depends upon the costs of causing this change. Isocost lines may also be added to each graph representing fixed expenditures for factors, with the slope representing the relative prices of the factors. There may be an infinite number of isocost lines in each graph, each one associated with a different total expenditure. As usual the point of primary concern is the position of tangency between an isocost line and the single isoquant associated with the path A_j. Isocost lines above a tangency level, such as I_3, are inefficient. The same change could be generated at less cost. Those everywhere below the isoquant, such as I_1, are insufficient to cause the change. The value of the isocost line at each such tangency determines the minimum cost to B of causing a shift in A's path to A_j. Let C_j be that minimum cost for each path A_j.

The value of the gain to B of that shift in A's behavior has already been defined by the variable G_j. Each possible exercise of power thus has associated with it a net value of causing the change, V_j, where

$$V_j = G_j - C_j \qquad (4.3)$$

In many, or even most, cases the value of V_j will be negative, that is, the costs of causing a behavioral shift will outweigh all potential gains. If, however, there are ever positive values for some V_j, then rationality requires B to exercise some power.

It is possible to map the variable V_j over the entire range of path options for A, creating a "power possibility function." This is done in Figure 4.2a The options are arbitrarily ordered in terms of the value of V_j with lowest values to the left. Here the curve is shown as smooth but, given the assumed discrete nature of the A_j, it is more likely discontinuous, which would affect the aesthetics but not the significance of the graph. The loss associated with the worst possible cases may be quite large; that is, there would be large costs in causing a change that provided little or no benefit. The graph for all possible human interactions will at least reach the zero level because that is defined as the situation if B does nothing; that is, A_0 is the status quo and can be achieved at zero cost.

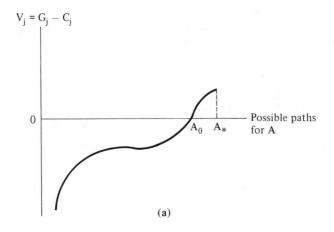

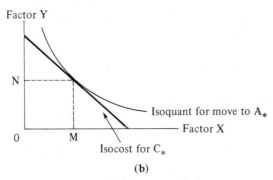

Figure 4.2. Maximizing payoffs from power.

For some possible interactions with some possible persons, this power possibility function will rise above the horizontal axis, indicating a positive payoff to the exercise of power. The path for A that is associated with the highest net payoff to B's exercise of power is furthest to the right and is designated A_*. As a rational actor, B will exercise power to move A to the path A_*. The optimal form of power to use has been predetermined by the tangency between the isocost line C_* and the single isoquant for A_*, the values of which were used to derive the power possibility function. Returning to the mapping for that particular path permits a reading of the most efficient technique for producing the change, that is, the best form of power.

This is done in Figure 4.2a, where the power possibilities curve reaches a maximum at the point associated with a caused shift to A_* Figure 4.2b displays the single isoquant for that move, the tangency

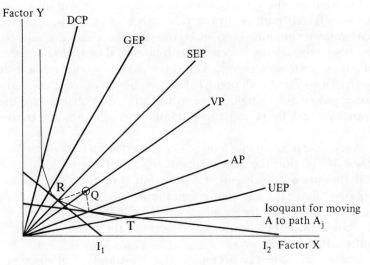

Figure 4.3. The choice of a power form.

with the minimum isocost line necessary to cause the move, and permits the determination of the optimal form of power. In this case the best technique to use is the one associated with using factors X and Y in proportion $0M/0N$.

Discrete forms of power

In Chapter 3, I specified several qualitatively very distinct forms of power. It thus seems inappropriate to specify smooth, continuous isoquants for producing shifts in A's behavior. A more realistic presentation would recognize that a selection of production technique here is likely a discrete choice. Unlike cutting cloth a bit more carefully, a decision to use value power, rather than simple economic power, implies a discrete shift of production technique. A linear programming approximation of a smooth isoquant may thus be preferable to the smooth isoquants of the previous section. Figure 4.3 is such an approximation displaying six distinct techniques corresponding to the forms of power defined in Chapter 3. As a rational actor, B will always be on one of the rays from the origin, or at the origin itself, indicating no interaction at all. The space between the rays is always inefficient, that is, uses more resources than are required to attain the given result. (This approximation assumes fixed factor proportions for each of the various forms of power exercise, which is probably restrictive but not terribly significant at this stage.)

On each ray there is a point associated with causing the shift from the unaffected path A_0 to the new, power-affected path A_j via that particular technique. Thus in Figure 4.3, the change would require the resource package associated with point R if caused via the exercise of simple economic power. The same change would require the resources associated with point T if caused by the exercise of ungranted event power. The single isoquant for any given change can then be approximated by taking those points on each ray and connecting them.

A particular technique may be eliminated from consideration at the stage of creating the linear approximation if the options on either side dominate it. In Figure 4.3 the point Q on the value power (*VP*) option is above the line connecting simple economic power (*SEP*) and agenda power (*AP*) *for the same gain*. No matter what the factor costs, it would always be cheaper to use one of the bordering techniques rather than value power.

Isocost lines are unaffected by the presumption of discrete techniques of production. They continue to represent combinations of factors that yield a given, total cost. The slope continues to be determined by the relative factor prices of the resources. Given factor productivity in the various methods (represented by the distance of the points from the origin), changes in relative factor costs may induce B to alter his strategy from the use of one form of power to another. Sufficient changes in relative costs will require it. For example, a change that shifts the minimum isocost line from I_1 to I_2 will induce B to move from reliance upon *SEP* to *AP*.

The switch to linear approximations of isoquants does not alter the remainder of the analysis. Minimum costs of producing a change in A's path are still determined by comparing the isoquant and the isocosts to generate values for V_j. The resulting V_j can be used to derive the relevant power possibility curve. The optimal choice of technique for the best, positive exercise of power (moving A to path A_*) is the same.

The special case – an initial statement

The relative productivity of techniques and the nature of factor costs will dictate whether power will be exercised at all, and the best form of power. That best route may, of course, be to combine resources into something worth trading with A, relying thus on simple economic power. There is no apparent reason to conclude *a priori*, however, that simple economic power will *always* predominate. If another form

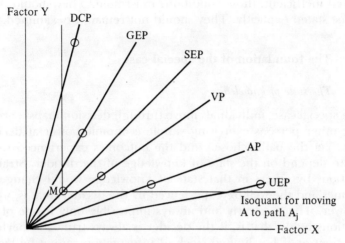

Figure 4.4. The special case.

of power generates better net returns, the assumption of rationality dictates that B will follow that route. Yet the vision of market behavior that dominates economics is that all interactions are based exclusively on that one form of power. It is thus making some extreme assumptions about the productivity of all other techniques of production at all times, in all situations involving markets.

Every time there is a positive return from exercising power as determined by a power possibility function, the best option must be such that simple economic power *always* dominates every other technique. Figure 4.4 depicts that presumption. The resources necessary to cause A to move to path A_* are noted on each of the rays from the origin. For every conceptual form of power except simple economic power, that point must be to the northeast of the point M on *SEP*. Thus each isoquant must reduce to a right angle through the point M on *SEP*. It will *always* be more efficient to use simple economic power. This must be true at all times and for all pairs of interactors for the special case to hold.

That is certainly one conceptual form for a power isoquant to take. It is hardly the only conceptual form. In order to make an *a priori* assumption that Figure 4.4 is appropriate for all human interactions involving markets, it is necessary for a number of prior conditions to be fulfilled. Economists rarely state these conditions explicitly. Indeed, they are perhaps not often aware that they are postulating them. Nevertheless, in order for all of the other forms of power to be forever

declared inefficient, those conditions must hold. They should, however, be stated explicitly. They should not remain unexamined.

The foundation of the special case

The state of knowledge

In the special case, individuals move through decision maps, encoun-
tering other persons exercising simple economic power at decision
nodes. Yet the paths chosen and the outcomes experienced would
seem to depend on the state of knowledge of the decider. Strategic
alterations by others in that state of knowledge would change the
outcomes and the welfare experienced by the decider, that is, would
be power. That is clearly and always impossible only if one of two
conditions holds, that is, if the decider is always truly and perfectly
omniscient or if her limited stock of information cannot be biased,
altered, or affected by any other person. Those are very strong conditions and deserve further consideration.

Omniscience – the possession of all data. Many forms of potential power
become ineffective if the potential subject knows everything. She can
evaluate, by herself, such things as the carcinogenic properties of the
additives in her food. She knows the length of life and future repair
needs of durable items she is considering acquiring. She knows the
future employment, wage, benefit, and promotion payoffs for each
possible career path. Her mapping is complete and accurate. It is not
simply estimated or perceived. It is true.

Most of the chance nodes on her tree then collapse to known outcomes. A normal decision tree allows A to assign probabilities to each
branch emanating from such a node. True omniscience, however,
requires much more. For many of those chance events the term "probability" is simply wrong. They are not really chance events at all. The
outcomes are outside her control, but not outside human control.
They are decisions that will be reached in the future by other persons.
"Probability" is usually defined "as the proportion of times that a
certain event will occur if the experiment related to the event is repeated indefinitely."[1] If the result is always the same, the proportion
is always 1, and the outcome is not probabilistic at all.

Because the chance nodes on A's tree are really often decisions

---

[1] Paul G. Hoel, *Introduction to Mathematical Statistics*, Wiley, New York, 1962, p. 4.

made by B, the outcomes will be probabilistic only if the decisions made by B are inconsistent and sometimes irrational. Economic theory implies that all human behavior is determinate and that, given the same constraints on B (and of course the same preference function), the outcome will always be the same. Thus there is no probability distribution at all. The single determinate outcome will always result, that is, its $p = 1$. It is predetermined with mathematical precision, but it remains not yet known by A.

Consider the case of a job candidate at a university assessing the "chances" of getting tenure. To be sure, there have been, and will be, other cases somewhat similar but never identical. To have a meaningful probability we would have to repeat the event over and over, rerunning world history time and again over the *same* choice. Unless the decisions made by the recommending department, the university committee, and the president, in the face of unchanging information, are random events (that is, those individuals do not engage in systematic maximizing behavior), the outcome would always be the same! She would not be denied tenure on some runs and granted it on others.

The problem for the candidate is not one of assessing a probability distribution. There is none. The outcome has a probability of 1. All other outcomes have a probability of 0. What appears as a probability is, in fact, ignorance of relevant facts. That ignorance may be veiled, but not avoided, by replacing objective with "subjective" probabilities that "reflect a purely personal degree of belief in the likelihood of the occurrence of such an event. They reflect the hunches people have, their 'feelings in the bone.' "[2]

This invention of a new form of probability may salvage the forms of decision trees. Unknown outcomes can still be included, and my ignorance can be subsumed under the less pejorative term of subjective probabilities. However, to be free of all potential power, A must

---

[2] Heinz Kohler, *Statistics for Business and Economics*, Scott, Foresman, Glenview, Ill. 1985, pp. 155–156. Of course what are regarded as random events in most textbooks on probability are themselves really misstatements of the issue. Under the normal laws of physics the number shown on a thrown die is not a random event at all, but a perfectly determinant one. Given the same face upward at the start of the throw, the exact same force applied in exactly the same direction, thrown onto the same surface, under identical conditions of temperature and humidity, the same number would appear each and every time. Variations in the outcome of thrown dice are not characteristics of the dice but of the thrower, who is apparently incapable of exactly duplicating all of the influences he or she imparts to the dice. The success of gambling casinos depends not upon the randomness of dice but the randomness of the throwers.

know more. A hunch or a feeling in her bones will not do. Omniscience requires that she know the total picture of constraints and preferences of each of the actors whose future decisions will affect her decision tree. The candidate will need to know what will be the actual criteria of the decision. Even if scholarship and teaching are the stated criteria, what do those terms mean to the individuals who will decide? Will they consider other factors – politics, personality, race, gender, or golfing skill? When chance events on her decision tree are decisions made by others, the normal concept of probability fails. The results are not undetermined. For her they are just unknown, but for omniscience to hold they may not be.

The implicit assumption then is that A knows B as well as she knows herself. If not, B may be able to shape A's subjective probabilities and hence perceived tree by affecting her stock of information. Of course, the converse must also be true. B must also know all there is to know about A's preferences and future behaviors. This complete store of knowledge about both self and all potential interactors must be given equally to all actors in the economic system. If some have complete knowledge and others do not, obviously the blessed ones will have a potential to use it in the exercise of power. All persons must be wholly omniscient. (I am obviously describing here a new race of beings, no longer "homo economicus," now "deus economicus.")

Omniscience – processing of all data. Not only must all information be known to all, each individual must be able to process this total body of data efficiently and accurately. There may not be differences in basic intelligence or in human capital. There cannot be experts and amateurs. All the actors in this drama must be globally rational. All possible options at all possible junctures must be under consideration. The decider must be able to hold in her brain all of this information and be able to process it intelligently and accurately. She must not restrict her considerations to any subset of options or event contingencies on the basis of rules of thumb, past experience, or easy availability of data. To know all but not fully understand it is to fall short of real omniscience.

Uncertainty – the acquisition of information. If the assumption of complete knowledge and understanding is too rigid, if ever A must start with less than perfect information, if she must ever choose on the basis of a perceived decision map, or if ever she must acquire information about the world from outside herself, then the presumption of the impossibility of power is in jeopardy. It can be saved only by imposing conditions on the processes of acquiring information that protect its total independence from human influence.

Information must be viewed as if all data exist, unowned and uncontrolled in a large heap. The process of acquiring data then is one of making trips to this pile and selecting, free of all human influence, the bits of data relevant to the choices that must be made. All data must be obtainable in unbiased form from nonhuman or completely disinterested sources. If that is not the case, if the information relevant to A's choices (for example, the likelihood of B's future behavior) is disproportionately in the possession of an interested human actor, then there is the potential for withholding, misrepresenting, biasing, selecting, or distorting the information as it is acquired from that human source. Strategically caused changes in A's perceived decision tree can result in altered choices and welfare, that is, can be an exercise of power. If all but simple economic power is to be assumed *a priori* impossible, such actions must be prohibited. Persons cannot control information. If actors are permitted to be less than omniscient and are allowed to acquire information from other humans, the presumption of no other form of power may be maintained only if one of two other conditions holds.

Uncertainty – the genetic need for truth. If interested persons do possess information relevant to the choices that A must make and if they recognize the potential for strategic use of that information, their failure to do so can be explained only on the basis of cost. If there is, innate to the human animal, a love of truth so great that any distortion, bias, or withholding of information from another human causes such psychological distress that, regardless of the other results, there is always a net loss of utility to the possessor of information, then all potential exercises of power become uneconomic. There is no gain to me from any possible path selected by A that would compensate for my internal pain, knowing that I had not been wholly truthful. That must not be true only of me, but of all humans. It must be part of that invariable and universal utility function that Becker postulates as genetically and identically determined for all people at all times. There would seem to be, in world history, ample evidence to call into question an axiomatic presumption of an inviolable love of truth. Perhaps there is another way to banish power.

Uncertainty – a perfect social right to truth. If an interested party such as B is not prevented from using information strategicially by an internal love of truth, the presumed impossibility of other forms of power can be maintained only if there are external forces so preventing him. There must be a socially enforceable and perfect "right to truth." Then if B misstates, biases, selectively provides, or in any way alters A's stock of information such that A makes a wrong choice (a welfare-reducing one she would not have made had B not so acted), she would have a legal cause of action. Note that this needs to be a total right. Not just restricted to severe fraud, it must cover all forms of information alteration.

Moreover, for the right to be effective it must be enforceable at zero cost, or absolutely all costs of enforcement must be transferable to the violator of the right. If B can reduce A's lifetime welfare even slightly by the distortion of her information stock and it costs A anything to bring an enforcement action, then A is still harmed even if B must compensate her for the damage done by the distortion. Only if the measure of damages includes a complete and accurate assessment of overt legal fees plus lost time, psychological distress, and emotional trauma from the incident and the enforcement action is A able to be returned to a position independent of the exercise of power by B.

Of course, A must not only have the right to an enforcement action. She must be assured of winning or else the expected value of that right is diminished. That, of course, implies that the court, unlike the now ignorant actors, will be omniscient in the sense of the previous sections. It must be able to ascertain what the objective truth really is and was. Finally, all violators of this right to truth must always have sufficient assets to satisfy all of the perfect compensatory awards granted by this perfect and omniscient enforcer of the rights.

The special case, limiting all power to simple economic power on the basis of the productivity of power forms, implicitly requires either omniscience on the part of all actors or forces that create an inviolable devotion to truth by all. These conditions ensure one of two things. Either (1) she has all knowledge and her perception exactly matches reality, and she *knows* that it matches reality so that B cannot generate distortions, or (2) there is the possibility of inducing a distortion, but any gains to B will certainly be lost to the inescapable pain of guilt or the perfect and sure exercise of A's legal rights to truth. Clearly, the costs of attempting to use such power would be too high to justify any expected benefits. Power other than simple economic power becomes uneconomic. One of these conditions regarding the state of knowledge is necessary for the special case to hold. Neither is, however, sufficient.

The nature of events

An *a priori* limitation to simple economic power also requires implicit assumptions about the ability of actors to affect the events relevant to other actors.

Ungranted event power – a complete system of rights. There must, of course, be no ungranted event power at all. If anyone has an ability to decide the outcome of events that will affect me, I am subject to the whims or, better, the strategic decisions of that person. If I willingly grant the power, I am perhaps made better off by some combined series of events and exchanges; simple economic power could be at play. If, however, I did not choose to give the power, there can be no presumption that it is to my benefit. Ungranted event power must not be allowed. There can never be a "mud farmer" waiting for unsuspecting "reivers."

Thus the total elimination of ungranted event power requires as a first step the complete specification of rights to *everything*, that is, that there be no externalities. It is now standard in economic theory that externalities result from an imperfect or incomplete specification of property rights.[3] We must know *ex ante* who owns the rights to shade and sun, the rights to construct or obstruct, and the rights to breath air and view gardens. We must know who owns the rights to technological processes, name brands, collections of words, and fashion "looks." We must know who owns the rights to market shares, ocean resources, and good ideas. There can be absolutely nothing in which the total package of rights is not completely fixed. That is the first condition. It is not the last.

Ungranted event power – the creation of rights. The absence of complete property rights does imply event power, but property rights themselves are also a form of event power. If my neighbor has the clear right to construct a tall building and cast shadows on my garden, *she* is now in control of that event. Indeed, she has even greater power than before, since now she may rely on the forces of a larger society to enforce her right to control that event. I may, of course, attempt to buy the right from her, but if I fail, she may cause me harm whenever she wishes. The resulting allocation of resources may be efficient. It will not be free of power.

---

[3] The classic statement of this principle is to be found in Ronald Coase, "The Problem of Social Cost," *Journal of Law and Economics*, Vol. 3, October 1950, pp. 1–44. This whole topic is discussed in much greater deatil in Chapter 8.

The comprehensive system of rights necessary to eliminate externalities still contains the potential for ungranted event power unless the rights were themselves established by unanimous consent. No one must disagree, or that person will have been subject to ungranted control over an important event, the definition of rights. Pure democracy with a decision rule of unanimity must prevail. That consensus must, in turn, be reached without any exercise of power regarding the state of knowledge under which each individual decides on her vote. Each generation must unanimously and freely accede to the system of rights so established. Any change in rights must be unanimously agreed upon. Any and all losers of rights will, of course, have to be compensated for the total value of the rights lost, for that is the route of simple economic power. If this is not so, then those who control the events of defining and/or redefining property rights are themselves exercising a form of ungranted event power.

Ungranted event power – the enforcement of rights. Incompletely specified rights imply event power. Less than unanimous agreement on the form of rights implies event power. Fully specified and unanimously accepted rights are sufficient to eliminate all ungranted event power if and only if (1) those rights are themselves perfectly enforceable at zero cost to the party holding the rights, and (2) the party violating those rights is never "judgment proof." If I have the clear legal right to unobstructed solar rays reaching my land and you do, indeed, shade my garden with a structure or a tree, then I must be able to return completely to the lifetime utility that I would have experienced in the absence of your violation. That means that any compensation ordered via an enforcement process must be comprehensive and perfectly accurate. It must cover all costs to me including lost time, legal fees, and aggravation. It means that you must always be able to pay that full compensation. Should I "win" less than the total damage, I am due less than your action cost. I am a net loser. If I can collect less than I am due, I am again a net loser. If you can gain anything at all from the violation of my perfect property rights, it may benefit you to do so.

Only if a comprehensive set of property rights is established and unanimously agreed upon via a process that is itself wholly free of any power, *and* all of those rights are perfectly enforceable at zero cost to the holder, is it valid to assert that ungranted economic power will *always* be uneconomic to exercise. Only then can B never alter A's decision path by controlling events without first getting A's con sent, that is, by offering something to A to make it in her interest. The shape of the map is established via the comprehensive system of rights. B can do nothing to violate A's rights. B can do nothing to redefine the rights in a manner detrimental to A, for her consent is required for all changes in rights. Ungranted event power is, then, unproductive indeed. If event power remains, it can only be willfully granted event power.

Granted event power. This form of interaction arises whenever a person willfully gives to another an ability to control future events. It becomes just simple economic power when that right of control is exchanged for something more valuable to the subject of the new event power. In that case it is, by definition, part of a positive exercise of power, but if and only if the exchange itself meets certain conditions. It must, in short, be part of a perfect contract. The contract must be complete, unambiguous, and totally comprehensive. There must be no uncertainty in the terms of performance that one party could exploit. There must not be any unforeseen contingencies that alter the required performance of the parties. The contract must be formed with neither party subject to any influence or control over her state of knowledge by the other. The truth or omniscience conditions of the last section must hold.

Such total contracts must be negotiable at reasonable cost and must be perfectly enforceable at zero cost to the nonbreaching party. If complete contracting is prohibitively expensive, then contracts will be incomplete. If enforcement is not perfect and costless, then performance is not assured. Anything less means that, through oversight, the pressures of negotiating costs, the lack of care, the failure to anticipate all possible adjustments, or pure stupidity, one party may grant to another an ability to exercise negative power, to seek benefit at the expense of the subject of that power. Then the assumption of rational maximization requires that the shortcoming of the contract be exploited. If these conditions fail, then complex forms of ungranted event power are possible. Thus the conditions must be assumed fulfilled if such power is presumed uneconomic.

For simple economic power always to predominate, for all other conceptual forms of power to be inferior, then all of the rigid conditions regarding the state of knowledge must be fulfilled *and* the conditions regarding control over events must be met. The simultaneous acceptance of both sets of conditions is implicitly necessary for specification of the special case. Even this, however, is still insufficient.

The nature of values

Finally, preferences must be totally devoid of all human influence. The general utility function specified in (2.1) must be such that for all humans at all times all $\partial U_i / \partial S_i = 0$. The long debate over the content of personality as a reflection of nature or nurture, phenotype or genotype, must be implicitly resolved in favor of genetic determination. Somewhere on the DNA helix are genes that establish inviolable preference functions. At conception, the lifelong shape of the function is given. Others may, over time, alter the constraints within which choices are made, but the basic function is immutable.

Economics thus merges with the new field of sociobiology. Sociobiologists like David Barash and Edward O. Wilson argue that genetic matter actually can control behavior. Sea turtles upon hatching invariably go toward the ocean. Their behavior is not random and is clearly not learned. It must be genetically controlled. Salmon return to the specific stream of their birth with no instruction, conditioning, or learning. The behavior must be genetically controlled.[4]

How then are variations in behavior explained? Why do subspecies in different environments display different behavior? The variations do not arise from learned responses by individuals but by adaptive selection by species. Genes control behavior. Differing genes compete on the basis of the suitability of behaviors in differing environments. The best suited genes enjoy reproductive success and come to dominate. Marmots in high elevations of the Olympic range, for example, maintain complex social structures and interrelate with other adults in large family groupings. Their lowland cousins, however, display extreme intolerance among adults and never live in large groupings. The sociobiological explanation does not depend on differences in learned marmot "culture" but on population genetics. In low elevations with plentiful food, marmots who are genetically driven to expel their young are more successful in spreading throughout a region. The alpine marmots, in a much harsher environment, with the same "expelling gene" are likely condemning their young to starvation, to say nothing of reproductive failure. Thus the difference in behavior is interpreted as being adaptive. The offspring of genetically intolerant marmots are successful in low-elevation environments; the offspring of tolerant marmots are successful in alpine environments. The behavior of the animals becomes different in the two regions because

---

[4] For an interesting and readable treatment of the field of sociobiology see David P. Barash, *Sociobiology and Behavior*, Elsevier, North Holland, New York, 1978.

of the differential success of genetic variations controlling social behavior.[5]

These are controversial hypotheses. They become increasingly so as they are applied to animals of higher order. The controversy really heats up when they are applied to humans. For example, principles of sociobiology tend to support the adaptive advantages of sexual promiscuity and aggressiveness on the part of men and sexual selectivity on the part of women. Survival of the genetic material of males is made more likely by maximizing the number of offspring. Biologically capable of fathering vast numbers of children, there will likely be more surviving offspring of males who are promiscuous and aggressive. Women, on the other hand, who are biologically limited in the numbers of children they may bear, will be more adaptively successful if they concentrate on the quality of their children, that is, are highly selective in the males with whom they mate.[6]

In order to assume total independence of human values from social influence, it is necessary to assume that humans are like alpine marmots, and the behavior of both is ultimately determined by genes. If that is indeed the case, then any attempt to alter the preference functions of other human beings will be infinitely expensive, given the current state of DNA recombination technology. Then, no matter how high the possible gains to a potential exerciser of value power, it will always be economically foolish even to try. Human values totally precede social contact. They are unalterably formed long before birth.

There are extraordinary philosophical consequences to this special case. The world is then populated by people devoid of free will and personal responsibility. People are genetically compelled to maximize a genetically given preference function. Since they control neither the preferences, the external constraints, nor the drive for maximizing behavior, they in fact make no real choices at all. They are merely responding to genetic preprogramming. That is an extreme vision of human behavior, but one that must be adopted if value power is to be impossible. (Gary Becker's view is even more extreme. The sociobiologists allow for variability in genotype and for species adaptation in response to environment. Becker dictates identical and immutable preferences for all individuals, indeed, for the human species over all time.) If preferences can change then in a determinate world, they are changed by something, perhaps even other humans. That must not be allowed, or the special case cannot hold.

[5] Ibid, pp. 57–63.
[6] Ibid, pp. 289–296.

The special case restated

What, finally, is the implicit foundation of this special case? The exercise of all forms of power, other than mutually positive, simple economic power, will always be prohibitively expensive if and only if for every pair of actors,

- each has absolutely perfect knowledge so that neither is able to alter the stock of the other in any fashion, and each knows that her information is perfect, or
- each has exactly the same stock of incomplete information, the same basic intelligence, the same human capital stock, and thus no ability to alter or distort the stock of information of the other, or
- information is differently held and understood, but no one will ever mislead anyone else because human genetics dictates a total adherence to principles of truth, or
- any attempt to use unequal information access to alter the behavior of another to her detriment will be unsuccessful because there is a complete legal right to total truth from all other human beings in all contexts, and that right is always perfectly enforceable at zero cost to the subject of power,

and simultaneously,

- all property rights in all conceivable things, processes, ideas, and so forth, are absolutely established, and
- all rights were originally created by a power-free process of pure democracy with unanimous agreement, and
- all of those property rights are unchangeable except via the unanimous consent of all parties potentially affected, and
- all of the rights are perfectly enforceable at zero net cost to the holder of the rights, and
- all contracting is so perfect that it is infallible, and
- all of those contracts are themselves perfectly enforceable at zero cost to the parties to the contract,

and simultaneously,

- human preference functions are absolutely free of all social influences, that is, they are genetically determined and totally immutable once established at conception.

The special case requires not just one or two of these extreme conditions. It requires all of them to hold simultaneously. It would appear, thus, as an extremely narrow special case. The conditions fall little short of absurd. Of course, Friedman's famous methodological argument about the realism of assumptions might render that absurdity irrelevant if the sole purpose of the model were to predict choices.[7] Here (and in many other cases) that is not the sole purpose. Here I wish to ask questions about the nature of human relationships in markets not unlike the ones that concern Friedman in his political writings.[8] I seek answers to questions about the potential role of power in human societies interacting to generate the material things required to fulfill their combined needs. The assumptions of the special case dictate the answers. I cannot justify absurd assumptions if they, in turn, seriously restrict the range of possible conclusions.

When the question concerns the qualitative aspects of human relationships, would any serious inquirer be willing to seek general answers within the confines of this special case? Certainly economists never set forth such extreme conditions in explicit form. They would perhaps be embarrassed to do so. It is not uncommon, however, for them to build a model world based upon individuals with

- given and fixed preference functions,
- given initial endowments of factors, and
- perfect knowledge.

In that form the special case seems a bit less special. It seems exceedingly common. Yet those shorthand presumptions, so useful for generating predictive models of individual choice, are in fact the very set of restrictive conditions that make it such a narrow special case in an exploration of power. Indeed, the central case there is here the special case. It is narrow in the extreme. It has already assumed away all potential for power. To use the special case to search for power would, of course, be absurd. "Assuming that it cannot ever exist I shall now proceed to find that it does not exist."

The special case relaxed

Relaxing the assumptions of the special case does not, of course, prove the existence or extent of power. It merely permits an examination of the potential for power. Traditional economists have, from time to time, relaxed some of these conditions, yet when they have, two interesting characteristics seem to follow them in their explorations.

[7] Milton Friedman, *Essays in Positive Economics*, University of Chicago Press, Chicago, 1953, pp. 3–43.
[8] Milton Friedman, *Capitalism and Freedom*, University of Chicago Press, Chicago, 1962.

First, they tend to treat the relaxation as if it were the special case, for example, models that treat the acquisition of information as a costly process tend to speak as if that is an interesting deviation from the norm of perfect information.[9] Probably the converse is true. In my experience, at least, perfect information is clearly a deviation from the norm.

Second, having been trained within the confines of the special case as adapted to questions about the Stuff emanating from social inter- actions, they continued to ask only those questions. Property rights are considered in the context of the impacts on efficiency of resource allocation.[10] The word "power" is never spoken. When the model is extended to administrative and institutional structures as substitutes for markets, questions of resource allocation are central.[11] Stuff mat- ters; relationships between persons seem not to be seen.

I now have a workable definition of power; I have categories of power to seek. I have a model of human behavior that dictates that power will be sought and exercised whenever it is in the maximizing interest of an actor to do so. I have specified the special case conditions necessary to forbid all such power. It is time to relax those conditions and to look at the possible role various forms of power could have in a more general world, inhabited, not by the genetically controlled dei economici of the special case, but by less perfect economic humans. That is the content of Part III.

Before beginning, a word of warning is in order. Trade-offs are a normal part of the world as viewed by economists. The central analytic focus is how persons deal with them. It should come as no surprise, then, that trade-offs are also part of theorizing. The methodology chosen for this exploration of power focuses on conscious maximizing choice. It treats the exercise of power as a decision of "production techniques." In so doing, meaningful insights may be gained, but some forms of power may yet be hard to find.

This is a theory of power suited to exploring its more overt forms. It is suited to an examination of strategic decisions made by identi- fiable individuals seeking explicitly and intentionally to change the behavior of other identifiable individuals. This is particularly so in Chapters 5 through 8. Social influences that are not fully understood by the exercisers of power, or that are perhaps not fully intended, will be harder to find with this technique. Broad-based power, perhaps without clearly identifiable subjects or exercisers, will be difficult to

---

[9] For a full discussion see Chapter 5.
[10] For a full discussion see Chapter 7.
[11] For a full discussion see Chapter 6.

uncover. The base elements of the theory are persons rather than tribes, groups, or classes. It is only power exercised by those persons that can be well examined here. Only in Chapter 9, amidst a broader examination of value power, will I be able to shed any light on some of the more subtle, and covert, possible manifestations of power. This book is obviously not the final word, but it should be able to add substantially to the discussion.

PART III

Power and markets

CHAPTER 5

Information, uncertainty, and power

The knowledge of the circumstances of which we must make use never exists in concentrated or integrated form, but solely as the dispersed bits of incomplete and frequently contradictory knowledge which all the separate individuals possess. . . .

. . . in any society in which many people collaborate, this planning, whoever does it, will in some measure have to be based on knowledge which, in the first instance is not given to the planner but to somebody else, which somehow will have to be conveyed to the planner.

Frederick A. Hayek, "The Uses of Knowledge
in Society"

Ignorance and independence

In the modern world, each of us is dependent upon others to fulfill many of our needs and desires. The self-sufficiency of Robinson Crusoe may still be popular in first-year graduate school classrooms, but it has little relevance elsewhere. Contemporary "survivalists," fearing a coming conflagration, stock up on manufactured weapons and commercially prepared and preserved foods. They transport these items in commercially acquired vehicles over government funded roads to rural areas selected on the basis of their social character. No one can start from scratch and create any semblance of a modern standard of living. Society is, by definition, "social."

What we need from each other, however, is less a sharing of effort than it is a sharing of information, of technology, of simple know-how. Adam Smith's ageless example of the division of labor is, in fact, long out of date. He described a factory where the processes of drawing wire, cutting it, sharpening one end, attaching heads, and placing finished pins in papers all become separate functions performed by separate persons.[1] In that example, however, the individual workers

---

[1] Adam Smith, "Of the Division of Labor," *An Inquiry into the Nature and Causes of the Wealth of Nations*, reprinted in P. Newman, A. Gayer, and M. Spencer, *Source Readings in Economic Thought*, Norton, New York, 1954, pp. 123–125.

could easily move from one function to the next because there was
no presumption of specialized knowledge or skill required for any of
the tasks. Indeed, he presumed each task to be mindless and repetitive.
There may be little problem in having a wire cutter attach pin heads.
There might be serious problems in having a software engineer perform brain surgery. Different complex tasks require vastly different
knowledge. We simply do not know how to do each others' jobs. Given
an unlimited supply of willing slaves waiting only for my direction, I
could never recreate a modern society, nor could any other mortal.
The information required is simply too vast.

Consider a simple *gedankenexperiment*. What would I need to know
in order to create for myself the experiences of a single morning? I
am writing these words in a simple office. They are appearing on the
screen of a personal computer driven by a word-processing program.
All of this is made possible by the development of collections of tran-
sistors, miniaturized into tiny silicon chips. If my life depended upon
it, I could not make even the grossest approximation of one.

The computer itself is powered by electricity generated some miles
from here and transmitted over lines composed of metals. The metals,
in turn, are refined from various ores discovered and mined from
the earth and processed into fine strands. I would not know how to
begin to undertake such production. The lines are covered with in-
sulating material manufactured from a petroleum base that, in turn,
is discovered by complex processes of geologic exploration. The crude
is pumped from the earth and transported, often via special pipelines
dependent upon the vagaries of fluid dynamics, to special sites to be
processed. How, I do not know.

The computer sits on a desk made of various wood compositions,
including veneered plywood shaved from whole logs. The walls are
covered with paints made from materials gathered throughout the
world. There are also several photographs made possible by a chemistry I do not at all understand. My clothing is made of fibers and is
processed with chemicals I do not understand. I have taken a short
break to consume prepared foods that may have long-term implications for the biochemical processes of my life itself, but I do not know
what they are.

I transported myself in a plastic, metal, and rubber vehicle powered
by an engine composed of several exotic alloys. It burned a fuel manufactured from that peculiar raw petroleum I did not understand
before. I have no idea why some of it becomes plastic insulation and
some becomes gasoline. I have been interrupted by the ringing of a
telephone that transported speech across the North American con-

tinent, partially over wires and partially by microwave radiation systems. I have no idea how.

My dependence upon others in this world is not simply one of our agreeing to separate our efforts into components that each of us is equally qualified to perform. My dependence is because I am qualified to perform so very few of the functions. What we need from each other more than anything else is knowledge.

It is not simply conjecture that leads to such a conclusion. Several attempts have been made to estimate the proportion of the total economic activity in the United States devoted to the discovery and distribution of information and knowledge. Fritz Machlup's was the pioneering effort. He identified six different categories of economically significant operations or activities involving knowledge, that is, its transport, transformation, processing, analysis, interpretation, and original creation or discovery. Using an analysis of industrial activity, he aggregated the resource costs expended in the United States for each of those activities in the public and private sectors. Using data from 1957–1958 he estimated that 29 percent of all of the economic activity in the United States was devoted to discovering and distributing information. Nearly a third of all the resources in the country were expended to overcome the fact that neither any individual nor the system as a whole had "perfect information."[2]

In more recent years there have been attempts to update Machlup's aggregate analysis. They tend to argue that he understated the role of a need for information in structuring economic activity. Some estimates have approached 50 percent of the GNP.[3]

The exact proportion of resources so devoted is not really the issue. What matters is that, in modern society, information is obviously not perfect, that its acquisition is extremely expensive (or that we, totally irrationally, are expending up to half of our scarce resources on something that is freely available at no cost). The presumption of perfect information in the special case should be suspect as descriptively accurate.

[2] Fritz Machlup, *Knowledge: Its Creation, Distribution and Economic Significance*, 3 vols. (Vol. I issued under title, *The Production and Distribution of Knowledge in the United States*), Princeton University Press, Princeton, N.J., 1962, 1982, 1984. The GNP share estimates are found primarily in Vol. I., Chapter 9, pp. 348–376.

[3] Cf. Marc Uri Porat, *The Information Economy*, Vol. I, *Definition and Measurement*, U.S. Department of Commerce, Office of Telecommunications, Washington, D.C., 1977, and Michael R. Rubin and Elizabeth Taylor, "The U.S. Information Sector and GNP: An Input-Output Study," *Information Processing and Management*, Vol. 17, 1981, p. 164. Machlup was planning to issue revised estimates at the time of his death, and posthumus publication has been promised by others on his research team. As of this writing they have not appeared.

When that assumption is relaxed, no one then acts on the basis of an "objective decision tree." We move instead through mappings defined by our *perceptions* of trees, which in turn depend upon the information that we do have. If that stock of information is in any sense socially affected, then so also is our subsequent behavior. Relaxing the implicit assumptions of omniscience or a perfect right to truth would seem to open the door to power. Even though economic theory occasionally opens that door, it seldom recognizes the intruder on the doorstep.

The economics of information and uncertainty

There is a large and growing literature on the economics of information, but it is a literature with a very strong and peculiar bias to it. It considers only half of the relevant issues. In his study Machlup defines a classification scheme for work in the economics of information.[4] He "finds" seventeen separate subspecialties of economics concerning decision making with incomplete and imperfect information. It is even interesting that thinking of economic behavior as if information is not a free good should be considered a realm of subspecialties. Why, one might ask, is not analysis of perfect information-based behavior considered the special case and ignorance considered the normal one?

Almost without exception, the concern of the analysts surveyed is the behavior of the decider who must operate without complete information. There is virtually no mention of any strategic behavior on the part of the possessors of information or other interested parties wishing to take advantage of that ignorance for their own ends. He provides a sample bibliography of work classified within his scheme of subcategories. The bibliography covers some sixty-four pages with approximately 400 total entries. Of that number there are perhaps two which deal with the strategic responses of interested parties to someone else's uncertainty or ignorance.[5] That is nothing short of astonishing. It indicates a continued *assumption* that people do not act on other people; they merely transact with them. These analyses of incomplete information seem to follow one of two branches. The first assumes individuals who are capable of globally rational decisions but are unable to acquire information costlessly.[6] Persons have an unlim-

---

[4] Machlup, *Production and Distribution Knowledge*, Chapter 10, pp. 313–334.

[5] Ibid., Chapter 11, pp. 335–402.

[6] For a survey of this literature see J. Hirschleifer and John B. Riley, "The Analytics of Uncertainty and Information – An Expository Survey," *Journal of Economic Literature*, Vol. 17, December 1979, pp. 1375–1421.

ited capacity to hold and process information, but the act of acquiring uses up scarce resources. Maximizing strategy thus dictates acting with some degrees of ignorance. The capacity for omniscience is unfulfilled because of the cost of acquiring data.

The second approach assumes individuals who are mentally unable to process unlimited quantities of data and hence are restricted to limited information on the basis of their own capabilities, that is, it assumes "bounded rationality." Individuals act with imperfect information because they are simply unable to hold and process very much of it. Past some point, even costlessly acquired data has no value because there is simply no "room" for it. Each approach is interesting in its own right. Each recognizes the significance of actors operating with varying degrees of ignorance as the normal state of economic affairs. Each has been primarily used to consider the resource allocative efficiency implications of imperfect information. Neither has been much used to explore the implications for the exercise of power.

Global rationality with costly information

Risk and uncertainty. A rational individual who is truly omniscient, who knows all of the characteristics of all possible options, who knows with certainty what events the future holds will, of course, always make the right choice. A decision maker who does not know all may make the wrong choice. Economic theory distinguishes between two forms of imperfect information, "risk" and "uncertainty."[7] With risk I may know the likelihood of storms, but I cannot know the weather next week. "[T]he individual chooses among acts, while Nature may metaphorically be said to 'choose' among states."[8] Once the probability is fully known, I can only await nature's "choice."

"Uncertainty," on the other hand, refers to a lack of complete information. More data collected in the present may reduce (or increase) the degree of uncertainty about future events. More data will not reduce risk, though I may have uncertainty about the degree of risk associated with a particular action. If I do not know the chances of a winter storm in the pass through which my load of fruit must go, I can reduce the uncertainty by acquiring information about the probabilities of various kinds of weather. I cannot, however, reduce the risk by acquiring more information.

I may, however, also be uncertain about wholly determinate events,

[7] Cf. ibid.
[8] Ibid., p. 1377.

that is, ones without any risk. Contemplating an increase in my price, I may be concerned about the response that will be forthcoming from my oligopolistic competitors. However, their response is not a chance event. My inability to predict the response is due to a lack of complete information about their situations, motivations, and chosen strategies. With real omniscience I could know how they would respond prior to their response. Recall the discussion in Chapter 4 of the term "probability" used to define the outcomes of what are really determinate events in the control of other actors. The problem there was really one of uncertainty rather than risk. True risk should be a fairly rare element in social interactions among rational maximizers. Uncertainty should be common.

The rational response to risk and uncertainty. Faced with imperfect information, the literature prescribes either "terminal acts" or "informational acts" (sometimes called "search behaviors"). The former establishes decision rules to be made in the face of risk, that is, it deals with adaptation to unavoidable risk. The latter, concerned with overcoming the problems of uncertainty, defines optimal strategies for seeking more information and for terminating search when it ceases to be efficient. Both lines of analysis focus on the behavior of the party making the choice under consideration, rather than the potential for another party to exploit that lack of information. The behavior of a potential subject of power is commonly examined. The behavior of potential exercisers is not. With true risk, in which nature "chooses" among states, power is rightly ignored. When the choice is made by humans, such oversight is dangerously distorting.

When uncertainty is recognized, the search literature defines optimal strategies for overcoming it. Actors engage in "search," acquiring bits of information sequentially as long as the costs of doing so are justified economically. The process implicitly views information as an unowned resource waiting patiently to be acquired by whomever is willing to pay the costs. Information is like a large pile of sand. Search is a process of making sequential trips with a bucket, gathering seemingly undifferentiated increments of data. There may be different probabilities of acquiring different bits of data or messages, but these probabilities seem not to be the result of strategic actions by other actors. Nature again "chooses." The issue under consideration is the optimal search by the decider, not the optimal alteration by someone else of the probabilities of the decider's acquiring different bits of data. The optimal search typically ends when the marginal benefit from an additional trip equals the marginal cost. The typical analysis ends when the optimal search does. The content of information acquired is in the hands of the searcher and perhaps chance events. It is an individual rather than a social phenomenon.

Social problems with the response – adverse selection. Occasionally analyses admit to the possibility of power, though often it is an unconscious admission. Consider George Akerlof's "adverse selection," or "lemons," problem. When, in a market, there is a range of quality but only the average quality is known and knowable by buyers prior to the transaction, owners of better than average items will be unable to realize premiums for those especially good things and will not be willing to sell. Owners of lower quality goods will have a strong incentive to sell, especially if they can get a price equal to the value of the average item. As a result, the best items are kept off the market and Akerlof describes a used car market of this type as "the Market for 'Lemons.' "[9]

It is interesting that even here, when power seems to leap off the pages to someone interested in seeing it, Akerlof seems to have little awareness that he has introduced such a phenomenon. As a traditional economist writing in a prestigous journal, he seems concerned only with the traditional efficiency questions. He notes in passing, in an almost parenthetical clause, that of course "dishonest" use of information can hurt those cheated but stresses that the real problem is that "dishonest dealings tend to drive honest dealings out of the market."[10] In other words, the final outcome is not Pareto optimal. That of course is true, but it is also a market in which the relationships between the trading parties is not the mutual gain of traditional theory.

Adverse selection has now found its way into analysis of insurance markets. If the insurer is unable to tell with certainty who are the good risks and who are the bad and the insured parties are better able to tell, then charging premiums equal to the average risk of the whole potential pool could induce more poor risks to buy than good ones. The biasing of the insured pool relative to the total population creates solvency problems for insurers.[11]

---

[9] George A. Akerlof, "The Market for 'Lemons': Qualitative Uncertainty and the Market Mechanism," *Quarterly Journal of Economics*, August 1970, Vol. 84, pp. 488–500.

[10] Ibid., p. 495.

[11] Cf. Richard Zeckhauser, "Medical Insurance: A Case of the Tradeoff between Risk Spreading and Appropriate Incentives," *Journal of Economic Theory*, March 1970, pp. 10–26, for example.

Social problems with the response – induced demand. There is, finally, a growing literature in the field of medical economics that also recognizes the power potential of technical experts who must make decisions for consumers. That literature is important and will be discussed in a few pages. It is important to note how special the case seems, however. It is a small subtopic in a specific subspecialty. It is even too specialized to appear in the bibliography of Machlup's three-volume survey. It is too special to be treated in microtheory textbooks.

Bounded rationality

The concept of bounded rationality. There is a locally famous engineering course at Stanford. At its conclusion each student is required to design and build a device to meet the performance specifications set forth by the professor. One year the requirement was to build a device to move, under its own power, up, across, and then down a piece of tubing in the shape of an inverted U. The day of demonstration was the cause for the fame. It always provided good theater. It had moments of high tension and always of surprise. No two devices were ever alike. One student had devised an electric-powered device with inside facing wheels set at an angle. The device crawled over the arc in a long spiral. Another student had devised a spring-powered, two-pieced, hinged vehicle that crawled across like an inchworm, first advancing the front and then drawing up the rear. The most extraordinary device was also the most simple. One student presented a simple balloon and some type of clip. He blew up the balloon, attached it to the tubing with the clip, and let go. As every three year old has learned to his delight, the device quickly traversed the required course, sounding the student's salute to the hours of labor his colleagues had expended on their more complex creations.

Each student was surprised by the solution to the problem proposed by the others. No student carefully considered each possible option, evaluated the payoffs to each, and selected the best. Each began seeking a solution and, for unexplainable reasons, each came upon a different one. But each discovered solution was "good enough," and at that point energy went to developing the discovered option rather than seeking superior ones. Even after a full course of instruction, with the same material, emphases, and exercises, each choose from only a few small branches of a much larger potential tree. They were simply unaware of the rest of the possibilities. They seemed not to behave as the model of Chapter 3 would predict.

Perhaps this process of limited decision making is common. Indeed, the second main approach to imperfections in information makes bounds on decision behavior its crucial assumption. It begins by drawing upon psychological literature that, in turn, argues that the human brain has a limited data processing capability. Studies indicate that some maximum number of "items" may be held in a human brain for simultaneous contemplation. Beyond that point, the addition of another item requires the forgetting, eliminating, or burying of one of the previous ones.[12] Humans cannot consider an entire decision tree for anything less than a very small decision. Life-scale decision trees are totally incomprehensible. Humans, in this view, are simply incapable of such global calculation and data management.

Herbert Simon considers a complete, global decision tree for something as simple as a game of chess. Here there are a finite number of discrete moves available at each point. Rules strictly define the limits of that choice set. Each move follows a set of discrete prior moves. All options available to an opponent are clearly specified. There is a single well-defined objective or payoff and a clear and distinct start and finish to the entire mapping. What results should be a complete and clearly specifiable decision tree. Simon notes, however, that such a tree will have approximately 10^{120} discrete branches to consider.[13] Not even the greatest chess master is capable of holding and processing that much data. It defies the capabilities of the human brain. What then are the chances of dealing with the complexity involved in living a life with far more options and far fewer clearly defined rules?

Failure to accept the limits of human capabilities leads, in this vision, to simply silly results. Suppose I were to prescribe the "optimal" defense policy in face of impending nuclear attack. My solution would be to have all Americans immediately induce psychic-powered transmigration of their bodies, relocating themselves at a velocity many times the speed of light to a distant planet capable of supporting human life. In the parlance of the television classic "Star Trek," we would all "beam ourselves up," just in the nick of time. This would unquestionably be an effective defense. The fact that it defies all known physical laws is its one drawback. The global rationality of

---

[12] Cf., for example, Kenneth Arrow, *The Limits of Organization*, Norton, New York, 1974, esp. Chapter 2, or several of the works of Herbert Simon collected in *Models of Bounded Rationality*, MIT Press, Cambridge, Mass., 1982, esp. Vol. II. J. Holland et al., *Induction*, MIT Press Cambridge, Mass., 1987.

[13] Herbert Simon, "Theories of Bounded Rationality," in C. B. Radner and R. Radner, eds., *Decision and Organization*, North Holland, Amsterdam, 1972, pp. 161–176, see esp. pp. 165–171.

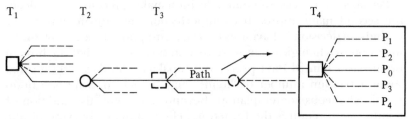

Figure 5.1. Decisions under bounded rationality.

conventional homo economicus is only slightly less in violation of all we know about physical laws. The proponents of bounded rationality feel that the difference is sufficiently slight that basing economic theory on global rationality is not much different from basing defense policy upon my proposed solution.

Bounded rationality and decision trees. Boundedly rational actors do not fit as well into the formal models of decision trees. They plan less and react more. Unable to perceive and manipulate complex trees, they are more likely to wait for events to develop that then compel some forms of reaction. They are unable to map extensive trees *ex ante*; they wait for particular branches to be revealed to them by unfolding events. They respond *ex post*. The response, rather than being globally rational, is more likely to reflect a sequential search for a solution, and the search will stop whenever a path that is simply good enough is discovered. There may well be, indeed probably will be, superior paths somewhere else, but boundedly rational actors simply cannot keep looking and analyzing. These actors satisfice rather than maximize. They do not fulfill the dictates of formal theory because they cannot. They do what they can. It is significant that Howard Raiffa, one of the major names in decision theory, notes that when he has been in major real-world decision situations, he has seldom been able to perform as his own theory would prescribe. He found that "simple, back-of-the-envelope analysis was all that seemed appropriate."[14]

Figure 5.1 is an attempt to compare boundedly rational behavior with globally rational behavior. Starting at the present, time T_1, the actor picks a path, not from among all possibilities, but from a limited

---

[14] Howard Raiffa, *The Art and Science of Negotiation*, Harvard University Press, Cambridge, Mass., 1982, p. 3.

subset. (Solid lines indicate choices under consideration. Dashed lines indicate choices that exist but are unknown to the decider.) Everything to the right of time T_2 is largely unknown and unanticipated. A path will be chosen and followed until unexpected events force a reconsideration. There may later, for example, at time T_3 be potential decision points when our subject could alter his path. However, absent external shocks, he will pass through those points with no concern for potential alterations in behavior. They were unanticipated before. They are unnoticed now. It will simply be business as usual according to standard operating procedure.

Future (and perhaps unanticipated) chance events may bring the decider into the area of the box at time T_4. The nature of the event outcome acts as a stimulus that causes a response in the form of a chosen change in path. The need to chose was not anticipated back at T_1. The presence of a decision node at T_4 did not become apparent until the decider actually reached T_4. Even then, the full range of options is not known. There are pictured four new paths, and all are assumed superior to continuing on the current path, whose payoff is denoted as P_0. They are not all equal, however. It is assumed that $P_1 > P_2 > P_3 > P_4 > P_0$. With global rationality all would be considered and P_1 would be chosen. In a model of bounded rationality, all will not be considered and evaluated. The stimulus will call forth search for a better option but not necessarily for the best. Once any one of these routes has been found and evaluated as good enough, the search ceases and the new route becomes standard operating procedure until new external events cause new choices to be made. Note, then, that the order in which the new options are discovered determines the new path that will be chosen. Any shaping of the subset under consideration will affect the choice made.

Power and the economics of information

Reading this literature with power in mind, the potential for its exercise seems to leap from the pages at every turn. Of course, ignorant people with limited capabilities of understanding the world may, at times, be prime candidates for manipulation by others. Yet it seems not to have occured to the authors to consider those implications of their work. They have abandoned the rigid form of the special case but have unknowingly maintained its restrictive focus. Historians of science often quarrel over the date of discovery of a crucial thing or fact. Scientists were able to isolate oxygen long before they recognized it for what it was. Discovery requires recognition.[15] The theory discussed here is in much the same state. Analysts of the economics of information have introduced power everywhere. Little recognized, however, it remains largely undiscovered.

Both of these special areas of theory leave us with actors struggling to overcome ignorance and limited knowledge of the choices and events that will shape their lives. They must navigate without perfect maps and with imperfect compasses. The choices they make will not be based on complete and perfectly specified decision trees. They will be made on the basis of *perceptions of segments of trees.* Any potential exerciser of power who can alter the nature or perception of the segment in contemplation can alter the behavior of the decider. If it is not prohibitively expensive to do so, the exerciser must. Only the special case of omniscience or a perfect right to truth clearly eliminates all such potential.

Incomplete information as potential for power

Both branches of the economics of information open the way for power of all forms to be exercised. Simple economic power is of course admitted. So also are the others. In this chapter I focus on the most overt exercises of power, that is, those with clear individuals exercising and subject to power. There is a literature associated with names such as Jon Elster and Timur Kuran that looks at broad social influences on basic values and preferences.[16] This literature suggests that the separation of persons into "exercisers" and "subjects" may be difficult, that the roles may overlap, and that power may be even more pervasive. Such forms are of crucial concern in a comprehensive search for power, but examination of that more sophisticated concept is postponed until Chapter 9. Here I will look at the possibilities for more overt exercises of power consciously undertaken by identifiable individuals and directed at identifiable others.

Economic behavior under uncertainty

The first approach to uncertainty in economic theory, that is, a concern for acquiring data in sequential search, may easily result in power

---

[15] Cf. Thomas Kuhn, *The Structure of Scientific Revolutions*, 2nd ed., University of Chicago Press, Chicago, 1970.

[16] Cf., for example, Jon Elster, *Sour Grapes: Studies in the Subversion of Rationality*, Cambridge University Press, 1983, or Timur Kuran, "Preference Falsification, Policy Continuity and Collective Conservatism," *Economic Journal*, Vol. 97, September 1987, pp. 642–665.

if one small modification in vision is admitted. Rather than information being a pile of sand awaiting all comers, view it as a result of the expensive endeavors of human beings. It comes into being in the possession of specific individuals who, having invested in its acquisition, should not be expected to give it away in disinterested fashion. Certainly this vision fits more closely with Machlup's catalogue of human effort devoted to information activities. If information is owned, it will be part of the strategic arsenal available to agents preparing to engage in social interactions.

Suppose B has much of the information relevant to the choice A must make. B may be the producer of a product, a politician running for office, a student seeking a better grade, a child worried about a broken vase, or any number of other interested parties. If B is able to separate the information into that which is favorable to his ends and that unfavorable, then changing the relative availability or cost of each should alter the composition of the stock of information upon which A will make her choice.

Some information may be hidden. Governments may classify it. Business firms may deem it proprietary. It may be withheld. Some information may be offered to others at subsidized rates. Advertising copy is generally selective in the information it offers. Some may even be expensive to avoid. Large billboards along my route home provide information I can avoid only at some inconvenience to myself. Commercials at a "time-out" with only seconds remaining in an important football game are hard for consumers to avoid. Indeed, the rising importance and success of the thirty-second political ad on television may be attributable to the fact that they can get across a "message" before the audience has the time to escape.

In an earlier book I called this the blind-date principle. My cousin is coming to town and would like a date for the weekend. I supply you with information that he has a spectacular personality, an exceptional sense of humor, and gorgeous, deep blue eyes. I neglect to mention that he has three of them, travels on a motorized pogo stick, and has several highly communicable diseases. By intentionally biasing the stock of information I can lead you to make a choice you might not have made in the absence of my persuasion. I have changed your behavior. I have affected your lifetime utility (in this case presumably negatively). I have exercised power.[17]

---

[17] A more detailed exploration of this blind-date principle, complete with graphs and an occasional equation, can be found in R. Bartlett, *Economic Foundations of Political Power*, Free Press, New York, 1973, Chapter 2.

Power with bounded rationality

If bounded rationality holds, that is, if persons can process only a small amount of information, if they continue along a path until pushed to change by external events, and if they adopt new paths in response to a satisficing strategy that depends upon the order in which they discover options, then there are three ways for power to be exercised. First, information could be used to alter the content of the body of data under contemplation. If I can determine what information you will have, I will help shape your limited perceptions of your decision tree. Second, information could be used as part of external pressures to force change. Boundedly rational deciders respond to external events, but they do not have complete information as to what those events are. External information can shape perceptions of reality as well as options. Third, it could be used to alter either the order or the valuation of responsive options discovered. Socially controlled information may affect the order in which good enough alternatives will be found. It can help to determine the *perceived* payoffs from options discovered. The potential for power is large.

Incomplete information and forms of power

Simple economic power. Occasionally a blind date turns out to be wonderful. Influencing the stock of another's information may sometimes be part of simple economic power. Announcement of a superior alternative to or a better price for a product clearly allows A to take a better path. Subsidized information (advertising) that emphasizes particular characteristics or quality advantages of certain items or brands may help consumers reach better decisions. It is interesting that there has developed a real, "respectable" literature on this area of influence in economics. There are analyses of "signaling," that is, giving consumers information on quality differentials. There are analyses that argue that the types of information that will be effective vary according to the nature of the product. All of these are, of course, power that is positive for both exerciser and subject.[18]

Decision control power. Altering the stock of information might become negative power for the subject. If the information subsidized is inaccurate, highly biased, selective, or even fraudulent, A may be

---

[18] See, for example, Phillip Nelson, "Advertising as Information," *Journal of Political Economy*, July/August 1974, pp. 729–754.

harmed. If the information withheld is important, the power may be negative. Providing free, but false information on a new vitamin-based cancer cure, thus delaying other forms of effective treatment, is clearly negative in terms of lifetime welfare paths. So is withholding information on possible toxic side effects of other treatments.

A crucial element in a current choice is the perception of future chance events, outcomes, and probabilities. Information about those often comes from other persons. They may be able to create inaccurate perceptions, and the inaccuracies may be long lived. As a simple rule, those engaged in low-cost repeat transactions without long-term consequences can minimize information distortions at fairly low cost via experience. Nonrecurring transactions, or ones in which the experience is itself difficult to evaluate, create a greater potential for significant and noncorrecting negative power to be exercised. In a case of unnecessary surgery, the patient will have absolutely no way of ever discovering whether she would have been better off without the hysterectomy. The motorist crossing the desert at 3 a.m. will never know if the fan belt replaced at the urging of the gas station attendant at the last fill-up was indeed defective (or indeed whether the "nicks" in it were there before the attendant's inspection). What would have happened if a different choice had been made? She will never know.

When the future "event" is in fact a future decision to be made by another person, the potential for decision control power via altered perceptions of the relevant tree should be clear. If B somehow leads A to believe that the chances of promotion are really quite good when B knows that he has never promoted a woman before and does not really expect to now, A may elect employment with him. With accurate information as to B's likely future behavior she might well have followed another path.

Agenda power. If the perceived tree varies from the objective, then actions that shape the perceived agenda are power. It may be positive power. It need not be. Under situations of bounded rationality and satisficing, any ability to affect the order in which good enough options are discovered is an ability to affect the choices that will finally be made. If the action substitutes a path barely good enough for one that would have been optimal, that action is an exercise of negative power. The *Wall Street Journal* recently reported on a series of recruiting practices in Japanese labor markets. Highly structured and seasonally limited, one of the tactics reportedly used is "taking hostages." Prime job candidates are required to spend days, at company expense, on special events such as trips to Tokyo Disneyland. The purpose of these extras is not to entertain, nor to acquire further information about job candidates, but to isolate those candidates from contact with other companies and other job offers.[19] The action changes the options under consideration on the decision trees of the candidates in favor of the choice the companies wish them to make. Because of the long-term nature of Japanese employment and the rarity of intercompany shifts, the impact of these alterations in the agenda may have significant lifetime consequences.

Event power. With imperfect information, one is not only uncertain of what may come to be but may also be uncertain about what has happened. As events unfold, what matters from the perspective of current choice is not what did happen, but what the decider perceives to have happened. To the extent that B can shape, via the use of information, what A thinks has happened, B has actually changed the character of the relevant events. It is again power that may be either positive or negative.

Value power. Deciders may not only be dependent on human sources of information for their perceptions about what has happened (or will happen). They may also be dependent on others to value specific outcomes. What is to be in fashion each year depends upon the actions of designers, the selections of critics, and the dissemination of that information to a larger public. Those seeking to evaluate the fashion "worth" of a particular item find that their payoffs reflect the information provided to them by others.[20]

On a grander scale each society expends large amounts of time, effort, and resources instilling in each generation an appropriate collection of political values. Conscious formation of political preferences is a significant part of all societies. Colleges are given substantial grants from rich alumni on the condition that they may be used to support lectures and a chair to promote free enterprise. Children in China are given substantial instruction in the advantages of socialism and the failings of capitalism. Given the extraordinary amount of resources devoted to such "instruction" in all modern societies, either they are all behaving irrationally, that is, wasting resources, or there are, in fact, real impacts on the political values of populations.[21] Con-

---

[19] E. S. Browning, "Interviewing for a Job in Japan Can Include Being Held Hostage," *Wall Street Journal*, September 10, 1985.

[20] G. Stigler and G. Becker, "De Gustibus non Est Disputandum," *American Economic Review*, March 1977, pp. 76–90, esp. Subsection V.

[21] See Bartlett, *Economic Foundations*, esp. Part IV.

trol of information and the exercise of value power deserve further elaboration. In Chapter 9 they receive it.

Factors affecting the potential for power

Imperfect information creates opportunities for the exercise of all forms of power. When information fails, simple economic power loses its clear monopoly as the sole form of interaction in markets. It is not, of course, clear that other forms of power are more important, or even that they are commonly used. As with all techniques of production, the optimal choice depends on the conditions of a specific situation. As an economic system develops, however, certain characteristics of market situations should have a tendency to increase the efficiency of other forms of power relative to simple economic power.

Delegated choices and the role of experts

In a technologically complex society there are a number of choices that cannot be made intelligently without a vast store of background data and understanding. Single choices may occur rarely but be of great significance when they do. The decider could attempt a hurried acquisition of all necessary knowledge, make a random choice, or choose to delegate the choice process to another person who has, or may have, the background necessary to make the right decision. If the expert to whom the choice is delegated has any interest at all in the outcome that would diverge from that of the decider, then rationality could dictate the exercise of power beyond simple economic power.

Consider medical care as an example. A patient experiencing chest pains and concerned about the implications might wish to diagnose the cause and find a treatment. He would, of course, first have to know what kind of raw data he should acquire to aid in the diagnosis. After substantial investment of time and perhaps money he might conclude that a certain battery of tests would help discriminate between various potential causes. He could, at least conceptually if not legally, "buy" the tests and the information associated with them. This would provide him with such things as a printed tracing from an electrocardiogram, the results of laboratory tests to determine cardiac enzyme levels in his blood, and perhaps x-ray pictures of his chest cavity. He would then, of course, have to undertake studies to understand the significance of the raw data. What does it mean to have a creatinine phosokinase blood level of 376? What do the peculiar wiggles on the EKG tracing imply? Are deep Q waves and elevated s-t segments significant? He might then decide to "buy" an echo cardiogram to see if any segments of his heart move paradoxically, of course having first discovered what all of that means. If the pains were, in fact, evidence of a current heart attack, he might find inconvenient the extensive investment in time and learning necessary to complete the diagnosis.

Alternatively he could leave the decision of which types of raw data to gather and the interpretation of their results to an expert, the doctor, with years of specific training in precisely such a technical area. There is little question that in complex areas it is often far more efficient to rely upon the specialized skill of an expert.

A potential for power arises, however, when experts have a personal interest in the outcome of the decision. If the doctor has a financial interest in the lab, has open spaces on the surgical calendar that are not contributing to revenues, or has other concerns, then she has an incentive to make choices for patients on other than purely medical grounds. This is not meant to impugn the character of doctors. I have the highest regard for them. I married one. It is merely an element in consistently applying the assumptions about human behavior adopted previously. Doctors are assumed not to be worse than the rest of us, but they are not assumed to be better either. This "doctor-induced demand" hypothesis is, of course, not new. For several years it has been subject to a good deal of discussion in the medical economics literature. In fact, it is one of the very few areas in which power strategies (though the term is not used) are ever discussed in the confines of neoclassical analysis. It seems to be regarded as something of a curiosity rather than an example of a phenomenon with a wider possible application.

It is not even agreed that it exists in the medical field. Some evidence indicates that it is important.[22] Other evidence indicates that it is not.[23] It is not my purpose here to resolve the issue once and for all. I cannot. What is significant is that highly trained public health profes-

[22] Cf., for example, Joseph P. Newhouse, *The Economics of Medical Care*, esp. pp. 55–61, or Joseph P. Newhouse, "The Demand for Medical Care Services: A Retrospect and Prospect" in J. van der Gaag and M. Perlman, eds., *Health, Economics, and Health Economics*, North Holland, Amsterdam, 1981, pp. 85–102, or Victor R. Fuchs, "The Supply of Surgeons and the Demand for Operations," *Journal of Human Resources*, Vol. 13, supplement, 1978, pp. 35–56.

[23] John P. Bunker and Byron W. Brown, Jr., "The Physician-Patient as an Informed Consumer of Surgical Services," *New England Journal of Medicine*, May 9, 1974, pp. 1051–1054.

sionals and econometricians are not sure if the treatment prescribed for particular patients is, in fact, appropriate. If they cannot tell after the fact, then it is likely that many patients are unable to tell *ex ante*. That is all that is required for a real power potential to exist.

Such power might also be used to serve a physician's legal security rather than his financial gain. There is at least anecdotal evidence of an increase in "defensive" medicine. As malpractice suits increase and average awards rise, doctors may insist on the most extensive diagnostic testing available even though it may not be medically indicated and may be expensive for the patient. In such a case the physician's interest is to overtest and perhaps overtreat to minimize his liability.

It does not matter whether all doctors engage in such demand-related alterations in treatment. It does not matter whether the average one does. What matters is that the presence of extreme technological complexity and the necessity of relying upon experts whose interests are not completely synonymous with those of the patient creates a situation of information-based power. Sometimes the exercise of power may be positive, but sometimes it may be negative. To conclude that because it involves a market, no power relation may ever arise between a particular doctor and a particular patient is what is unjustified. The issues must be joined. If they are rational, doctors will at times make choices distorted toward their own interests.

If the power potential exists for doctors as experts, then why not for auto mechanics, computer repair firms, investment counselors, real estate agents, college professors, Pentagon procurement officers, lawyers, dentists, architects, entymologists, and the myriad other experts who offer advice, perhaps linked with the sale of services?

As a society increases in complexity and generates more choices that must be made with the aid of expert advice, it simultaneously is increasing the role that can be played by the exercisers of power. When the main market choice is which bunch of carrots to purchase from stalls in the central square, the potential for negative power is minimal. *Caveat emptor* is sufficient to negate such power. When it is which set of long-term contracts will best provide for the health needs of retirement years, the potential for power based upon control of information has become more significant. It is simply impossible for the average buyer effectively to beware.

Complex processes and products

The industrial revolution has made everything more complex. In an era of self-sufficiency, products and production processes were of necessity relatively simple. Each consumer/producer understood the nature of production he undertook. Each could evaluate the quality of similar products produced by others. The very growth of technology that led to specialization and the transfer of most items to market-based, rather than own-based production, meant a lessening of the proportion of relevant information owned and available to buyers. Of course, sellers also have less information as to the needs and priorities of final users than was the case when people produced for their own needs.

As the complexity of products and processes increases there is an increasing asymmetry in the ability of parties to a transaction to evaluate precisely what it is that they are trading. As a result the potential for the exercise of all forms of power increases.

The content of food. As the last century was closing there was a basic change underway in the production and distribution of food to substantial portions of the U.S. population. Urban growth was shifting from medium-sized cities to a few truly dominant ones. Steel frames for tall buildings and the invention of the elevator permitted the development of vertical space. Intracity transit systems allowed a horizontal expansion, and the creation of electrical generating capacity freed manufacturing from geographically established sources of power. This also meant that neither self-sufficiency nor local production of food was any longer viable. Food processed, preserved, packaged in large-scale operations, and transported for a national market became the norm.

There were, undoubtedly, many advantages to this new system, but there was also a shift of power away from purchaser and toward producers. The information and knowledge necessary to evaluate the results of these new, complex processes was simply not available to the average consumer. Opening sample cans of various brands and subjecting them to detailed laboratory analysis prior to consumption was not a realistic option.

A number of processors took advantage of this potential for the exercise of power and provided selective information to consumers regarding the products offered for sale. Through mislabeling consumers were often induced to "select" paths through a decision tree that they would not have taken if the stocks of information upon which they based choices were not consciously manipulated by interested parties. Negative power was a common result.

Perhaps most of the losses in the food labeling situation were aesthetic. The appearance of an occasional rat in canned beef probably does not reduce the protein content or create a major hazard to health. The fact that the "wine" purchased was actually made from tannin and coal tar may not really harm the consumer. The fact that several heavily marketed tonics, often consumed in quantity by members of temperance societies, were in reality largely alcohol may not have caused physical harm. With other products, a lack of care in content may cause irreparable damage.

Elixir of Sulfanilimide. The development of new pharmaceuticals has been of unquestionable benefit to humans. Diseases that used to kill vast numbers of people have become minor inconveniences. But drugs offered for sale with implicit or explicit promises of effectiveness may also harm those taking them. Consider a tragic example.

In 1937 the Samuel E. Massengill Co. introduced a new form of the new "miracle" sulfa drugs. Produced and marketed as a solution to the problem of making antibiotics available for patients, especially children, unable to swallow pills, Elixir of Sulfanilimide was introduced. A product of the company's chief chemist, Dr. Harold Watkins, the drug was distributed throughout the country. The only flaw in the marketing strategy was that the dissolving agent, diethylene glycol, was highly toxic. Reports began to come in of children who died after suffering initially from strep throat, developing terrible pains and cramps, and suffering unrelieved for one to three weeks. One hundred and seven such deaths occurred before the last of the product was withdrawn from the market. (The Pure Food and Drug Administration was able to recall the product only because it was inadvertently mislabeled. "Elixir" implied the presence of alcohol and, as none was present, the administration was empowered to act on false-labeling grounds. It had no authority at the time to halt marketing of the drug simply because it was deadly.)[24]

It would seem that, had all information been available to the parents of those children, their choices might have been different. There was real negative power exercised across a market that was precipitated by inequality in information. It is not clear how much information Massengill actually had as to the toxicity of its elixir. At times it claimed to have undertaken clinical tests prior to distribution and other times it admitted a failure to conduct such tests. Massengill clearly concealed some relevant data, either that the solvent was toxic, or that no tests had been done to determine if it was.

---

[24] Cf. Charles O. Jackson, *Food and Drug Legislation in the New Deal*, Princeton University Press, Princeton, N.J., 1970, esp. Chapter 7, pp. 151–174.

MER/29. In other cases there is clear evidence that drug manufacturers knew that a product was unsafe and chose to suppress that information, *also knowing that some parties would likely be harmed.* The classic case involves a drug with the commercial name MER/29. Produced by Richardson-Merrill, it was required to meet FDA testing regulations prior to marketing as an aid in the control of serum cholesterol levels. The regulations were partially a result of the Elixir of Sulfanilimide scandal. The FDA now required proof of safety and efficacy before a new drug could be marketed. Internal monitoring of test data yielded substantial evidence of severe side effects, but Richardson-Merrill employees chose to falsify the data presented to the FDA. Based on reported rather than actual data, the FDA approved the marketing of the drug. Richardson-Merrill then undertook a campaign to convince doctors (experts) of the advantages of this medication over others. The ads, needless to say, did not mention the negative data discovered in testing but hidden from the FDA. In use, however, over 500 patients taking the drug developed cataracts and various degrees of vision loss. In case after case, courts found that Richardson-Merrill had acted with dangerous disregard for truth and safety.[25]

This case obviously involves a complex exercise of information-based power. The decision to employ the drug was, in most cases, made by an expert (the prescribing physician) on the basis of information provided by other experts (the FDA) and interested parties (Richardson-Merrill). There are also complicating factors in terms of who knew what within the corporation. It is sufficient to note that as products or processes develop that are too complex for final consumers to evaluate effectively and efficiently, new power potential is in the hands of those able to perform the evaluation. If those parties are themselves interested in the outcome of consumer choices, they will on occasion exercise that power.

The Copper 7. Information-based power in markets dominated by complex products and processes need not be limited to the ultimate consumers of those products. Another case of alleged obfuscation of important data involves a form of IUD produced by G. D. Searle and Co. and sold as the "Copper 7." At the time of this writing the case is still under investigation and adjudication and hence the final determination is unclear. There is apparently strong evidence that Searle

[25] *Toole* v. *Richardson-Merrill,* 251 C.A. 2d. 689 and *Roginsky* v. *Richardson-Merrill,* 378 F. 2d, 832, are two of the important cases in this area. The example is also discussed in Christopher Stone, *Where the Law Ends,* Harper & Row, New York, 1975.

marketed the product under a claim of the incidence of pelvic inflammatory disease of less than 1 percent, while its own internal data indicated a rate as high as 3.4 percent.[26] There is evidence that the FDA and prescribing physicians were misled, to say nothing of patients receiving the device.

There were obvious negative utility impacts for those women exposed to a much higher risk of serious disease and sterility than they might have been willing to accept. There are less obvious potential losses as well. Monsanto subsequently acquired G. D. Searle & Co., buying not only its assets but also all of its potential legal liabilities as well. There is evidence that Searle withheld from Monsanto the same information it withheld from consumers, thus hiding millions of dollars of potential liabilities.[27] Negative decision control power may well have been exercised over the management (and stockholders) of Monsanto as well as over unsuspecting women and their physicians.

The Pinto. A final example of the potential for negative power is another spectacular case. In the testing stage of development of the Pinto, the Ford Motor Co. became aware that the design of the car created a real hazard for occupants in a rear-end crash. A protruding bolt would likely puncture the gas tank, which could easily lead to fatal fires following relatively minor collisions. Ford, in internal analysis, determined that this would result in 180 deaths by burning and an equal number of nonfatal, but serious burnings. Ford engineers estimated that preventing these deaths would require a modification costing approximately $11 per vehicle.[28] In other contexts the cost estimates for correction were $4 to $8 per car.[29] This was known at the very highest executive levels of the Ford Motor Co., yet they chose neither to correct the problem nor to notify buyers of the defect.[30] Nowhere in the company's ads for this car was there mention of the

---

[26] Bill Richards, "Monsanto Inherits a Problem in Searle," *Wall Street Journal*, October 28, 1985.

[27] Ibid.

[28] The earliest public revelation of the problems with the Pinto was an article in *Mother Jones*, entitled "Pinto Madness." Published in the September/October issue of 1977, pp. 18–32, it included the table from an internal Ford memo, entitled "Fatalities Associated with Crash Induced Fuel Leakage and Fires" (p. 24). The table concludes that the lives lost were of less value than the cost of correcting the defect.

[29] *Grimshaw* v. *Ford Motor Co.*, App. 174 *Cal. Rptr.* 348, p. 370.

[30] In Grimshaw, the jury was so affronted by what it considered wanton disregard for public safety that it initially awarded punitive damages of $125 million in this single case. On appeal the judgment was reduced to $3.5 million in punitive damages, but the appellate court found that the evidence overwhelming supported a finding of a conscious decision at the very highest levels of Ford to market the car, knowing of the fuel system defect.

real possibility of horrible death resulting from a minor rear-end crash because of a design defect. Knowing of the potential, some of the ultimate victims might still have chosen to accept the risk. Others, however, might not have.

Institutionally structured environments

Chapter 6 will explore some of the causes and implications of organizational forms of coordinating human behavior. It is an empirical fact that most of the production of these complex products takes place in response to administrative directions within organizational structures. People are employed in factories, offices, stores, schools, and farms. Unless their employment contract is absolutely comprehensive and completely enforceable, they must, in practice, delegate much of the responsibility for creating environmental conditions to others.

Unable to evaluate fully all of the conditions of the broad environment created by such institutions, those within them are dependent upon others to create acceptable situations. While it is relatively easy to tell when a local environment is noisy, it may be difficult to tell when it contains intolerably high concentrations of many toxic chemicals. It is very difficult to determine if the automatic sprinkler system will work under actual fire conditions. (Indeed, in a recent case a contractor was sued because he simply glued unplumbed sprinkler heads to the ceiling of a building.) It is hard to know if the structure in which you work (or live) is adequate to withstand a moderate earthquake. All of those are relevant questions, yet in most cases the information must come from parties who have a conflict of interest. No one quite trusts the description of a blind date. Life in any organization is partially a blind date.

Consider two illustrative anecdotes. They do not prove the pervasiveness of power. They demonstrate only the possibility of power. Reaching a conclusion about power in any other context requires an examination of the variables associated with that case.

Asbestos. As early as the 1930s top executives of the major firms producing asbestos became aware of serious health hazards for exposed workers. They responded with a conscious decision to withhold that information from the public and exposed workers. They did nothing to reduce risk or to warn those at risk. Control over the information meant an ability to change the lifetime welfare of other persons. The information could have been shared, and either compensating wages would have had to be paid or adequate precautions would have had to be undertaken. In either case, the costs to those who decided to withhold the information would have been high and the benefits low. There was a potential for negative power to be used; it was unquestionably exercised. Key executives both controlled important events and shaped workers' perceptions of those events.[31]

Murder in the workplace. A second case involves the Illinois company, Film Recovery System. Three executives of the company were found guilty of murder by a Cook Country judge in the early summer of 1985. The judge was convinced that the defendants knew that the manner in which they had organized production was exposing workers to toxic levels of cyanide and that they willfully concealed from employees the dangers they faced. The victim in the murder, a Polish immigrant with very little command of English and certainly no training in industrial engineering, chemistry, or medicine, was in no position to evaluate the risks and dangers created for him by decisions made at other levels of the organization. Unaware of what to bargain for and in a weak bargaining position, he could hardly have contracted for levels of safety at the time of his employment. Assuming that death by cyanide poisoning at age fifty-nine constitutes a reduction in the value of a lifetime utility stream relative to not so dying, there was an exercise of negative power. It will be hard indeed to devise a legal remedy that could now "make him whole."[32]

Responses to the exercise of power

Increased reliance on delegated decisions, increased complexity in products and processes, and increased organizational control of environments – all these act to increase the potential for the exercise of negative power. Markets, as such, offer no perfect defense against this evolving potential for power. Those subject to it, those who feel its negative impacts, if rational maximizers themselves, will act to escape its effects or to limit its exercise whenever it is economic to do so. Interference in markets, rather than being an introduction of

---

[31] There are a vast number of cases involving liability for manufacturers of asbestos. One of the significant ones which ultimately has been upheld on appeal is *Fischer* v. *Johns-Manville Corp.*, 472 A.2d 577. At trial the jury found willful concealment of information from employees and the public and awarded substantial punitive damages as a result. The New Jersey appellate court agreed that the evidence was conclusive that knowledge of the health dangers had knowingly been surpressed by key executives in the firm and the industry.

[32] Cf. *New York Times*, June 15, 1985.

power, may well be an effort to reduce levels of real power in unrestricted exchange.

As Albert Hirschman noted, an actor feeling a negative impact from some other person may either "exit" or raise his "voice" in protest. Which technique is chosen is, of course, a matter of the relative costs and productivity of the two in the particular situation.[33]

Exit – the market solution

Exit is the technique of expressing dissatisfaction in a competitive market. I discover that the milk you sold me is spoiled, and therefore I take my business elsewhere. That is incentive for you not to lose my repeat business by providing fresh milk. But exit loses its effectiveness if there are few good options or if repeat business was unlikely anyway. To take your business from the investment counselor who has squandered your hard-earned fortune with the stern warning that he will never do that to you again seems a bit weak. To tell the surgeon who unnecessarily removed most of your organs that you will never do business with him again makes for a weak exit. (If he removed enough, you may already have exited.) To tell the auto company whose poorly designed car burned your family to death that you will not buy from it any more seems ineffectual. To tell the employer who knowingly subjected your now dead father to fatal toxins in the workplace that he will no longer work under those conditions seems fairly mild. The fortune, the organs, and the family are already gone. They may not be taken again. Exit, to be effective, implies being able to cause future customers to exit before the negative power is exercised. Without the possibility of recurring damage to the same individuals, control is possible only if the damaged parties are willing to raise their voices.

Voice – the political response

In any political system it is possible for rational individuals to "produce" political influence. There are always ways to affect the political process.[34] Many such political developments may be viewed as responses to the development of new forms or degrees of power in evolving markets. The creation of new power in the national markets for processed foods at the end of the nineteenth century did not go unnoticed by those consuming the foods. The failure of exit as a limit

[33] Albert O. Hirschman, *Exit, Voice and Loyalty*, Harvard University Press, Cambridge, Mass., 1970.
[34] Cf. Bartlett, *Economic Foundations*.

to this power also became apparent. In a rapidly urbanizing environment, few could realistically return to the farm. They could not, themselves, evaluate the real content of packaged foods. They could not rely on the entry of pure food competitors since all firms' labels assured consumers of purity in the product. The relevant information to a market decision was all in the hands of one of the parties. That gave new power. Buyers sought to use the power of government regulation to alter this new power that the market had permitted.

They were ultimately successful, compelling Congress to pass the Pure Food and Drug Act of 1906. It is important to recognize the character of this political conflict. The passage of the act did not introduce power into markets. It merely changed the form and distribution. Technological change had granted new powers to the parties of an economic transaction, powers that were not simple economic ones.

Voice – the judicial solution

Much of the evolution in legal principles has been in response to evolutionary change in the forms of power arising in markets. Specific cases like those cited in the last section give rise to legal responses that act to alter, but not eliminate, the power exercised.

Medical malpractice. A physician, because of the necessary reliance on his judgment by patients, is given an inescapable legal duty not to abuse that trust. Should he damage the patient via unnecessary surgery or surgery done improperly he is liable for damages. That is certainly one limitation on the exercise of power by physicians. It raises the costs of using imperfect information to gain a market advantage. It does not eliminate it, however. First, of course, in the presence of insurance that is not experience rated, the actual costs to the power-exercising doctor are substantially reduced. Moveover, the threat of malpractice actions may result in overtesting and treating in the form of defensive medicine. The result is not physical damage but a higher than necessary medical bill. Limitations on one area of power exercise may in fact encourage its exercise in another.

The law increasingly recognizes the potential for experts to abuse their privileged positions (exercise negative power) and is establishing new forms of malpractice for different classes of persons to whom decisions are delegated. There are now malpractice actions of lawyers, therapists, and even clergy. Trust officers, investment counselors, and perhaps even real estate agents have varying forms of fiduciary duties. The power of the law is made to intervene to reshape negative power arising in markets.

Products liability. The increased complexity of products and of processes also has caused the law to redefine the duties of truth and care that it imposes on actors in a market. The classic principle of *caveat emptor* has fallen from judicial grace.

Not long ago the duty to provided a safe product was considered a contractual duty. If an injured person had not engaged in direct contract with the party responsible, there was no grounds for suit. It was that exact principle that gave rise to the common practice in the automobile industry of selling cars first to independent dealers who in turn transacted with the public. Thus isolated from direct dealings with consumers, the manufacturers were free of liability for injuries, even from defective products. There was power in markets unconstrained by law.

Courts' recognition resulted in a series of cases such as *McPherson* v. *Buick Motor Co.* (217 NY 382, 111 N.E. 1050) that restructured, not introduced, power. While Mr. McPherson was driving his new Buick down a clear road, the automobile suddenly collapsed when one of the wheels shattered. Mr. McPherson was thrown from the car (seatbelts having not yet been invented) and injured. He sued Buick, who argued that, because he had bought the car from a dealer rather than the manufacturer, Buick could not be held liable. Under established principles of law, Buick was correct, but the justices redefined the power by expanding the scope of obligation to all potential users of a product, regardless of contract relationships.[35]

Such laws may serve to affect the power in markets that arises from unequal access to important information. It will eliminate that power from active exercise only if the costs imposed by the law are always and everywhere prohibitive. The very fact that all of the examples in the previous section come from cases in which the damage was already done and courts were being used as the vehicle to discover the previously inaccessible information is evidence that the costs are not prohibitive. The Pinto was designed long after the McPherson case was decided. The data for MER/29 were falsified long after the law made it clear that it was illegal to do so.

---

[35] A larger discussion of the progression of cases creating a tort liability for manufacturers can be found in H. Berman and W. Greiner, *The Nature and Functions of Law*, 3rd ed., Foundation Press, Mineola, New York, 1972, Chapters 5 and 6.

Conclusions

There is a tendency to attribute to timeworn adages more than is their due. Compressing complex ideas into few words often results in distortion. "Knowledge alone is *not* truly power," for power connotes the presence of a social relationship between persons. In isolation knowledge is only productivity. *It becomes power only when other persons do not have it!*

As economic systems evolve and information increases in scope and complexity, as it is increasingly fragmented into the "dispersed bits" that Hayek noted in the quote opening this chapter, power enters. It enters whether or not markets are present. The rational individuals upon whom economic theory is based must be expected at times to exercise that power. Markets alone are no perfect defense. Indeed, many of the political and legal "interferences" with markets may be seen as responses to, rather than introductions of, power into economic relationships. Whenever knowledge is a scarce good, it confers potential power upon its possessors.

The subjects of that potential power may seek to escape its negative effect in still one more way. They may choose to replace market interactions with administrative structures, creating institutional relationships designed to overcome the worst effects of unequal access to important information. Administrative structures may be still another response to power. That possibility is examined in the next chapter.

CHAPTER 6

Power and organizations

The previous chapter opened with two quotes from Frederick Hayek on the problems of consolidating information from a multitude of sources. No system of coordinating human behavior into a coherent whole can proceed without mechanisms for gathering information on what is and dispersing information to others about what to do. Hayek and many others have concluded that the mechanism best able to do this is the market. Relative prices are summary statistics carrying an astonishing amount of information about market demands, costs, and technology. Indeed, the logic expressed in formal microtheory models leads to the unavoidable conclusion that markets are the most efficient means of structuring human effort. Decentralized decisions in response to these prices is proven to lead "as if by an invisible hand" to a socially optimal outcome.

That leaves a perplexing question, however. If markets are clearly better than all other alternatives, then why are they so little used? Most of the production in this world takes place under a system of administrative authority with hierarchical patterns of control. Goods may ultimately reach a market, but only after extended stays in organizations in which human behavior is coordinated by administration. This fact is often obscured in the specified drama of economic theory in which one important category of actors consists of business "firms," usually discussed as if they were individual entrepreneurs. To these mythical creatures are attributed the human characteristics of rational maximization. They are assumed to have fully specified goals and to adopt maximizing strategies.

On the surface at least, that description bears little resemblance to the administrative actors of the real world. General Motors is a real world firm. It is not a small concern. Its total output exceeds the GNP of all but a handful of the world's countries. It controls vast quantities of raw materials; handles some of its own shipping; produces automobiles, household appliances, locomotives, aerospace devices, and financial services. It shifts capital, labor, and other resources between countries and among uses on the basis of internal administrative directives. It is a structure related to markets but that is itself clearly not a market.

General Motors has no mind that can be said to be unwaveringly focused on profit. It has no mind in which complete data resides and in which the necessary calculations are made. In fact, it has no mind at all. It is a figment of legal and theoretical imagination to speak of it as a "person." It is, in fact, a collection of thousands upon thousands of individuals organized administratively. It is the result of a conscious decision to replace markets with these other structures. But why do such organizations exist if markets are clearly superior? How can they survive if market organized competitors could outperform them?

The economics of organizations

These questions have obviously not escaped notice by economists. There is a growing literature worthy of review. I shall not undertake an extended tour, however, but merely point out a few significant landmarks, paying them passing notice. Each, without noting it, has argued that organizations arise as means of controlling the kinds of power that were discovered in the last chapter. They all speak of the problems of "costs" in imperfect markets without emphasizing that these costs are under the explicit control of other human beings, that is, that they are power.

Ronald Coase and the costs of markets

In 1937 Ronald Coase asked "why coordination is the work of the price mechanism in one case and of the entrepreneur in another."[1] His answer was simple: "There is a cost of using the price mechanism,"[2] a cost seemingly arising through deviation from the special case of Chapter 4. Specifically, when there are imperfections in information and it is costly to overcome them, or when transactions and negotiations become costly, the market may become inefficient. This approach is at once a salvation of microtheory methods and a challenge to its conclusions. Markets are avoided as organizing devices for the best of all possible reasons, because they are at times inefficient. Rational maximizing choices are still the basis for human interactions. The outcome of market-coordinated behavior, however, will no

[1] Ronald Coase, "The Nature of the Firm," *Economics*, New Series, Vol. 4, 1937, pp. 386–405, reprinted in G. Stigler and K. Boulding, eds., *Readings in Price Theory*, Irwin, Homewood, Ill., 1952, pp. 331–351, at p. 334.
[2] Ibid., p. 336.

longer necessarily be perfect in a Pareto-optimality sense. With imperfect information about an uncertain future and bargaining via
costly and therefore incomplete transactions, the final outcome may
be far less than perfect. Intrafirm, administrative control allows more
flexibility, control, adaptability, and lower probable costs in such cases.
Firms are *chosen* over the market as part of cost-minimizing strategies.

Kenneth Arrow and the limits of organization

Kenneth Arrow has undertaken a number of studies into market
imperfections and organizational responses. His most accessible statement is a series of lectures given at the University of California in
1971 and later published under the title *The Limits of Organization*.[3]
Arrow, like Coase before him, perceives organizations as devices to
overcome the problems of costly information and expensive transactions associated with real-world markets. Humans are unable to
devote total personal resources to the acquisition and evaluation of
information. Human minds are unable to assess, evaluate, and calculate properly all that would become important to a complex choice.
Therefore, a division of labor is called for with information entering
organizations at entry points, that is filtered, manipulated, processed,
and passed forward to higher levels. There it is further aggregated,
processed, and passed on until the very highest levels are reached.
There paths are selected and organizational strategies are set. Organizations are, therefore, best thought of as conscious investments
in information channels, which are designed to minimize the costs of
search behavior.

However, the best laid organizational plans are simply pieces of
paper until the actors within the organization carry out their various
parts. By definition, they do not act in response to impersonal market
variations in prices. They act in response to more detailed directives.
Those at the top could, conceptually, take all of the information gathered and processed in the ultimate decision, collate and return it to
all below, and try to *persuade* each participant of the wisdom of following the plan. There are, or course, two problems with this. First,
the individuals within the organization may have different final goals
and hence disagree as to the best choice. Second, the whole process
would be horribly expensive and inefficient. Hence Arrow's conclusion is that the efficient organization is one that acts to create infor-

---

[3] Kenneth J. Arrow, *The Limits of Organization*, Norton, New York, 1974.

mation channels to the top but utilizes authority to fulfill the decisions made.

This would seem to make organizations superior to markets whenever information is costly and processing it is limited, but this is not the conclusion that Arrow comes to (or wishes to come to?). His lectures note the significance and importance of organizations, but he is writing to explore their limits. All capital investments, once in place, are less adaptable than at the design stage. Ideas and approaches become physically solidified. So it is with Arrow's organizations. The structure of information channels creates, in effect, the agenda of the organization. It determines what types of data will be found, filtered, and presented favorably. In a fluid environment, organizations become less able to adapt. They become rigid and inflexible, and like all nonadaptive organisms, they face the possibility of "adverse environmental selection," that is, death.

Still, once the world of the special case has been abandoned, there are costs of interacting in markets that sometimes become so prohibitive that markets themselves must be abandoned. Arrow never uses the term, but what organization is seeking to escape is often the uncontrolled exercise of "power."

Armen Alchian, Harold Demsetz, and team production

Armen Alchian and Harold Demsetz take a different approach, arguing that the real cause of organizations is a peculiar form of production function.[4] Whenever there exist team production functions such that the contribution of individual workers are inseparable from those of others, it becomes impossible to measure the marginal contribution of each. It is thus impossible to pay according to results. If two men are lifting a heavy log, it may be hard to determine which is bearing a higher share of the load. If either refuses any input, the output of both is zero. If one undertakes a minimal effort but shifts most of the burden to his partner, the log is raised, but an outside observer will not be able to assign specific efforts to each.

Thus Alchian and Demsetz argue that the function of a business firm is to overcome the contracting difficulties when information on individual effort is impossible or at least expensive to acquire. The firm substitutes monitoring of behavior for metering of output in determining wages and controls. The firm is to be viewed, not as the

---

[4] Armen Alchian and Harold Demsetz, "Production, Information Costs, and Economic Organization," *American Economic Review*, Vol. 62, December 1972, pp. 777–795.

apex of a hierarchical pyramid, but as the central actor in a series of simple, bilateral contracts between individual workers and the employer.

Once again, however, organizations are viewed as a necessary response to problems of specific individuals having control over information and events crucial to a potential exchange partner. Even for those individuals who would certainly reject the terminology, firms are a response to the introduction of power into markets.

Oliver Williamson and organizational failures

Oliver Williamson's book *Markets and Hierarchies: Analysis and Antitrust Implications* is a rich mine of insight into the economics of organizations.[5] In it he assumes "bounded rationality." As seen in the preceding chapter this approach starts from the empirical findings of psychology and concludes that the human brain is very limited in its ability to hold and process complex information. In interactions this becomes a potential threat to either party when there is substantial "information impactedness" or unevenness in the possession of crucial data. When coupled with "opportunism" or a strategic potential to exploit that information advantage there is the potential for loss. Though he does not use the term, he is here admitting "power" to the model. Finally, he assumes a world of costly transactions. Writing a complete contingency contract for all potential states of the world and reaching agreement upon it is perhaps an impossible task in his theoretical world.

A market then is likely to approach a small-numbers situation because knowing of all possible transactors, evaluating them carefully, engaging in detailed negotiations, and so forth, will quickly become prohibitive. Thus a relatively small number of trading options will often become the relevant choice set.

In simple market exchanges there are now identifiable individuals willing and able to exploit uncertainty for their own advantage. With imperfect contracts, unfolding events will give to parties unforeseen chances to exercise event power for their gain at another's expense. To the subjects of that power, such exercises are real costs. Organizations again become devices to minimize those costs associated with

---

[5] Cf. Oliver Williamson, *Markets and Hierarchies: Analysis and Antitrust Implications*, Free Press, New York, 1975, as well as his "The Modern Corporation: Origins, Evolution, Attributes," *Journal of Economic Literature*, Vol. 19, December 1981, pp. 1537–1568, and his *Corporate Control and Business Behavior*, Prentice-Hall, Englewood Cliffs, N. J., 1970, and his *The Economic Institutions of Capitalism*, The Free Press, New York, 1985.

market transactions in such an imperfect world. The elements of the organizational structure in particular situations are best understood in terms of attempts to overcome these failures. Williamson never uses the term "power," but his whole analysis argues that organizations exist as consciously devised mechanisms for the control of power arising in imperfect markets.

Organizations as responses to power

The work in this area always speaks of the "costs" of using markets. That term itself obscures much of the real nature of the problem. Nature dictates that one cannot grow wheat without land, seed, and water. These are real costs that cannot be avoided. They are constraints that must be faced, but they involve no exercise of power. When another human being has the ability to hide crucial information from me, when she has the socially sanctioned authority to shape events that affect me, those are also constraints, but they are qualitatively different. They are not from the hand of nature but are the work of humans. I have distinguished those social relationships from other constraints under the name "power." All of this work recognizes those social constraints. None of it wishes to recognize the qualitative differences between natural and human impacts, however. Power has been found, but not yet "discovered."

What it has stressed is important. When the special case is relaxed, as it readily is in real-world markets, then nothing more than a drive for efficiency is required for the substitution of organization for markets. Humans interact in contexts other than pure market exchange. Efficiency dictates that they must. Empiricism demonstrates that they do.

What the work has overlooked is also important. Administrative structures may be viewed as attempts to escape from the new forms of power that imperfect markets permit. Yet even the escape may be illusory. The substitution of administrative structures may, itself, create new manifestations of power.

Organization and agency

If organizations exist because it is impossible to coordinate behavior perfectly via markets in a world of imperfect information and costly transactions, it seems a bit disingenuous to assume away those conditions inside the firm or organization. We should not, then, speak of firms as single persons. They are collections of persons in a formal structure of roles and authority. They are structures of actors who are charged with making choices for the benefit of others. In the language of law, many of those in organizations are no longer "principals" but "agents."

The concept of agency

Formal economic theory is built upon a presumption of individuals acting on their own behalf. The traders of the traditional market model are trading for themselves. In a world of organizational structures, agency relationships become ubiquitous indeed. Economic theory expects Robinson Crusoe. Economic reality more often finds Jack (of beanstalk fame). Consider the difference. Crusoe has bananas and wants pineapples. Friday has pineapples and wants bananas. Crusoe trades directly with Friday and each has his own interests at heart. This is a trade between principals. The presence of a bilateral, voluntary trade indicates that both think they are made better off. If each had sent someone else to make the trade for him, an agent, the outcome would become less certain. The agents would make the decisions for the principals. If logical consistency is to hold, the agents must ultimately be driven by their own self-interest, not that of their principals. The final trade might not then be in the best interest of both principals.

Jack was given instructions by his mother to go to market and, *on her behalf*, trade her last cow for food. Jack, granted this authority by his mother, chose instead to trade for a handful of "magic" beans. In that case the trade ultimately worked out well for both Jack and his mother (if not for the giant). That was perhaps a serendipitous result. There are undoubtedly cases when an agent's substitution of his own preferences or judgments have been less beneficial to the principal. The creation of an agency relationship is definitionally a creation of *power* granted by principals to agents.[6] Using agency relationships to escape from the power of market imperfections has merely changed the locus and form of power. It has not eliminated it after all. With the replacement of markets by organizations, Jack is as common as Crusoe. In a modern society in which self-employment is the exception, production is dominated by large organizations, and govern-

---

[6] Most economists writing about this problem continue to speak of it as one of agency costs. There are losses associated with the use of agents as an institution. They seem not to recognize that the agents are persons and hence it is also a power relationship. Cf., for example, John W. Pratt and Richard J. Zeckhauser, eds., *Principals and Agents: The Structure of Business*, Harvard Business School Press, Boston, 1985.

ments and organizations buy vast quantities of outputs, agency is common to us all. Purely individual production is relatively rare.

To the extent that those rational, maximizing, *self-interested* agents have any discretionary authority, they have the potential for exercising even negative power. That potential is negated if and only if there are mechanisms that

1. reveal to agents a complete specification of principals' preference functions, *and*
2. reveal to principals the complete processes of agents' thoughts and actions, *and*
3. provide perfect incentives for agents, under the complete and costless control of principals, to maximize the principals' utility.

Without those controls agents may distort outcomes from the principal's perspective.[7] Of course, if all of those mechanisms were present, principals would be sufficiently omniscient and omnipotent that the market failures that generated the need for organizations and agents would have all disappeared. *The very presence of agency relationships is evidence of imperfect agency relationships!*

Harvey Liebenstein has observed that "once agents enter the scene there is no need for both parties to gain in order for transactions to take place."[8] That is a dramatic conclusion. *If agents are involved, parties to even a bilateral, voluntary exchange (that is, the ultimate principals) may be harmed by the transaction.* If true, the whole structure of welfare economics and much of the normative case for the superiority of markets sit upon a most unstable foundation. Market trades may be the result of the exercise of even negative power. The agent may choose to pursue his own ends at the expense of his principal.

Defining the principal

Recognition of the discretionary power of agents is not the end of the story. In order even to define negative or positive power there

---

[7] The usual economic response is to attempt a specification of complex payoff functions that will lead to a coincidence between agents' and principals' incentives. In many cases, however, the complexity of contracting necessary to develop those would only seem viable in a world of perfect information and minimal transactions costs, that is, one in which there would be little need for agents. Cf. Kenneth Arrow, "The Economics of Agency" in Pratt and Zeckhauser, *Principals and Agents*, pp. 37–51. Arrow notes, after seeking such functions, that the contracts in reality seem to be based on custom rather than the economist's prescriptions.

[8] Harvey Leibenstein, *Beyond Economic Man: A New Foundation for Microeconomics*, Harvard University Press, Cambridge, Mass., 1976, p. 161.

must be a well-defined preference function for the "principal." If my boss does not know what she wants me to do, how can I know? I have assumed that all natural persons have preference functions, and if the principal is such a person, I can speak of the agent following or deviating from the dictates of that function. But what if there is no real principal? Many of the major actors in a modern society will, in fact, be organizations rather than persons. IBM is an actor, as are Procter and Gamble, the AFL-CIO, the National Association of Manufacturers, and NORML. In both legal and economic theory terms, these are "individuals" who must have a preference function against which to judge the behaviors of agents.

Does IBM have a utility function? What would that mean? What or who is IBM? If IBM has a preference function, it must in some sense derive from real people, but which ones and how? In legal terms IBM has many principals who are its stockholders, and thus, perhaps, there must be a mechanism for aggregating the preferences of each of the individual stockholders into a single, well-defined and unambiguous function, that is, there must be a "social welfare function" for the collectivity of stockholders.

Kenneth Arrow's "impossibility theorem" has already proved that *there is no way to aggregate individual preferences into a collective preference that meets very minimal rules of collective rationality.*[9] In short, what is required to speak of the preferences of a collective principal (for example, a corporation), Arrow has shown to be impossible. There will often be no well-defined preference function for the ill-defined principal of a large and jointly owned firm! There is thus little likelihood of all agents perfectly following a nonexistent function. Even if the agent is responding to the preferences of some subset of principals, by acting as the simultaneous agent of all, she will be violating the preferences of others.

Where then does that leave us? Efficiency dictates that transaction costs, imperfect information, and opportunistic behavior lead administrative organizations to control the power they imply. However, the formation of organizations with their agency relationships, by definition, creates other forms of power.

Layers of agency

The larger and more complex the economic organization, the more important the role of agents. General Motors, Exxon, American Tele-

---

[9] Kenneth J. Arrow, *Social Choice and Individual Values*, 2nd ed., Yale University Press, New Haven, Conn., 1963.

phone and Telegraph, as well as Stanford University, the United States Army, and the American Baptist Church are simply formal aggregations of agents. *All* of the acts within and between such organizations are undertaken by agents, and all therefore have a wide potential for various forms of power. Indeed, with various levels, subagents are simultaneously agents of superior agents and of ultimate principals. Unless the chain of information and control is perfect throughout, subagents may be impelled to follow the interests of superior agents rather than principals. As the organization increases in complexity, so does the structure of power within it. The importance of agents increases; the control of agents diminishes. "The possibilities for nonoptimal agent behavior expand enormously if we think of a hierarchy of agents, all of whom can contribute or engage in transactions."[10]

Organization, agency, and the growth of power

An organization is a structured relationship of subagents, superior agents, and principals. Each of those is, in turn, a maximizing individual traversing a decision map that is now formally interrelated with the maps of all of the other individuals within the organization. The structure of the organization also determines the nature of the tree interrelationships. These structures thus change the productivity of various methods of exercising power. The points on the linear programming approximation of an isoquant back in Figure 4.3 must be affected by the presence and form of these structures. In many cases, simple economic power no longer clearly dominates.

Decision power

Each principal or superior agent may grant one or two forms of potential decision control power to lower agents. In Arrow's terms, the creation of information channels is a process of giving to someone else responsibility for undertaking your "search." The content of the information you receive is now explicitly in the hands of another person. That is clearly a form of decisional power. It may be positive, negative, or neutral *if* the principal, as a natural person, has a well-defined utility function. If the principal is a fictional aggregation of individuals, it has no such guiding function, and the power may well be positive for some of the component persons but negative for others.

[10] Leibenstein, *Beyond Economic Man*, p. 162.

Within a formal structure, the principal may also be delegating explicit authority to make actual choices. Rather than merely giving up control of the search process, a principal may give up control of decisions. Agents may even be able to make decisions without notifying principals. That introduces a degree of decision power that is more extreme and more explicit than previously considered.

Event power

Agents can, of course, exercise positive power, and obviously principals expect them to or they would not consent to the relationship. The whole reason to employ agents is that they are expected to perform functions that further the productivity of the organization. Much of the granted event power is over the specific functions of operating the organization. After all, someone must produce the product. However, with imperfect control of agents, they may undertake actions that become events that do not further the (still undefined) goals of the principal. An obvious example arises under the legal doctrine of *respondeat superior*, whereby the actions of the agent are attributed to the principal. Thus a principal is "vicariously liable" for damage done by her agents.

A doctor is liable for the actions of her nurse, her receptionist, and the person who shovels the walkway to her office. A bus company is liable for actions taken by its drivers, mechanics, and dispatchers. A manufacturer is liable for actions taken by her designers, engineers, assembly workers, distributors, and inspectors. A bank is liable to its depositors for funds embezzled by its employees. The stockholders of Richardson-Merrill were liable for damages when laboratory personnel falsified animal test data on MER/29.[11] In each case the development of an agency relationship gives to the agents the power to cause harm to the principal. Pursuing their own ends, they may create substantial costs for principals.

Agenda power

If bounded rationality is added to the model, then agency adds a new element of agenda power. Anyone who affects the order in which options are discovered determines the outcome of the choice. By shaping the agenda considered, the agent is exercising power. If it substitutes a good enough outcome for the optimal outcome, it, in

[11] *Roginsky* v. *Richardson-Merrill, Inc.*, 378 F.2d 832.

fact, lowers the lifetime welfare of the subject. Agents are the ones who likely (1) interpret external events and thus create the recognition that a choice must be made by the organization and (2) discover and present responsive alternatives.

Value power

Those who run organizations have long recognized the potential for value power and have been concerned about it. Theorists of organizational behavior have long focused on issues of corporate culture and processes of socialization that take place within organizations giving to its members a shared sense of values and priorities. That culture is sometimes called on to control agents' power.

In his explorations into principal–agent relationships Kenneth Arrow is a bit discouraged because the careful incentive functions that economic theory would seem to prescribe for such contracts bear so little relation to the contracts in the real world. The real basis of behavior, he speculates, may instead be in social relationships that create values later affecting agents' actions. Behavior may result from "systems of ethics, internalized during the education process and enforced in some measure by formal punishments and more broadly by reputations. Ultimately, of course, these social systems have economic consequences, but they are not the immediate ones of current principal-agent models."[12]

Complex power in complex organizations

Power as defined in Chapter 4 involved relationships between persons, but in the everyday sense of the word. Though the law defines corporations, whether commercial, religious, or educational, as persons, here that obscures the reality. The corporation is made up of real persons in agency relationships. To see the power in any situation it is necessary to go inside the organization in search of the behaviors of natural persons.

In the preceding chapter I discussed several examples of information control that seemed to involve negative power, yet in each such case the organization was treated as if it were a person exercising power. When the organization is recognized as a set of structured agency relationships, untangling the structure of power becomes even more complex.

[12] Arrow, "The Economics of Agency," p. 50.

G. D. Searle and the Copper 7

G. D. Searle, of course, could not falsify, obscure, or fail to disclose any data regarding the Copper 7. If that was done, it was done by agents of Searle. The principals (the stockholders and the women using the IUD) played a very limited role. Who, in fact, defined the elements of that exchange? Somewhere within the organization there were specific individuals who had the authority to acquire, collate, analyze, and pass on relevant information about the incidence of complications. It is not at all clear how far that information rose through the ranks of various agents. It is certain that it did not reach either of the ultimate principals. Other agents of Searle in the marketing division engaged in a vigorous "blind-date campaign" aimed at doctors, stressing the advantages of the IUD without mentioning the real data on complications. Notice that agent control over information was shaping the perceptions and decisions of other agents within the organization, and was also being used to affect actors outside of it.

Doctors, in turn, operating as "expert" agents for patients, made decisions based upon the information made available to and through the organization. Finally, patients, principals of the doctor agents, were party to the transaction when they "made the choice" to accept that form of birth control. Only when the real data were belatedly discovered did the real principals find out about the nature of the transaction. Women discovered that they faced a much higher risk of serious problems. Stockholders discovered that they faced serious legal liabilities for damage. *Some* agents knew that all along and exposed both other agents and ultimate principals to possible losses in utility because of their control of information and decisions.

The story does not really end there, or course. In fact, where it does end is still undetermined as of this writing since the courts are just beginning to deal with it all. Agents of Monsanto (top management), operating on the basis of information and perceptions generated by other agents within Monsanto, and perhaps some external "experts" acted for their principals (the Monsanto stockholders) to acquire Searle. Agents within Searle, who now could obscure the fact that other agents had previously obscured data about medical complications, could shape the perceptions of the Monsanto agents.

Untangling this web will be difficult indeed. Identifying the specific individuals who exercised power will be complex. Many lawyers will, I am sure, devote substantial portions of their careers to just those questions (acting, of course, as agents for various principals). What is clear is that the complex organizational structure with its uncertainty and agency was involved in a series of transactions in which some parties were harmed. It was real, living human beings who had and exercised that power. It was real, living human beings who were its subjects. It was exercised because of and through organizational structures. The fact that the final principals transacted across a market did not fully protect them from the exercise of negative power.

Richardson-Merrill and MER/29

Richardson-Merrill was legally liable for damages resulting from the sale of its drug, MER/29, because "it" falsified laboratory data in the testing phase to hide evidence of potentially serious side effects. But of course Richardson-Merrill did no such thing. Agents of the corporation did it. The decision was initially made by laboratory technicians in response to directives from their immediate supervisor.[13] They in turn were responding to their own and their immediate supervisor's perceptions of a "good" choice. They had the power to shape the perceptions of other agents within the company and thus of the evaluating agents in the Food and Drug Administration, who in turn shaped the perceptions of the commissioners who approved the drug. That in turn was a major factor in shaping the perceptions of physicians who decided to prescribe the drug. Confidence in those physicians was a major factor in patients' taking it. For Mr. Roginsky, whose serum cholesterol level could have been controlled by other medications, the ensuing vision loss would seem to be a reduction in his lifetime utility because of the exercise of power through that chain. He was one of the ultimate principals to the transaction and was inarguably harmed.

The other principal, the collection of stockholders, then faced the possibility of harm. When a court of law decided they were vicariously liable for the actions of these subagents within the corporation, they faced the costs of compensation as well as possible punitive damages. One or both of the principals in that transaction were inevitably going to be made worse off because of the power of those agents that in turn arose from the nature of the organization in which they operated.

Agency power and the failure of legal control

Power arising from relaxing the conditions of the special case has so far called forth two types of social response. The first has been the

[13] *Roginsky.*

generation of legislative and judicial controls on the exercise of power via the state. The second has been the private response of creating administrative structures to replace the market when the costs of being subject to power become too great. The two responses are not independent. They are certainly interrelated; indeed, they may often be in conflict. The nature of state-based controls affects the possible forms of organizations. The presence of large organizations changes the political environment in which many of the legislative controls are developed. The nature of large organizations may also alter the ability of the legal strictures to be effective limitations on market-based power. In Chapter 8 I will return to the question of organizational impacts on political outcomes.[14] It is appropriate here, however, to discuss the impacts of organizational structure on the effectiveness of judicial controls.

Law as a cost in the exercise of power

In the preceding chapter I noted the development of legal rules via common law processes that created duties and liabilities for parties to market transactions. Those rules are nothing more than a change in the minimum costs of using various methods of power. In the isoquant map of Figure 4.1, C_j represented the lowest possible cost of causing A to change paths through her decision map. The imposition of new legal liabilities changes that cost and alters the productivity of various possible power techniques. Indeed, for most practitioners in the new field of "law and economics," that is precisely the crucial element of legal decisions. It is not that they redistribute costs of past actions. It is that they establish incentives for future behavior.[15]

In order for those new incentives to be effective, however, they must ultimately be felt by the *real* persons who possess the potential power and who would otherwise exercise it. A cost borne by someone else matters little in my decision calculus. Effective legal controls on power must impact the appropriate real persons within their multi-leveled agency structures.

---

[14] For a more complete analysis of this see also, R. Bartlett, *Economic Foundations of Political Power*, Free Press, New York, 1973, or R. Bartlett, "An Economic Theory of Political Behavior: Firm Size and Political Power," in John J. Siegfied, ed., *The Economics of Firm Size, Market Structure and Social Performance*, Bureau of Economics, Federal Trade Commission, Washington, D.C., 1980, or R. Bartlett and W. Patton, "Corporate 'Persons' and Freedom of Speech: The Political Impact of Legal Mythology," *Wisconsin Law Review*, Vol. 1981, pp. 494–512.

[15] See, for example, Richard Posner, *Economic Analysis of Law*, Little, Brown, Boston, 1972.

Christopher Stone and law in an organizational world

The development of organizations as a response to power thus complicates the use of legal rules as a control of power. In legal terms the actors are the corporate persons. In real terms the actors are its *agents*. Corporations, whether commercial, educational, or religious, never, ever do anything. They are figments of the social imagination. Agents of the corporation undertake all of the real actions. Agents alone can exercise the power from which law is perhaps the only protection. The costs imposed by legal principles must then affect the incentives of the specific agents who are in a position to exercise power. An organizational barrier now stands between the real possessors of power and legal controls. The consequences of its existence must be considered.

Christopher Stone has written an analysis of legal rules applied to complex organizations. Writing as a lawyer, he does not use the language of economics, but the analysis is closely parallel. His concern is still with the incentives that legal rules generate for real human beings acting not as principals, but as collections of agents inside corporate structures. His conclusions are given away in his title; the corporate form is *Where the Law Ends*.[16]

The common law is best adapted, perhaps, for dealing with questions such as "Did your cow eat my corn; if so who was responsible, and who should pay compensation to whom?" It provides compensation for past wrongs and establishes incentives for future behavior. What Stone is concerned with is the effectiveness of the incentives when organizations are involved and agents are acting for mythical principals.

Individual agent costs. If liability is to be imposed, upon whom should it fall? "Piercing the corporate veil" and imposing liability on individuals who may have unjustly exercised power is one possibility. In the Richardson-Merrill case, the court found that there was no knowledge for the falsified data at the very top levels of the company. The decision to exercise the power began within the testing laboratory itself. However, holding only those persons liable would not seem to provide optimal incentives. They were all virtually judgment proof, that is, had vastly insufficient resources to provide compensation. Moreover, excusing top executives creates positive payoffs to managers who

---

[16] Christopher Stone, *Where the Law Ends: The Social Control of Corporate Behavior*, Harper & Row, New York, 1975.

"don't want to know" how results are generated. Holding the top executives responsible for something about which they knew nothing, however, seems to violate a shared sense of fairness. Surely, agents of Richardson-Merrill exercised significant power because they held those agency positions, yet what legal incentives fully capture the situation?

Richardson-Merrill as an organization benefited from the actions of its agents. To limit liability to those lower-level persons gives it a risk-free payoff. If there are costs to the exercise of power, individual agents bear them. If there are benefits, the organization enjoys them. That would seem to generate an incentive for internal organizational elements that would encourage the exercise of power.

In the asbestos cases, the intraorganizational site of the exercise of power was clearly higher. The decision to withhold information on potential health hazards was made at the very highest levels of organizations.[17] Unfortunately, most of those executives have now gone on to their final reward (or penalty). The decisions were made as much as fifty years ago. The damage is only now becoming apparent to many of the subjects of that power. Not even the long arm of the law can impose real liability on the exercisers of that power. They are beyond its reach. It clearly provided no deterrent to their actions.

It may even be that there is no identifiable individual who is clearly responsible. Consider a hypothetical case. Suppose some persons in the engineering division had knowledge that a brake system must use exactly the materials specified or failure could occur. Other individuals in manufacturing, without this knowledge, substituted a material that in earlier designs had been acceptable. The manufacturer did not know that his substitution was unsafe. Indeed, he had been doing that in similar models for years. The engineers did not know what was in the brakes. Their design was flawless. In no human brain did information simultaneously exist that the brake was using that material and that it would therefore be unsafe. There is no real person who knew. Only the corporate "one" did. Real persons are at fault in the design and operation of the information systems, perhaps, but establishing specific agent liability would be difficult. Establishing it in a fashion that would provide effective future control would be even more difficult.

For legal liabilities to be effective controls on agents, they must involve real costs. Yet the agent is operating not for her own benefit, but for corporate purposes. If she is found liable, there may be strong

---

[17] *Fischer* v. *Johns-Manville Corp.*, 472 A.2d 577 (N.J. 1984)

incentives for the organization, or some of its other agents, to provide indemnification. Even if formal reimbursement from corporate funds in prohibited, subtle indemnification in future salary and bonuses could eliminate any real cost to the agent. Such after-the-fact protection would not seem at all unlikely. All decisions on reimbursement will be made by other agents rather than the nonexistent principal, that is, by parties who may well identify with the problems of the liable agent. "There, but for the grace of a greedy attorney, go I."

Corporate liability. Perhaps, then, the principles of vicarious liability should be strictly applied and the corporation itself should bear the costs of exercising negative power. There are, of course, two problems with that approach. The first is that those who bear the costs did not exercise the power. Just as corporations never act, they never bear costs. All such costs are ultimately felt by real persons. Who ultimately bears the costs of liabilities imposed upon the corporate entity? Even that is uncertain. The stockholders may well find their wealth diminished in a case of sufficient magnitude, but the stockholders may simply be the pension funds of retired schoolteachers and families planning to send little Janey to college. If the judgment damages the profitability of the firm, employees may find their wages affected and in extreme cases may find their jobs in jeopardy. But, of course, neither of those groups acted at all. Their behavior is unrelated to the damage done and hence the liability can act as no incentive to controlling their exercise of power. The act for which liability arose was independent of the judgment and control of the persons bearing the burden. It may provide compensation after the fact, but it does not create incentives for *agents* to avoid such behavior.

The second problem with vicarious liability is that juries may feel a sense of injustice imposing costs on persons who, in reality, did not *do* anything. In the MER/29 case, the final award of damages was limited to $20,000 because, as Judge Friendly said,

a sufficiently egregious error as to one product can end the business life of a concern that has wrought much good in the past and might otherwise have continued to do so in the future, with many innocent stockholders suffering extinction of their investments for a single management sin.[18]

Those exercising the power are free of its costs. Vicarious liability completely shifts the burden from the agents making the decision to exercise power. In the case of asbestos, the top executives knew that they would not be personally liable for nondisclosure of dangers and

---

[18] *Roginsky*, p. 841.

probably knew that the corporation itself would not be liable for many years if ever. Executives, whose careers are relatively short and whose rewards are based on immediate performance, would, if rational maximizers, be little deterred by possible costs to the corporation decades in the future.

The viability of legally imposed costs as a control over the power of imperfect markets is affected by the nature of the organizations that exist. These organizations themselves may be viewed as responses to market power. As a result, power arising from imperfect markets, and attempts to void it, may be responsible for much of the broader institutional structure of the whole society.

Conclusions

Organizations may indeed, as the growing economic literature argues, be responses to problems that arise when markets fall short of the special case. They may indeed provide partial solutions to some of those problems. They are not, however, sufficient to recapture the powerless Eden first lost when the tight boundaries of the special case were breached.

They are themselves structures of imperfect agency and therefore power. They grant power to many of their members, power dependent upon institutional position. The very use of agency is sufficient to conclude that agents are under imperfect control. Finally, the existence and special form of organizations undermine the ability of judicial institutions to use legal process to control that market-generated power.

This is not, of course, to argue that the development of organizational structures has, normatively, been a "bad" thing. There are undoubted social benefits. Among their advantages, however, is *not* an ability to attain the pure and powerless world of market theory. Their existence places us in a complex and normatively ambiguous world. In imperfect markets there is real power. When organizations are substituted for those markets, there is real power. There is power within. There is power without. There is seemingly no escape.

CHAPTER 7

Power in the employment relation

For his book *Working*, Studs Terkel interviewed scores of people about their activities "at work."[1] Virtually all worked for someone else. Virtually all felt that someone had "power" over them. The dissatisfaction of having a "powerful boss" seemed a common factor in the oft expressed discontent of employees at all levels. They all perceived real power in the employment relation.

In the previous chapter power arose from principals' imperfect control over agents. It was power exercised by agents with principals and superior agents as subjects. Yet the workers in Terkel's book felt themselves to be the subjects of power, not its possessors. It is the potential for power in the employment relation that needs attention now.

The employment relation

There is substantial disagreement among economists over the role of power in employment relations. Standard textbook theory sees nothing distinct in labor markets. Labor is simply another factor of production, allocated among uses via market forces. The fact that labor not only is owned by individuals but lies inextricably bound within their minds and bodies is simply irrelevant. There is nothing intrinsically different about buying labor or pig iron. Both are simply marketed factors of production.

Simon and others have argued, however, that there is a distinct power relation in employment.[2] Individuals agree to act under the direction of another, in service of ends established by the other. Rather than agreeing on specific pay for a specific product or result, in employment there is an agreement to permit the direction of work effort by another person. What is "exchanged" is not product or output, but effort or input. It is not thing for thing but acceptance of control

[1] Studs Terkel, *Working*, Pantheon, New York, 1974.
[2] Herbert Simon, *Administrative Behavior*, 2nd ed., Macmillan, New York, 1961. Cf. also his *Models of Man*, Wiley, New York, 1957.

for a price. To reach agreement on all the unknowns in a dynamic production situation becomes prohibitively expensive (if not impossible). Formal contracts specifying complete performance details are simply unattainable.

The result, says Simon, is a special employment contract, exchanging a fixed payment for the *authority* to direct that effort as the employer sees fit, perhaps with some established and bargained-for limits. The employment relation is a contract over (limited) authority and thus is, in human terms, a special contract. Labor is different from pig iron after all.

For Marx, of course, power in the employment relation is predominant. On the short-term, individual level, the decision to accept any one contract of employment seems perfectly free, but in the long-term, systemic view it must be recognized as "wage slavery." For labor as a class it is work for wages or starve. In that coercive relationship workers are harmed both by being "exploited" (an income distribution issue) and by becoming "alienated" (a philosophical one). Power in that relationship is the key to understanding the oppression of capitalism.[3]

Marxian economics is well outside the mainstream of neoclassical economics. Armen Alchian and Harold Demsetz are not. For them, not only is there no exploitation or alienation, there is no power or authority in employment at all. Even Simon's view is false. There is only obfuscated simple economic power.[4] Comparing employment with the relationship between a grocer and a shopper, they argue that there is no essential difference in the two situations. A shopper may "order" the grocer to stock particular brands of milk and may "punish" the grocer for failure to comply by discontinuing purchases. An employer may "order" an employee to undertake a particular task and may "punish" the employee for failure to comply by discontinuing purchases of labor. In both situations they see a series of spot contracts under continual renegotiation, and the only authority is an ability to discontinue trading in future periods. Each directive from a super-

---

[3] There are a number of good sources explaining the basic Marxist position. See, for example, Karl Marx, *Capital*, Vol. I, in a variety of editions, Paul Sweezy, *The Theory of Capitalist Development*, Modern Reader, New York, 1942, or Ben Fine, *Marx's Capital*, Macmillan Press, London, 1975. For an excellent, though a bit turgid, discussion of alienation see Fredy Perlman, "Introduction: Commodity Fetishism," pp. ix-xxxviii in I. I. Rubin, *Essays on Marx's Theory of Value*, Black and Red Press, Detroit, Mich. 1972.

[4] Armen Alchian and Harold Demsetz, "Production, Information Costs, and Economic Organizations," *American Economic Review*, December 1972, pp. 777–795, esp. pp. 777–778.

visor is a new offer for a new spot contract. Each act of compliance is but an acceptance of the new contract. Either party may chose not to renew at any moment. There is no special ability to do harm to anyone, and firing a worker is not different than switching milk purchases to a different store. The employee has simple economic power because he can offer to work, the employer because he can hire. *Failure to exercise that power causes no harm relative to a no-trade position.* They are in exactly the same relationship as the grocer and his customers. In both cases one party to a series of past, spot contracts opts not to continue them into the future.

For Alchian and Demsetz, the firm is not even a hierarchical arrangement but a series of independent, bilateral contracts made between a central figure, the entrepreneur, and a series of surrounding contractors, neither with any real authority over the other. Labor is, after all, just exactly like pig iron.

Punishment as negative power

For Alchian and Demsetz, the employment relation involves real power only if there is some means whereby an employer can punish an employee, that is, if there is a potential for negative power in an employment relation. To be assured of perfect powerlessness, there must be no possibility of negative power. What conditions would have to hold to deny that possibility?

Contract independence

Alchian and Demsetz's lack of punishment potential implicitly assumes that the spot contracts are independent of each other and that they do not alter other outside options. Failure to renew should simply return the ex-employee to the utility path that would have been followed if no contracting had ever taken place.

Figure 7.1 displays the condition of independence graphically. The vertical axis measures utility experienced by an actor, G, and the horizontal axis measures time. Time at the origin is the instant just prior to the formation of any possible initial contract between C and G. The top path, U^*, measures the utility experienced if an initial contract is formed and is renewed indefinitely. The lower path, U', reflects the utility experienced if no trades were ever made. The difference between the two paths is, at each point, the net gain to G from the trade.

The no-punishment argument assumes that, if an initial contract is

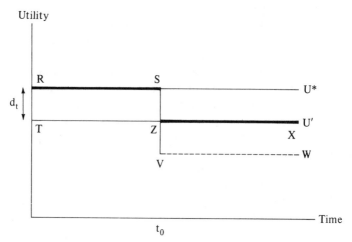

Figure 7.1. Power to punish.

made and G starts along the higher path, whenever C chooses not to renew, G simply and costlessly drops down to path U' and follows it for the rest of her life. That lower path waits, unaffected by the contracts with C, to accept G whenever she arrives.

The vertical distance between the two paths represents the net gain from contracting in each period. $RSTZ$ is the net gain to G from the sequence of contracts. After t_0 there is assumed to be no residual impact. C made superior offers in the past. He now ceases to do so. The relationship has been only beneficial to G. She may miss the gains but has not suffered losses. Only simple economic power is involved.

This condition may also be seen in a decision tree. Starting at the left, a series of spot contracts would define a path of choices, events, and payoffs. If at some later chance node (a decision node for C) C refuses to recontract, a new branch is defined. If C's refusal is to be wholly devoid of negative consequences, then the structure of the tree must, at that juncture, be *exactly* what it would have been at that time had the initial contract never been formed. The decision node must be identical to that which would have been. C's decision must only eliminate the single best offer. It must not change the options and payoffs from contracts with third parties. There must be no carryovers or lingering effects.

If, instead, the act of embarking on the upper path in Figure 7.1 changes future options, then C may be able to impose losses on G relative to a no-trade position; that is, C may be able to punish. Suppose that at t_0 expulsion from the contracting path requires G to follow a path that falls below U' for some period, or even permanently. Then there are later losses associated with the initial gains. If those losses ($XZVW$) exceed the gains ($RSTZ$), then the net impact of the relationship is in fact negative.

One could argue, of course, that if G knew fully the subjective probability of an end to recontracting and knew the consequences of such an outcome, she might nevertheless enter the relationship, feeling that the short-term gains outweighed the risk of future losses. There are a number of reasons why that interpretation of events does not allow an escape from power and punishment in employment. First, lack of that perfect knowledge was one of the reasons why the employment relation came into being. Perfect knowledge of future contingencies would allow complete performance contracts. A series of unknown, renegotiated spot contracts becomes unnecessary. Second, as argued in Chapter 4, "subjective probability" is simply a euphemism for ignorance. If there is risk based on *subjective* probability, there is by definition incomplete information, much of which may well be in the possession of C. Then the whole range of power associated with the blind-date principle applies.

Finally, even if a choice were made, based on discounted present values of expected future gains and losses, that alone is insufficient to *evaluate* the utility impacts on G. As argued in Chapter 2, such discounted values may have predictive power about choices, but they do not have evaluative power. Even if she did make the choice freely at t_0, it could still lower her lifetime utility.

In short, Alchian and Demsetz's analysis is based on an unstated presumption that we can all "go home again," that we can forget the past, that our future choices are unaffected by our past ones. Our decision trees, like our utility functions, are wholly exogenous. Cessation of current interactions with other persons does not alter future fate.

They assume, implicitly, absolutely perfect and wholly frictionless labor markets in which each unit of labor is paid the value of its marginal product. That value should become equalized in all modes of employment. Any "owner" of labor who cannot sell to one employer should be able to sell to another at virtually the same wage (since the value of marginal products is equalized by market forces). Since markets are perfect and frictionless, the change in jobs will be instantaneous. There will be no search costs. The new job will be the best available anywhere in the world. There will be no temporary loss of income. In Figure 7.1, TZ will be imperceptibly above the U' path and G may instantaneously and costlessly shift to that path at any moment.

Each potential employer will know the true quality of G. G will know the true value of all potential jobs. The market will assure that the now lost job had no perceptible premium over any other. Individuals are but nondescript owners of a factor. They have no personal stake in any particular employment. There are no secondary effects to consider. If there were any, they would have already been covered by perfect and complete contracts covering all possible contingencies. They restrict labor markets to those of the special case, thus removing punishment by restricting their vision, rather than by deriving conclusions.

Evaluation of punishments

A punishment will involve a caused reduction in another's lifetime utility. Economic theory is clear that the true significance of events cannot be determined until they are translated into impacts on experienced utility. Utility is ultimately a personal sensation. Although it may depend upon changes in objective phenomena, it is a subjective response. Therefore, the measure of harm done depends not upon the evaluation of armchair economists but on the responses of those feeling it. Thus if loss of a job causes an ex-employee to question her self-worth, if it leads to sufficient emotional tension that it causes family breakups or even suicide, or if it leads to a loss in perceived social status, those are real costs. It matters not whether Alchian and Demsetz would think such emotional responses justified. If those costs are felt by persons within employment relations, they are crucial to evaluating power impacts.

In evaluating effects it is also important to recognize that, at some point, increasing the size of an impact alters its character as well. If I can prevent you from eating a single sandwich, I have an impact on your welfare. If I can prevent you from ever eating again, the impact is both larger and qualitatively different.

Changes caused by an exerciser of power may be part of a complex function with a series of thresholds. Past some size limit, new secondary changes begin. A small reduction in income may have no other effects. A large reduction in income may affect social relations, self-esteem, and so forth. A complete search for possible negative impacts must be prepared to find qualitative shifts, that is, new secondary impacts, as the size of observable quantities changes. That search must consider all potential impacts, direct and indirect. It must recognize that the importance of each is ultimately subjective.

Simple punishment in imperfect labor markets

Relax now the assumption of perfect, costless knowledge. Allow labor markets to operate with both ignorance and friction. Permit unemployment to exist and perhaps persist. Introduce space and distance. Make laborers social humans as well as simply factor owners. The impossibility of negative power or punishment is then less obvious. Consider but a few possible elements of employer power that are not necessarily present between the grocer and the milk consumer.

Labor market costs

Search and transaction costs. Assume that there is, somewhere, a job path equal to the one from which G has just been expelled, that is, that following it will make G, over her lifetime, just as well off as she would have been on the original path. With global rationality, G may ultimately find the next best job, but only after real search costs and income interruptions have been experienced. Under bounded rationality there is no reason to assume that G will ever find it. There is certainly no guarantee and ought to be no expectation that G will find it quickly and costlessly. Thus the interruption in income becomes an unrecoverable hole in lifetime earnings and lifetime utility. Had G followed that second path instead of the first, she would have had a higher lifetime welfare, and C's ability, once G is on the original path, to expel her is a form of granted event power.

Obviously, if G never finds her way back to an equally good path, assuming one exists, she will have been made worse off. If she would have been more likely to find the U' path at the time represented by the left axis in Figure 7.1, she has made herself vulnerable by accepting the event power of C.

Performance proxies. With imperfect information, potential employers cannot accurately assess all the characteristics of all possible employees. In the absence of information produced by own experience, employers must rely upon work history as an externally produced indicator of probable job performance. To the extent that being fired is a signal that G must carry with her into the market, that may reduce the quality of the jobs made available. If she is able to hide that particular job experience, she is also hiding the positive experience aspects of that position, and perhaps raising questions about the hole in her employment record. C's ability to fire is an ability to return G to the labor market with a published statement of her incompetence. That is a potential ability to alter the agenda of job opportunities available to G in the future.

Of course, if all potential future milk purchasers were to require from me a written evaluation of the quality of C's milk in the past and a formal explanation of why I refused to recontract with that grocer, then perhaps I as a customer have the same ability to punish the grocer. If that is not present in the retail milk market, there is a qualitative difference here.

Idiosyncratic human capital. Much work effort may be viewed as an investment in this human capital, that is, skills that reside in the worker. If, however, much of this human capital is firm-specific, it will not be transferable to other firms and certainly not to other industries. Given finite lives, changes in learning abilities over the life cycle, and a boundedly rational ability to hold only limited information and skill, it is clearly impossible to return to the options at the beginning of Figure 7.1. At t_0, G is no longer the same "commodity" on the labor market. Indeed, she may now be a respository of obsolete technology and capital. The ability to fire is the ability to create instantaneous, human capital obsolescence of some degree. A fired route scheduler for the airlines is, in real markets, just that. She is not simply an available employee. She is an available, potential employee who (1) was fired and (2) brings a good deal of human capital regarding route scheduling for airlines as done by C's company. Those may not be exactly the qualities other employers are seeking.

G's acceptance of the job with C is an acceptance of C's authority to determine the way in which G will herself be altered over time in human capital terms. It is also a granting to C of event power to determine whether that capital, once in place, will be an asset or a liability for G. If my purchase of a quart of milk each week in any way materially changes the ability of the grocer to sell milk or other products in the future, then the prospects for punishment are the same in both cases. If it does not, they are not.

Social costs. Once does not drop off her labor at the job each morning and pick it up in the afternoon. She interacts with other persons. On many jobs, important social relationships are formed. Other employees become friends. Termination of the contract with the employer is also termination, or at least alteration, in the set of social relationships. That may be of little significance in some cases. It may be important in others.

In a society that defines individual worth in employment terms, termination may also be an alteration in the way in which G is treated by people wholly unrelated to her past job. Answering the inevitable query "What do you do?" by admitting unemployment will yield a different response than claiming the executive vice-presidency of the local bank. If admitting that Randy Bartlett did not buy a quart of milk this week causes the grocer to lose social status (and well it should), then Alchian and Demsetz are right. The ability to punish is the same.

Geography. In microeconomic textbooks, all production seems to take place on the head of a mythical pin. It is a hard fact of life that production in the real world involves geographic space. Even when the information and friction problems are overcome, the new job may be far from the old. Removing your teenage children from their high school, giving up a network of friends and family, selling the home in which your grandfather was born, and moving to a new section of the country may involve some net utility loss, even if the new job pays the same wages as the old. Again, if my failure to buy the milk leads to these results for the grocer, I also can exercise negative power.

Subjective evaluations. Professionals concerned with the psychological impacts of job loss readily attest to the utility consequences. Psychologists who study the impact of job loss conclude that it is one of life's most traumatic experiences. Perhaps there is an untapped mine of psychological research into stress induced by the failure to sell a quart of milk to a single customer. I look forward to it.

The president of the Association of Executive Search Consultants offers advice through the *Wall Street Journal* to executives who have been fired to "get your mourning out of the way and get on with it."[5] Another expert in the field notes that losing a job has "many of the characteristics of a divorce."[6] If the persons losing the jobs evaluate the experience as similar to a divorce and go through a period of mourning, their utility losses are real. Theory grants the right of valuation to the fired worker, not to the armchair theorist.

[5] "Advice on What Not to Do as the Search Continues," *Wall Street Journal*, November 19, 1985.
[6] Ibid., p. 33.

Secondary market effects

Alchian and Demsetz perceive employment as a series of spot contracts with no justifiable expectation by either party that the contract will be renewed in succeeding periods. Markets, however, do recognize a real, "bankable" expectation of continuing employment relations.

Employment and income expectation as an asset. Past employment, particularly employment with a single employer, creates, in market terms, a real asset in the form of an expectation of future income. In the process of financial intermediation, lenders seek to loan funds to borrowers in exchange for a right to future income. In order to reduce their risk they may also seek collateral in the form of a lien on an asset, but they will always require a reasonable expectation of future income. The best indication of future income is the stability of a past employment relation. Termination of employment thus carries the secondary effect of exclusion from financial markets, or at least inclusion on less favorable terms. To the extent that the expectation is really bankable, it is a real asset, and hence the power to destroy that asset is the power to harm.

Interrupted income as a loss of wealth. G may undertake debt financing in order to acquire durable assets earlier in time than is possible with self-financing. She wants a loan to buy a car, a home, a television, or new boat. Because the expectation of future income is not completely free of risk, lenders also demand the additional security of a lien on the home, auto, consumer durables, or boat. Interruptions in the flow of income may lead to a loss of title in, and use of, those things. In the fired employee's mind the utility gained from having those things now exceeds the financial costs of being in debt; that is, there is real consumer surplus being enjoyed. On a balance sheet the car and the loan may cancel each other out, but since the borrower opted for the car, that was clearly preferable to her. There is thus a real loss in welfare, defined in utility terms, when the mortgage is foreclosed even though the indebtedness is canceled. The power to interrupt income may thus also be power to reduce wealth.

Future access to capital markets. Uncertainty makes it very difficult for lenders to know the character of the people to whom they may loan money and, more importantly, the probability of being repaid. Although employment history is one indicator that may be used, credit experience is another, and one that is readily available from credit rating services. Interrupted earnings that cause a failure to meet payment schedules and ultimately result in the reclaiming of security for a loan may also reduce future access to capital markets, even if G is employed at that future time. That also is a loss of real welfare relative to continued employment. Capital markets expect the employment contract to be ongoing. If it is not, they do not perceive it as a mere readjustment in a series of spot contracts. They perceive it as evidence of personal failure.

Imperfections, organizations, and internal labor markets

There is a further complication to consider. By the end of the preceding chapter, departure from the special case had led to a most complex world. Information problems, unequal access to important data, limits to human computations, and imperfections in contracting had resulted in a world where administrative organizations often supplanted markets as coordinators of human activity. Rational, self-interested maximizers created those organizations in response to the potential exercise of complex forms of power in the imperfect markets of that complex world.

Many of the employment relations with which I am here concerned fall under the umbrella of, and are affected by, the character of those institutions that have thus arisen. Many of those organizations are not obviously based upon team-production functions with a single entrepreneur at a central hub directing all of the others.[7] Many involve layers of agency, perhaps with no single well-defined entrepreneurial principal at all. Organizations in the real world have evolved peculiar forms of labor practices, perhaps as the best response to all of these market complications and the resultant power. They may also, however, act to redefine the power to punish that is under consideration here.

Internal labor markets

In the late nineteenth century the nature of labor relations in many of the rapidly expanding industrial areas underwent a significant change in form. Early factories often saw a system of labor contracts with independent foremen who, in turn, contracted with the factory management. The foremen supplied their own work force and paid each employee a separately bargained wage. Both foremen and firm

[7] This is the concept of the firm put forth by Alchian and Demsetz in their "Production."

were principals. Firms, as such, had few "employees" other than staff and administrative personnel. By the end of the century employment relations were changing and the firms themselves began to take a role in selecting the individuals who would become production workers. Large-scale enterprises began to centralize administration of human resources and make it an overt management function. Individual employees were not then hired on the basis of separately negotiated contracts, but were hired to fill defined positions on distinct job "ladders," at wages associated with specific rungs, and subject to particular patterns of promotion over time. Formally structured agency layers came to predominate.[8]

Since then these patterns of filling employment needs, known as "internal labor markets" have become widespread. Virtually all large organizations in both the profit and nonprofit sectors employ these kinds of arrangements in acquiring human labor as a factor of production. While the particulars vary from organization to organization, there are some general characteristics that seem to define internal labor markets as a class of structures. These include the following:

1. Entry-level positions. There are certain well-defined points of entry onto job ladders. Virtually all positions on rungs higher than entry level are filled by promotion within the organization. There are often well-defined job tracks and career paths. There is little outside search for superior candidates to fill open slots higher up the ladder.
2. Compensation tied to jobs rather than persons. Levels of compensation tend to be tied to specific job categories, and individuals with clearly differing productivity in the same categories will be paid the same. Compensation for superior performance may be rewarded by accelerated movement up the job ladder rather than by current income.
3. Creation of work rules and personnel procedures outlining criteria for hiring, firing, evaluation, performance, and so forth.

These are peculiar systems to arise in market societies, for they seem to defy the rules of market transactions by restricting options, not paying for current performance, and creating expectation "rights" to continued employment. Why would these restrictions ever develop in interactions among rational transactors?

---

[8] For a fascinating volume describing internal labor markets in a variety of settings see Paul Osterman, ed., *Internal Labor Markets*, MIT Press, Cambridge, Mass., 1984.

Internal labor markets as a response to market failures

Oliver Williamson argues that such restrictions arise via his theory of "institutional failures."[9] Building upon the interactions of his four key elements – bounded rationality, information impactedness, opportunism, and the small-numbers problem – he explains the predominance of these arrangements as a rational response to the inefficiencies associated with real-market problems.

Employers are unable to acquire perfect information about all potential employees. Because of bounded rationality they cannot effectively evaluate more than a small fraction of the potential candidates. Much of the information they need about job skills, personal characteristics, attitude, and potential is disproportionately in the hands of the applicants. If applicants respond opportunistically and shape that information to meet their own needs, the employer is unable to ascertain with certainty the real potential of the employee. Who at an interview ever stresses their weaknesses and areas of incompetence? Who does not "pad" their potential? If all candidates do that, then it is expensive, if not impossible, to determine which candidates are, in fact, most qualified. Certainly the firm may incur some costs of verifying information by checking references, past employers, and the validity of academic records, but even there the candidate can control to some extent which information will be "checkable."

By hiring only at specific entry-level positions the firm is able to acquire information by experience with individual workers. The information is "internal" to the firm and hence will not be biased by an outside source. Unable to evaluate productivity effectively prior to own experience, firms will pay equal wages to all occupants of a particular rung on the job ladder. Because paying at a level appropriate to the highest productivity worker would be inefficient, the level of pay, according to Williamson, will be below that level, perhaps at the average. Highly talented workers will accept that exploitation (payment at less than current worth) because they know that they are superior and will be rewarded over time. Workers who ultimately prove out will be compensated for the early exploitation by payment in excess of current value when they reach a higher level on the employment ladder. This premium is in part payment for past underpayment and in part payment to hold workers with idiosyncratic job skills.

---

[9] See Williamson, *Markets and Hierarchies*, The Free Press, New York, 1975, esp. pp. 57–81.

This pattern is easy to see in a college faculty. Not trusting outside experience and evidence, many colleges prefer to hire only at the bottom and to promote from within based upon own experience. Faculty are paid according to rank rather than current productivity. Reward for "output" comes in the form of more rapid promotion and higher wages at higher rank. I teach no more courses, no more students, and no more effectively than I did as an assistant professor without tenure. I publish at no more rapid a rate. In effect, I did the same job for far less real compensation then than I get now. There were, when I was a junior faculty member, several senior faculty (not in my department, of course) who, in fact, taught far less and published far less frequently (in fact not at all) than I, yet were paid much more. Their premium was in part based on compensation for past underpayment. That reflects perhaps a rational response to being unable to predict the future productivity of faculty. It is certainly not, in the marginal productivity scheme of formal theory, compensation according to current marginal contribution.

It is perhaps instructive that major research universities often follow a different pattern of hiring and promotion. Since teaching is, in fact, of very little relevance to job performance, while publication in prestigious journals is paramount, job performance can be judged by outside information. Filling the top ranks from outside the university is then common. In a college where classroom teaching is considered very important, it is not clear that what is considered effective in one context will be so in another. I have noted over the years, for example, that every graduate student from a major midwestern university who has applied for a job has won that university's "distinguished teaching award." It is hard to know exactly what to make of that. Own experience with teaching is more reliable, and promotion from within the rule.

Note how these structures reflect Williamson's theory of market imperfections. Since information impactedness and opportunism make it difficult to evaluate outside candidates, outside information is used only at the lowest entry levels. Internal information is gathered by experience for promotion up the ladder. Since bounded rationality dictates only a small search for each position, search is restricted to that subset already within the institution. Because the same problems make it impossible to pay entry labor according to productivity, average-level wages are used, and the best labor is compensated with more rapid advancement to the next level and higher wages there. For potential employees, the undercompensation will be made up over time if performance is indeed above average.

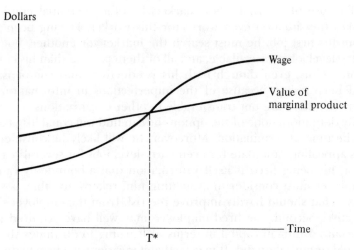

Figure 7.2. Compensation in internal labor markets.

Internal labor markets and the power to punish

Recall the essential characteristics of internal labor markets:

- Hiring only for specific entry-level positions
- Wages attached to job categories
- Entry wages set at average productivity with compensation in the future to high-productivity workers in the form of rapid advancement and premium wages
- Well-defined rules for promotion, retention, and termination

These introduce potential negative power in the form of an ability to impose lifetime losses at least at certain junctures in the decision path of affected individuals. If Williamson et al. are correct and internal labor markets generate a time path of compensation that underpays at early stages and overpays at higher rungs, then there is substantial vulnerability as the employee is reaching the crossover point. Figure 7.2 shows one such hypothetical situation. The vertical axis is measured in dollars and the horizontal in units of time. I have assumed that the actual value of contributed output of a hypothetical worker rises over time in a linear fashion. Actual compensation also rises, but in early periods it is below the worker's value while in later periods it is higher. A worker fired just as he approaches the crossover at time T^* will have been, even in traditional microtheory terms, exploited.

The use of internal labor markets by other potential employers makes the situation even worse for this worker. Having been fired from his first job, he must search the market for another, but only entry-level jobs are available, and all of them pay less than his current value. Thus, even though both his productivity and compensation had been rising, because of the imperfections in information and markets, those are not transferable to other organizations.

By definition, none of the options he can find will equal his position at the time of termination. Moreover, he will likely be considered a less appealing candidate for even entry-level jobs for several reasons. First, his being fired is itself information that a boundedly rational employer must consider in evaluating him relative to other possibilities. That should hardly improve the risk from the employer's perspective. Second, the fired employee may well have acquired some specialized human capital in terms of learning to do things the way his old organization did. It may be that it is easier for a firm to develop new "capital" rather than retool old. Third, since the employee had progressed beyond entry level in the old job, but only entry level is available in new ones, he may be considered overqualified. Obviously, this creates a catch-22 for the employee; having been fired he is a bad risk, but having been successful prior to firing he is too talented.

If the fired employee does find a new entry-level job, it will require an additional period of compensation at a level below the value of his contribution. Thus termination from the first job lowers the lifetime welfare of the worker on a pure income basis. If the psychological and search costs are added, the damage is simply increased. Note that the employer, in firing, to some extent also determines the agenda that will be relevant in the coming periods. That act "publishes" to the labor market information that lowers the expected value of the employee in the eyes of other employers.

The decision of the employee to accept that first job in the context of an internal labor market is an act that endows the employer with significant granted event power. It is analogous to the decision of the hypothetical farmer (back in Chapter 3) to plant tomatoes. But in the case of the tomato farmer, he sought to control the exercise of power by creating a formal, comprehensive, and enforceable contract specifying limits on that event power. Here, however, Williamson's argument is that the whole reason why there are organizations and internal labor markets is that such comprehensive contracting is impossible. To assume it as a solution would be to assume away the initial problem. If that is the solution, there was no problem. If there is a problem, that cannot be the solution.

The employee is forced to rely, then, to some degree on simple trust. If she does her job, the boss will do right by her. Maybe she can rely on the self-interest of employers who will be unable to use the advantages of an internal labor market (in overcoming blind-date problems) if it becomes known that they often renege on the implicit promise to compensate talented labor with future premiums and promotions. If this becomes known, they face an adverse selection problem in that employees who believe themselves to be better than average will not accept employment, whereas those who are below average can still gain on the early rungs of the employment and compensation ladder.

It was perhaps the inadequacy of that control and a failure of pure trust to contain abuses of that power that led to an acceptance of the formal personnel rules and procedures that now characterize many internal labor markets. Firms may have come to accept those rules (though after a serious struggle for power) because it acts as a signal to talented employees that the event power will not be unconstrained. It will not, however, necessarily be eliminated.

Organizations, agency, and the power to punish

Internal labor markets are only a part of the complications in this more complex case. Because the ultimate employer is an organization rather than a natural person, the problems of agency and imperfect agent control also enter the picture. Now the decision on hiring or firing has been delegated to an agent, a real human being with control over other humans because of her position within an organization. If, as I have argued, the granted event power in the employment relation must be given in part on the basis of trust, then locating this power in an agent makes that trust less effective as a control for at least two reasons.

First, if part of the basis of trust is the self-interest of the employing organization, that is, it is in *the organization's* interest to be able to hire over time a better quality of labor, it is not necessarily in the interests of the agent who, in fact, makes the choice and has the power. There are imperfections in the control that organizations as principals have over the actions of agents. There is likely no such thing as a coherent preference function for the collective principal. That principal has little knowledge of the activities of specific agents and little or no ability to impose direct sanctions.

The agent in whom this power becomes vested may substitute some criteria other than productivity for the organization. The hypothetical tenure example in which deciders added criteria of social compatibility, methodological purity, political ideology, or sexual availability would be a classic case. The agent may have a very different time horizon and be much more concerned with very short term elements than long-term productivity since she will, in turn, be moving along a career ladder and will need to find appropriate performance signals. Whistle blowers who attempt to stop illegal or unethical practices undertaken by other *agents* of an organization may benefit the organization over the long run but damage the involved agents. When those agents have any form of job authority over the whistle blower there is ample anecdotal evidence that they do not use it to reward her for her concern with long-term corporate welfare.[10]

Second, the person who grants the event power when she accepts employment grants it to the mythical principal and has no way of knowing which real persons will be the powerful agents when the crucial time comes. The trust must be that an undefinable principal will delegate authority to top agents who can be trusted to further delegate it to other unnamed agents who can be trusted to delegate it to still others. By definition, there is no complete contract to cover all this. The employee is accepting an ambiguous contract based on her perceptions of what will be deemed sufficient performance, how that performance will be evaluated, and by whom. If, when the time comes, the actual contract as interpreted by the now powerful agent differs, the employee is definitely not returned to the starting point to begin again. Her lifetime utility has been reduced by the unanticipated and uncontrolled exercise of power by the agent.

When the employee, or now ex-employee, learns that the trust has been violated, there is often no recourse. Precisely because it is not a formal, enforceable contract there is imperfect legal recourse. Because of bounded rationality and internal labor markets it is not simply a matter of telling the true story to alternative employers. The termination is a real and uncorrectable loss.

All of this becomes exceedingly complex if different forms of power are exercised over time. When the first choice is made to accept the job offer, control over information or any other technique might be used to induce G onto the path that then grants to C later event power. The sum total of the human interaction must be considered. It is not always a sequence of isolated and wholly independent events.

---

[10] For a series of case studies of organizational response to agents who may, in fact, be following principals' interests see Alan F. Westin, *Whistle-Blowing*, McGraw-Hill, New York, 1981.

Conclusions

An employment relation is an agreement on the part of the employee to take some degree of direction from the employer. On the surface, this is a form of authority or power. Alchian and Demsetz have argued that, for this power to be real, there must be some way for the exerciser to punish the subject, and they see no such way. That conclusion inevitably holds, however, only if the special case holds. All transactions must be costless, all information must be perfect, and all contracts must be globally complete and perfectly enforceable at zero cost. In addition these spot contracts must be between principals rather than agents, and organizational structures with institutional practices such as internal labor markets must be forbidden.

That is an interesting world. It is one often visited by economists. (Indeed, some seem to be most uncomfortable outside its borders.) It is not, however, the world in which real people live. That world is populated with uncertainty, costly transactions, imperfect contracts, and complex social institutions and organizations. Those elements create a possibility for real punishment to be inflicted by one human upon another. There is also, therefore, the possibility for one human who extracts a price from the other to refrain from exercising the power. The size of the price depends upon the scope of potential punishment.

This is, again, not an argument that every employment relation is built upon the blatant exercise of uncontrolled, naked power. Quite the contrary. It is an argument that various degrees of power are possible in real world employment relations, and a conclusion that they are paramount or trivial can never be made on the basis of simple abstract argument. A labor market need not be a defense against all power. It will not be inevitably a focus of power. Each situation needs to be examined in its own light and context. What I have attempted here is to provide some of the tools and a framework for doing so. I argue only that reaching conclusions about real cases without using those tools is irresponsible. Ideology may wish to do so. Serious inquiry will not.

I can now go further still. I have reached a juncture in the argument where the conclusions of the past three chapters should be considered together. When the special case fails, market interactions can involve the entire menu of power. Changes in environmental conditions such as the complexity of traded products inevitably alter the potential for the exercise of power. Many of the legislative and judicial efforts to define the "rules of the game" may be seen as responses to the chang-ing structure of market generated power (Chapter 5).

The failure of the special case also eliminates the clear presumption that markets are always the superior (that is, most efficient and *pow-erless*) method of organizing human activity. In many cases adminis-trative organizations may themselves be the response of rational maximizers to potential power in markets. Thus power arising in imperfect markets may well be a factor in determining the whole institutional structure of a society as well as its political policies and legal rules (Chapter 6).

Finally, that response, in the form of organizations with their re-liance on adminstrative practices and layers of agency, changes the nature of the employment relation. In the less than perfect world outside the special case, there may often be a real power to punish (Chapter 7).

There can be no markets separate from the other institutions of society. *Ceteris* is never *paribus*; it is always endogenous. Rational, max-imizing individuals will insist upon it. The nature of real-world mar-kets with the imperfections inherent in them means that other institutions will exist and will be systematically linked to existing mar-kets and their specific imperfections. One crucial element defining society, both within and without its markets, would then seem to be a pervasive system of power. The analysis is not yet complete, of course. I have so far concentrated on what may occur when people attempt to exchange the things to which they have rights in a market setting. I have yet to consider the nature and source of those very rights. These, too, may involve real power.

CHAPTER 8

Rights and power

In the world of Robinson Crusoe property rights play no role. Property rights are an instrument of society.... An owner of property rights possesses the consent of fellow men to allow him to act in particular ways. An owner expects the community to prevent others from interfering with his actions.

Harold Demsetz, "Toward a Theory of Property Rights"

Societies as systems of rights

Markets are always part of a larger social context, entwined in a social system with other endogenous institutions. The sum of these institutions and the self-interested, maximizing individuals who interact within them may, in fact, be much of what constitutes a society. There is at least one thing more. A society is also a system of *group* defined and defended "rights." These rights in turn define *who may do what, with what, to whom, when, and why.* There are several things to note about this definition. The use of the word "may" implies some kind of permission. As every parent knows, things are done without permission, but without an established right there is the expectation of some external punishment. The definition speaks of control over resources, of purpose, and of action. In the language of Chapter 2, it directly implies both event power and agenda power. If I have the *right* (social permission) to do something, and it affects you, I have event power over you. If I have the *right* (social permission) to prevent you from doing something, I have agenda power over you. Rights may take many specific forms, but without the element of social definition and enforcement, there can be no real rights. Persons may use things and may have hopes about how they and "their" things will be treated by other persons. They do not, however, have rights.

Individually determined rights

Carry the neoclassical fixation with asocial individuals to its most extreme level and assume fully formed individuals, separated from all

141

institutions. This mythical state of nature so beloved by philosophers might be called a situation of "individually determined rights." There is no agreement about rights. There is no real society. There are only isolated individuals free of obligation to others. (There is, of course, no historical validity to such a presumption. Long before humans became human, their ancestors were social animals with social structures. Asocial humans are the artificial constructs of eighteenth-century philosophers and twentieth-century economists.)

In the absence of social controls each person may do to any other whatever she can get away with. There is no social structure or mechanism to grant or deny permission. Any strategy is to be judged only on the basis of personal costs and benefits. There are no costs to consider except those that can be imposed by other asocial individuals acting in an individual capacity. My property is whatever I can hold against intruders. Anything I can take by force is mine. Anything I can acquire in any other fashion is mine.

Thomas Hobbes speculated that life in such a setting would be "nasty, brutish and short." Ethnologists studying animal behavior would undoubtedly agree. This is the set of "rights" common among animals. The territories, kills, food sources, and mates of animals are theirs only until a stronger animal comes to claim them. Then their rights are extinguished. Without a larger social order to enforce the rights, they are individually determined, and individually extinguishable.

Anthropologists have yet to uncover any human collections based upon these asocial rights. People cannot live effectively with each other under such a system. Potential societies with such a basis would be ill equipped to survive. Groups of people with ongoing interactions and some self-concept of community inevitably have complex systems of rights that carry *social* sanctions. Without socially determined rights, there is really no society.

Socially determined rights

True rights imply social enforcement. There must be a higher force to which an individual can appeal for their defense. That appeal may be explicit in the form of a legal proceeding. It may be implicit and involve the unrequested support of others. These rights cover the entire scope of human interactions. They involve the use of property in its narrowest terms. They also involve much more.

In a modern society, the law is a source of many, but not all rights. In the United States today, patients who go to the doctor have a right to treatment that is not malpractice. Sinners seeking counsel with clergy have a right to confidentiality. A party to a contract to buy his ancestral home may, with specific performance, have a right to have title transferred to him. Anyone walking down the street has a right to be free of physical assault. Employees have the right to be free of unwanted sexual propositions on the job, but not necessarily at the ball game. Citizens have the right to be free of discrimination based on race when it is practiced by any agent of government (unless, of course, there is an "overwhelming and compelling state interest" in doing so). They may be discriminated against by private parties, except in some circumstances. I can refuse to rent a room in my home to a member of a minority group. I cannot refuse to rent an apartment in a multiunit complex. Parents may not beat their children, yet under ancient Roman law they could have them executed. Divorced parents could, until very recently, "kidnap" their own children despite custody orders of courts. They cannot kidnap other people's.

What is property and the extent of the rights associated with ownership are also socially determined. The owner of land has the right to use it as he pleases, unless it conflicts with zoning regulations, environmental laws, nuisance actions, public condemnation proceedings, or prior contract obligations. He may erect an ugly building there and force others to look at it. He may grow weeds and let the seeds float through the air onto a neighbor's immaculate lawn. He may thus use it to do some things, but not all things, to some people. He has rights. The inventor of a new product may prevent others from marketing it in the United States, but not necessarily in all other countries. The composer of a song may prevent others from copying it or performing it commercially. He may not prevent people from singing it for their own pleasure. They too have socially defined rights.

Who may do what, with what, to whom, when, and why is a complex issue, defining in essence our relationships to each other. *All of these rights have a social basis.* They are not the product of individual bargains; they are the product of group processes. Even individually bargained contract rights are of no real value without the enforcement powers of social structures behind them. They become rights only when they become social. Markets, as collectivities of individual bargains, are impossible without well-defined, socially established rights as a precondition.

The scope of society

Societies have boundaries. When they are reached, rights cease to have meaning. Conversely, the limits to a given "society" may be deemed to lie, geographically or conceptually, where the rights end.

They are an artificial construct of a self-conscious collection of persons. The rights to freedom and property defended by the social organization of the west African tribe became meaningless at the slave market in New Orleans. Ownership of horses in Native American tribes could only pass within the tribe by a sanctioned transfer of rights from one member to another. Between tribes, forcible transfer was not only accepted, it was expected. A warrior who stole horses within the tribe was dishonored. One who stole outside the tribe was honored.

The history of nation-states includes many examples of acquiring territory by conquest and returning it via sale. Henry VIII took Tournai in what is now Belgium as a prize of war with France. Having forcibly driven out the French, he ruled it as his own for several years. In 1518, however, he sold it to François I of France. Neither monarch seemed concerned about the validity of the title. Neither seemed to notice that it had been stolen from France by force. Neither, as an experienced monarch, harbored any illusions that Henry might not reconquer it at a later date if it became advantageous to do so. Neither was noted, however, for such a casual attitude toward his property rights within the confines of his own country.[1] An individual taking crown property within France and attempting to sell it back to the monarch would have faced substantial social sanctions. An external power could do so with impunity, for there were no supranational social institutions to defend rights. If nations can be viewed as individual actors (which I do not believe they can), international rights are closely analogous to individually determined ones. There is no overriding social mechanism of enforcement. Whatever I (England) can get away with I shall do.

Forms of rights

Rights may take many forms, but only a few are consistent with the type of exchange characteristic of markets. What types of rights are possible, and how do they affect the functioning of markets? How do the forms of rights in markets affect the potential for power?

Entitlements

Some rights are attached to specific individuals because of their status. They are attached to those persons as long as the status continues.

[1] Jasper Ridley, *Henry VIII: The Politics of Tyranny*, Viking/Penquin, New York, 1985, esp. Chapters 4 and 7.

They may not be separated from the individual in that specific social role. They need not be sought or desired by the persons having them. They are socially granted. Children are entitled to support from their parents, and that is a right that may neither be bargained away nor sold. It is vested in them as a result of their status. The right to vote in contemporary democracies is similarly an entitlement. It is vested in the person and is not subject (legally) to sale or purchase. In many communities, residence in a jurisdiction entitles one to public library or special park usage. It is a right that is not directly purchased. It may not be sold. It is extinguished when the person moves outside the jurisdiction. Because they are not transferable, entitlements are obviously inconsistent with the development of markets.

Entitlements as use rights to property

In the case of property, entitlements become "use" rights attached to individuals. They may use property in certain specified ways but may not transfer that right to someone else. Clearly, feudal society was based on a system of use rights concerning land, with various parties having differential rights to use different areas. Serfs had a right to cultivate certain fields and to graze livestock in certain pastures. They could not, however, sell or otherwise transfer that right. Native Americans had similar rights to land and territories. Any member of the tribe could use the resources for his own benefit, but failure to use the resource personally ended any claim. The rights were not transferable. Property was "owned" in common. Individuals had use rights only.

The same general principle holds in many modern churches. Each member of the church has certain rights to the use of the church property by virtue of membership. It is not a right that may be sold or otherwise transferred. It is generally conferred as a condition of membership. When membership ceases, so does all authority over the property.

These rights are inconsistent with markets, which become possible only when the system of rights to property is expanded to permit transfer at the will of the holder. Nothing less will allow markets to operate.

Full exchange rights

The Uniform Commerical Code defines the sale of goods as the "passing of title from the seller to the buyer for a price."[2] Markets, which

---

[2] Uniform Commercial Code, Section 2–106.(2).

are the location of such passings, thus require social systems that define and defend identifiable rights that are vested in specific individuals and are transferable to others as specified by the initial holder. Without such fully vested and socially defended exchange rights, the concept of market trades simply becomes meaningless. Anyone who pays a price for the title to land under a system of nonexchangeable rights is close kin to the apocryphal bumpkin who "bought the Brooklyn Bridge." No one can really sell something he does not own. Until there are social sanctions defending full exchange rights for property there can be no real markets.

Obviously there can be no such rights in the hypothetical state of nature previously discussed. There must be collective mechanisms for defining and defending these rights or we are back at the "individually determined rights" (read "might makes right") of that case. Markets absolutely need social structures. They require an organized community making decisions about the nature of rights – in short, a society.

Economists of all persuasions have recognized this at least in terms of the class of rights relating to property. Milton Friedman realizes that his capitalism is not really possible without state enforcement of private property rights and privately established contract rights.[3] Marx saw stages of social history largely defined by the socially established system of property rights. What is actually traded in markets is rights. The special case was based upon implicit assumptions about the presence of developed markets, and hence about the nature of the system of rights and the social processes of defining them.

The economics of property rights

If rights can have many forms and if markets' functioning depends on the nature of the rights established, then two key questions stand out. Where do these social rights come from, and where do they lead? Economists have concentrated substantial attention on the second, for it involves analysis of resource allocation, an issue with which they are comfortable. They have incompletely addressed the first question, for a complete analysis would include a search for power, an issue with which they are not. There are classic articles addressing the sources of rights, but they have asked primarily why rights might come about. They have ignored how.

[3]   Milton Friedman, *Capitalism and Freedom*, University of Chicago Press, Chicago, 1962, Chapter 2.

Ronald Coase and the problem of social cost

Coase argues that externalities are not really failures of the market, but failures of the society to fully specify private exchange rights to all valuable resources.[4] If private rights are fully established and transaction costs are not prohibitive, then resource allocation will be efficient, and the final use of resources will be independent of who has ownership. If the resource has more value to one potential user than another, then that user will determine its use whether he must buy it from another or whether that other will be unwilling to bid enough to buy it from him. Externalities will be internalized. Resources will always flow to their highest and best use. Appropriate forms of rights promote efficiency. Property rights have a clear function. They make the world a better place. That is perhaps why they have come about. It says nothing about how.

Harold Demsetz and the Montagnes

Demsetz extends Coase's view and argues that an implicit awareness of the allocative function of rights *is* the reason why they came about. For him, a perhaps unconscious drive to internalize externalities is the actual historical force behind changes in the forms of rights. Private property was a rational response to externalities.[5] He borrows from an anthropological study done by Eleanor Leacock of the Montagnes Indians on the Labrador Peninsula in the seventeenth century.[6] Demsetz explains changes in the form of property rights as a response to changes in market opportunities due to contact with European fur traders.

Before European contact, all members of the tribe had equal (communal) rights to all beavers and all territories. Any hunter finding a lodge of beaver could (had social permission to) kill them all for whatever purpose he so chose. The increasing value of furs in exchange with Europeans created a problem of the "commons." A hunter who harvested each beaver he found gained a benefit. A hunter who acted to conserve the beaver population may only have provided gain to another future hunter. Thus each hunter had an

---

[4] Ronald Coase, "The Problem of Social Cost," *Journal of Law and Economics*, Vol. 3, October 1960, pp. 1–44.

[5] Harold Demsetz, "Toward a Theory of Property Rights," *American Economic Review*, May 1967, pp. 347–373.

[6] Eleanor Leacock, *American Anthropologist*, Vol. 56, No. 5, Part 2, Memorandum 78, 1954, p. 9.

incentive to overhunt, and none had an incentive to preserve the population for hunting in future periods.

The Montagnes did develop a different set of rights, and Demsetz argues that it was because they recognized, even if they did not articulate, this tragedy of the commons. Individual territories became the exclusive province of individual hunters. Beaver left to multiply in a lodge could later be claimed by the hunter with a right to that territory.

The new rights were restricted, however. They involved use rights to land for the purpose of taking beaver pelts for sale. The hunter did not own the land. He could not sell it, or even sell the right to hunt beaver on it. He could not prevent anyone from using it for any other purpose. Other hunters could take deer, squirrels, or rabbits as they wished and could cross it or camp upon it as they wished. A hungry hunter could kill and eat any beaver. The right was only to exclude others from taking beaver pelts for sale to European traders. The externality involved only the rate of harvest of beaver pelts for sale. Demsetz concludes that the rational maximizing Montagnes developed these new rights explicitly focused on that specific inefficiency.

Richard Posner and kinship obligations

Like Coase and Demsetz, Richard Posner can lay claim to Founding Father status in law and economics, the subfield of economics that has generated analysis of rights. He has also sought an explanation for the absence of vested exchange rights in primitive cultures. While surveying anthropological case studies he noted the widespread presence of systems of kinship-sharing obligations. A successful member of the society is obligated to share the fruits of his hunt or harvest with other members of his kinship group. Alternatively stated, members of the kinship group have a right to a share in the bounty of the successful member. There is no formal contract and no formal trade. There is no specific debt to be discharged in the future. There is only a reciprocal obligation to share if the situations are ever reversed. This right is not, however, marketable. The successful hunter cannot buy back the right to a share and cannot dispose of the surplus in any other fashion. The party entitled to a share cannot sell that right to someone else. The right is embodied in the person and is part of a nontransferable kinship status.

If private exchange rights are so clearly superior, why have they not been adopted in these societies? Posner is concerned with why rights exist, not how they come into being. Thus his answer is that under certain conditions they are not superior.[7] He builds a model with minimal production, no means of storing surpluses, no mechanism to enforce contracts, and limited ability to trade with other groups. Kinship obligations replace exchange rights because they are the most efficient form of "insurance" available. People have chosen these rights as part of a constrained-maximization strategy. Efficiency dictates the size of the optimal kinship group under varying conditions. Posner is therefore certain that, whenever technological constraints change in these "primitive" cultures, rational maximization will result in different forms of socially defined and defended rights. He is clear on why rights may change. He is absolutely silent on how.

Conclusions

The role of rights as a necessary precondition to markets has thus come to be recognized by those at the very heart of neoclassical economics. The forms of rights will inevitably affect the allocations of resources, and therefore who will get what. Demsetz at least recognizes that the system of rights has strong implications for who will win and who will lose, that "rights convey the right to benefit or harm oneself or others."[8] Neoclassical economists have asked how the forms of rights, socially chosen, will change outcomes. They have asked why different forms of rights might be chosen. They have paid little attention, however, to the historical processes of this "choice."

If rights are granted by God or nature, then no human had a hand in the choice. If they are accepted unanimously, then all humans benefit from a Pareto-superior decision. If the definition of rights contains no negative power and if the processes of trading rights involves only simple economic power, then and only then is the special case fulfilled. The market world is a powerless world. If, however, the processes of choosing or redefining rights involve the endogenous exercise of power by those who will later participate in their exchange, then the process of defining rights is relevant to even the *efficiency* of the outcome. If market transactions are to be free of the taint of negative power, no one must be harmed by the actions of another, either in defining or trading rights! I need to know, then, *how* rights are established.

[7] Richard Posner, *The Economics of Justice*, Harvard University Press, Cambridge, Mass., 1981, pp. 150–163.
[8] Demsetz, "Toward a Theory", p. 347.

The creation of rights as the exercise of power

The vision of property set forth by Demsetz and Coase as a prerequisite to efficient resource allocation relies upon an argument that externalities should be internalized. Earlier I noted that traditionally defined externalities are, in fact, a form of event power, and thus their prescription for eliminating this event power is to create well-defined, private property rights. The prescription does not, however, eliminate the problem, for *the act of creating property rights is itself an externality under the classic definition.*

Consider Demsetz's example of the hunting rights of the Montagnes. Under the old system of common rights *all* hunters had a right to take any beaver they found. When exclusive rights are granted to a single hunter, all of the others have, by definition, been excluded from a right they previously had, that is, they have been harmed. They have lost something of value to them, *and they are not compensated for the loss.* There is thus, by definition, an externality. Demsetz offers us no vision of the *process* of changing the form of rights. There is simply "an emergence of new property rights [that] takes place in response to the desires of interacting persons for the adjustment to new benefit-cost possibilities."[9] This makes the process sound like one of group consensus; it seldom is. If this emergence is to be Pareto optimal, absolutely no individual may, by his own subjective evaluation, be made worse off. Each loser of an old right must willingly agree to the loss or be fully compensated. If anyone is compelled to accept the loss, the creation of the new rights is not Pareto optimal. Negative power has been exercised.

When Demsetz presents his summation of the study done by Leacock, he exercises a bit of information power of his own. His concern is with the future results of the change in rights for resource allocations, so he tells us only the information relevant to that. Leacock, with an anthropologist's concern for impacts on community, adds other information left out of Demsetz's summary:

This is not to say that individual land holding patterns develop smoothly and easily as soon as the fur trade becomes the economic basis of Indian life. On the contrary, the Indians show considerable resistance to giving up the communal for individualized patterns of living.[10]

Some members of the tribe are forced to accept the loss of their prior communal rights. Someone in the social structure has had the ability

---

[9] Ibid., p. 350.
[10] Leacock, *American Anthropologist*, p. 9.

to exercise negative power, removing old options from the resisting members of the tribe.

Demsetz is not alone in focusing on the effects of rights to the exclusion of the process of forming rights. Coase followed a very similar path. Both recognized, but heavily deemphasized, the wealth and welfare implications of the processes of forming rights. It is as if they were to shout, "Well-defined rights lead to efficient resource allocation, and the specific assignment of rights does not change the outcome," only to add in a barely audible whisper, "though of course the distributions of income and wealth will differ." That whispered, parenthetical phrase contains a great deal of power.

Andrew Schotter uses game theory to analyze social rules that exist to control social behavior.[11] One of his examples involves the hypothetical case of two ranchers who must take their animals to one of two separated mountain pastures, one of which is clearly superior to the other. If they both go to the superior one, its superiority is lost. If either goes to the inferior one, the other rancher derives the benefit. It is a real allocative-efficiency, social-coordination problem. Schotter solves it as most neoclassical economists do, by making an assumption, that is, "property rights *evolve* to solve this simple coordination system" (emphasis added).[12]

How do they "evolve"? Does one rancher shoot the stock of the other? Does he shoot the other rancher? Do they hire private soldiers to defend the pasturage as was common in the American west? Do they flip a coin, consult an oracle, ask their priest, or hold a race to the better pasture? Does one finance the election of legislators favorable to his interests and then turn to the legislature for resolution? These are not irrelevant questions. Someone is going to gain. Someone is going to lose. There may be an exercise of *power* in the *process of establishing rights*.

History is replete with examples of the processes whereby the form and holding of rights is altered. Indeed, this "emergence" of new rights is what the conflicts in political history are most often about. Consider the development of private rights to land in England. Under feudalism, serfs had a socially determined and defended right to the use of various lands for crops and grazing. Those rights survived for many generations. With the rise in the value of wool, there were potential gains to be made by converting that land to sheep farming. The serfs, however, did not have exchange rights to the land, only

---

[11] Andrew Schotter, *The Economic Theory of Social Institutions*, Cambridge University Press, 1981.
[12] Ibid., p. 44.

use rights. Their rights could not be purchased, nor could any of the serfs have bought the rights of others (either legally or pragmatically given their income constraints). The transactions costs of gathering these rights would, in either case, have been prohibitive anyway. To take advantage of these potential profits (which, of course, were signals of improved efficiency in resource allocation), new forms of rights had to "evolve." In this case rights "evolution" meant burning the homes of the serfs, killing their stock, and on occasion killing them. After decades of this violent "emergence" of the new rights, Parliament ratified the change with the Acts of Enclosure in the eighteenth century. The new rights may have been more efficient when traded, but the process of their emergence was in no way Pareto superior.[13]

The expansion of the territories of the United States during the middle years of the nineteenth century is another example of changing the forms of the rights within a social group. It also involved changing the nature of the group empowered to make the social decision about forms of rights. The lands of the Great Plains were clearly occupied long prior to European expansion. Rights to the use of that land were also clearly established within the boundaries of the social groups living there. In most cases the form of the rights was communal use rights. Whichever member of the tribe was using a resource was entitled to it until he stopped using it. Then any other could use it at will. There was no concept of exchange rights in resources at all. The relevant society had not defined them as such and certainly would not defend them. Members of other tribes were not granted even use rights though certain leaders of the tribe could grant temporary use rights to members of other tribes. The full exclusionary powers of the group would be brought to bear on transgressors. In short, there was a well-developed system of socially defined and defended rights.

As contact with white society grew, new concepts of rights made their way into the region. Whites wanted the fully exclusionary, fully exchangeable rights in land common to their society, even though this concept made no sense to the current occupants. Insistent upon having their way, they sought to acquire what to them was wholly unowned land, and indeed in their sense it was. In an interview late in life, John Wayne adopted much the same attitude arguing that it was acceptable to take the land by force because "there were great

---

[13] For a dramatic description of the process of enclosures see Karl Marx, *Capital*, Vol. I, Part 8. For somewhat less dramatic descriptions see W. E. Tate, *The Enclosure Movement*, Walker, New York, 1967, or J. A. Yelling, *Common Field and Enclosure in England 1450–1850*, Macmillan Press, London, 1977.

numbers of people who needed new land, and Indians were selfishly trying to keep it for themselves."[14] Native Americans, however, perceived those incursions as clear violations of the communal tribal rights systems that defined their society. The path to resolution was clear. Decide which system of rights will prevail via resort to force. A new system of rights "evolved." Externalities were internalized. Hundreds of thousands of Native Americans died, and those remaining were either removed to or contained within specific reservations. Later trades of the rights so established may have been Pareto superior. The process of their "emergence" clearly was not.

The formalities of transforming title in this case carry still another element in rights transformation. The winners of the wars demanded that rights to the land be exchanged for a price, despite the fact that such transactions were not part of the social structure of rights of the losers. Treaties were signed *by tribal chiefs* transferring all use rights *of all members of the tribe, present and future*, to the United States or its designees. Tribal society had previously, through some social process, established a series of rights that did not include either exclusion or exchange. At the moment that the treaties were signed, two transformations of rights took place. The first was an instantaneous creation of *exchange* rights within the tribe that eliminated the use rights held by members and made them into exclusionary, exchange rights held by chiefs. Up until that moment each hunter had rights to use the land. At that moment he lost those rights, but not by a process of willfully giving them to the chiefs. They were compelled to grant them and the chiefs were compelled to take them. Enforcement of the instantaneous transfer was made possible by the presence of the United States Army.

The second transformation of rights was that those newly created and vested exclusionary and exchange rights were transferred to the United States government. In effect, the chiefs were required to sell something that they did not own. The expanding society of whites extended its system of rights to include a new group and redefined the relationships within that group as well as between groups. New rights did indeed "emerge," but some fairly significant welfare-affecting processes would seem to be subsumed under that simple and seemingly innocuous term.

The point to be made here is fairly simple. Rights are socially determined. They do not descend like manna from heaven; they are a human creation. The creation, or alteration in the form, of rights

---

[14] G. Barry Golson, ed., *The Playboy Interview*, Playboy Press, New York, 1981, p. 269.

(unlike the exercise of exchange rights in a market) likely creates winners and uncompensated losers. Unless everyone agrees to the change in the form of rights, some persons must have the *power* to compel others to accept new rights against their will! Without *that* power and its exercise there can be no "emergence" of new rights. It is simply a logical impossibility and an historical nonentity.

The point may be simple but its implications are not. It means that no real, normative statements can be made about any structure of rights, at least if traditional economic concepts are used. The Coase–Demsetz argument is that well-defined property rights are more efficient and hence implicitly preferable to other forms of rights. Yet even that conclusion is not really supportable for it takes a small piece of the total social process and uses it to draw welfare conclusions about the whole. The base-level definition of "efficient moves" in economic theory is that a change in resource allocations is better if and only if at least one party is made better off, and no one is made worse off. The Coase–Demsetz view is that private property facilitates these Pareto-optimal moves. They are wrong. It facilitates some such moves only by first making moves that are not Pareto superior.

What is involved is a sequence of moves, one altering rights and the next trading within the new system of rights. Unless each move is Pareto superior, then the whole series of moves cannot be said to be so. Hence it cannot even be said to be more efficient. If it is better, it is better under some standard that abandons the foundations of welfare economics and substitutes some undefined method for judging the relative worth of various individuals. The two sets of rights are clearly different, but one cannot, using accepted economic concepts, be said to be better than the other. They are merely different. That has enormous implications.

- If an externality is a form of event power (and a threat to future efficiency in resource allocation), *and*
- if such externalties can be internalized (and the power neutralized) only by creating vested exchange rights in individuals, *and*
- if these rights can be created only by exercising event power over the *process* of rights determination, *then*
- *the only way to eliminate power in one form is through the exercise of power in another!*

Market exchange is not possible without the prior exercise of power to create exchange rights. Markets do not eliminate power. Creating private exchange rights does not eliminate externalities. It simply moves them to different times, places, and contexts. There is no clear moral superiority to one form of power or the other. All perfect market transactions in perfect situations harm no one, *except* those harmed in the process of defining the rights later exchanged. To say we must impose losses on one group of people at one time to prevent other losses to other people at other times may be an inevitable choice of social structures, but it absolutely negates any reliance on Pareto optimality and efficiency as foundations for making that selection. Societies require rights. Rights require winners and losers. They simply do not permit universal gain. The powerless world of the special case thus depended on that set of unstated assumptions about the nature of rights and the processes of defining and redefining them. The failure of those conditions is a failure of the conclusion of perfect powerlessness.

When are rights defined?

It is, of course, possible to avoid the above argument by claiming that all rights predate human society, that is, that they are somehow given by the laws of nature or determined by nonhuman forces. If that is the case, then under my definition of "power" as the ability of one human to affect the lifetime welfare of another, there was no power in that process. Changes in rights and tornadoes are beyond the human pale. There are those who begin from such propositions. In Locke's famed State of Nature, noble savages live "in a state of perfect freedom to order their actions and dispose of their possessions and persons as they think fit, within the bounds of the law of nature, without asking leave or dependency upon the will of any other man."[15] For Locke, persons had rights and property before they had society.

More recently Robert Nozick has built a moral case for a minimal state arising from a similar State of Nature. Entitlements (rights) come from nature and precede society. "Things come into the world already attached to people having entitlements over them."[16] The process of setting rights is not a human or historical one.

Even overlooking the complete lack of evidence for a past State of Nature, the entitlements of which Nozick and Locke speak are in no sense practical rights. Persons may of course have possessions absent social structures but, as Demsetz noted in the quote opening this chapter, they do not have real rights. A person in a State of Nature

[15] John Locke, *Second Treatise of Government*, Section 4.
[16] Robert Nozick, *Anarchy, State, and Utopia*, Basic, New York, 1974, p. 160.

is entitled to his possessions just as a hyena is "entitled" to meat from a kill. It is his only until the lion choses to take it.

The inevitability of power in rights definition may be minimized, though not entirely avoided, by arguing that it occurred only in the distant past. Its current importance is small. That is, however, a conclusion based upon a false proposition. The definition of rights is inevitably an ongoing phenomenon that consumes the efforts of many of the "best and brightest." Changes in technology, both Demsetz and Posner agree, require and result in changes in rights. Only technologically stagnant societies may forgo the painful processes of rights redefinition.

Consider two examples. The communications revolution of this century has thrown established principles of property into complete confusion. Television signals are now transported by bouncing microwave radiation off satellites high above the earth. The signals not only pass through space, upon reflection they pass directly through millions of homes. If the "content" of the signals could be contained within a theatre "owned" by the broadcaster, rights long established would conclude that he could exclude from seeing the show anyone who did not pay to be admitted. He has excludable and exchangeable rights to the content of programming.

Here the signals are not contained in a theater. They are beamed, uninvited, into private homes. Statutes dictate that anything of value sent by mail that is not explicitly requested by the recipient may be treated as a gift. Does that mean that the satellite-reflected, but unrequested television signals that reach my home should be treated as a gift? As soon as I acquire a home antenna dish that permits me to transform the signals into television pictures I have decided that the signal is mine. The broadcasting company argues that I am intercepting and stealing its signal. The practitioners of law and economics analysis will argue that the rights ought to be shaped in such a form as to minimize total costs to society. I am merely arguing that the process of redefining rights is, in this case, very current and that it will result in winners and losers, compared to the status quo.

The rising costs of energy and the development of new building materials have changed the face of many southwestern cities. Large towers of reflective glass have risen higher and higher. The glass reduces the cooling costs of the building by reflecting solar radiation away from the structure, but away where? All of it is reflected onto other property, and even other structures that in turn face the possibility of higher cooling costs as a result. Who is entitled to what in this case? How do the entitlements of Locke's and Nozick's mythical

State of Nature permit us to resolve this without reliance on human-structured redefinition of rights?

In a technologically dynamic society, based in large part on market exchange, the definition of rights is under continuous pressure to adapt. It is not simply an aspect of the transition from feudalism centuries ago. It is a major element of contemporary society. Rights are defined and transformed every day. Power is thus also exercised.

The ongoing process of rights definition

How is that power exercised? What can be said about relationships between rights determination and rights exchange in markets? First and foremost is that they are not independent processes carried out in separate segments of the world. That point is made most persuasively by Warren Samuels.[17] He looks at a case involving a conflict between owners of ornamental red cedar trees and apple trees. There is, apparently, a form of cedar rust that is harmless to the cedar trees but that in a later stage is damaging to apple trees. Who was to have the rights? Could orchard owners compel cedar owners to remove diseased trees, or could cedar owners harbor the infection and put orchard owners at risk? Both the state legislature, and later in enforcment the state court, decided that apples took precedence over red cedar. Samuel's point is not just that a fixation of rights will allow externalities to be internalized. That is only part of the question. He really wants to stress that the choice of with whom the rights will be fixed is made by a set of institutions that are endogenous to society, not by something or someone outside of society. Those institutions will have to be concerned with the political and economic power of the affected parties.

The Coase–Demsetz position is, in effect, that the rights could be fixed randomly and it would not matter, for resource allocation would not be affected. The Samuels position is that they are not, in fact, fixed randomly but by processes that are as much a part of social interaction as market exchange. He does not use the term, but he is arguing that a significant part of the *combined* process of rights determination and exchange is based on "power." As with most insightful analyses that ask for an expansion of vision, it has been widely noted whereas its implications have been largely ignored.

In many countries the determination of rights results from the

[17] Warren Samuels, "Interrelations between Legal and Economic Processes," *Journal of Law and Economics*, Vol. 5, October 1971, pp. 435–450.

interactions of legislatures and courts. It is worth considering, then, whether power, as I have defined it, can ever be exercised through the medium of these institutions.

Legislative process

Statutes are the formal outcome of legislative processes. In terms of the hierarchy of authority in the United States, statutes take precedence over all other authority except the Constitution itself. What a legislature says are rights are indeed rights, though in many cases it is a court that decides exactly what the legislative language means. Clearly, the legislature has power. Just as clearly, if any other actors in the system can affect, alter, or influence the choices of competing rights made by a legislature, those actors have power, and it is a power beyond simple economic power.

Several years ago I wrote a book almost as long as this one.[18] It was an economic analysis of legislative and electoral processes, examining the rational, self-interested behaviors of actors in various roles in a political-economic model. I will not attempt to reproduce the entire argument, but will limit myself to a few salient points relevant here. Those interested in the full development of the analysis are referred to the earlier book.

The first major point is that *elections themselves are of very little significance in the determination of specific policies and statutes.* There are any number of technical difficulties that mean that the outcome of a vote may bear little or no relationship to the desires of the voters. Votes do not allow an expression of the intensity of preferences. If voters engage in strategic behavior the outcome may be simply false. If voters have widely different preferences, then the outcome may be purely random, depending upon the order in which options are considered.

These are embarrassing technical problems, but they are only the beginning. In elections we do not even vote for policies or policy preferences, we vote for candidates. It is impossible for an individual to express an opinion on a wide multitude of policy options via the mechanism of a single vote. That is made worse by the fact that rational strategies for candidates who truly wish to be elected dictate avoiding taking concrete stands on issues lest they alienate some group of voters. Vagueness is a better winning strategy than specificity.[19]

The problems really begin when it becomes apparent that the voters do not themselves have any idea what it is they are voting for anyway.

[18] Randall Bartlett, *Economic Foundations of Political Power*, Free Press, New York, 1973.
[19] Anthony Downs, *An Economic Theory of Democracy*, Harper & Row, New York, 1957, esp. Part II.

In his classic analysis of democratic institutions Anthony Downs demonstrated most persuasively that it is irrational to be an informed voter.[20] It is costly to acquire information and the possible benefits of investing in it are equal to the change in personal welfare that would result from voting for the correct policies times the probability that the well-informed, single vote will change the outcome. In virtually all situations the payoff from becoming informed is not significantly different from zero. It may be immoral to be an ignorant voter but it certainly is economic. The empirical evidence is strong that here economics prevails over ethics.

Legislatures, then, even if they wish to be guided by the collective preferences of the public, can have no idea what those are from the electoral process. There is then, I suppose, a certain appealing symmetry in the second major point. *They also have no real idea what it is they are doing.* If a legislature is to be small enough to be an effective decision-making body, it will be far too small to be an effective implementing and evaluating body. Most of the actual things done by government will be done bureaucratically in hierarchical, multilayered agency organizations much like those discussed in Chapter 6.

Awash in this sea of uncertainty, rational legislators wishing to maintain office will be subject to nonvoting forms of influence, either as selective information as to what is or ought to be happening, or as resources with which to provide voters with selective information as to how helpful they have been. *Thus actual policy choices, including those that shape and define rights, are the results of the patterns of political influence that are produced by actors within the system.* As rational actors, they only produce influence on issues important to them.

If any actor can ever (1) produce effective political influence over legislative processes causing a "favorable" redefinition of rights and then (2) trade those newly defined rights, the final outcome reflects real event and agenda power over ultimate trading partners. Though indirect, the impact is very real. In a world of complete omniscience, given factor endowments and rights, costless information, and perfect contracting – in short, in the world of the special case – this power need not be considered. In our somewhat less perfect world it is worth an occasional look.

Judicial process

The other main process by which rights are shaped is the adjudicative process of the courts. Issues reach a court only in the form of a "ripe"

---

[20] Ibid., esp. Part III.

controversy between parties with a well enough defined personal interest to have standing. The parties adopt an adversarial stance, with each attempting to build a more persuasive model of events and to establish a more persuasive perspective on that model based upon statute and precedent. The outcomes of the cases thus depend upon the skill of the adversaries and the human characteristics of the judges. The parties to the controversy may not be totally incapable of affecting either variable.

Certainly the market would indicate that attorneys have very different skills and abilities in persuading judges of the relevance of both facts and principles of law. Some may bill for thousands of dollars per hour and find ready buyers. Others would be priced somewhat out of the market at those rates. Assuming buyers will pay those premiums only for increased results, there must be productivity differences. The ability to find and hire such talent may affect the outcome of the rights-determination process.

Judges do not appear on this earth with a mandate from heavenly authorities to assume the bench. They are made judges by human institutions. It is customary in the federal judiciary for senators from the affected state to recommend the candidates for federal district judgeships. It is sometimes the custom that a relevant bar association will provide the list of candidates. Judges are appointed by a political executive and approved by a political legislature. At either of those stages political tests may be imposed that affect the nature of the judges who ultimately will sit. In interesting cases the media may highlight the characteristics of potential candidates. If, via the production of political influence, interests or actors whose rights may be affected by legal process can influence the selection of judges, that is again an exercise of power. When President Reagan sought to shift the U.S. Supreme Court to the right via his nomination of Robert Bork, an outspoken conservative, Congress and liberal organizations mounted sufficient opposition to prevent his confirmation. One becomes a judge via a political process.

Some judges, of course, are elected. In some leading state jurisdictions such as California even the Supreme Court justices are subject to election, recall, and reelection. Then, all of the processes that make legislative elections subject to political influence also apply.

Conclusions

The institutions that determine rights are, as Warren Samuels argues, an integral part of a larger society. Those who make the rules and those who play the game are not part of different systems; they are not different species:

> In every case the logical and substantive nexus of the matter is the role of law in the restructuring of private power, which is to say, the response by or use of government to and by those who would use government to restructure the distribution of private power, or use government for some other purpose.[21]

If net gains can be made by acting to affect the process of rights determination, consistent maximizers will do so. If the neoclassical model is to be consistent, only cost restraints will prevent that route from being followed, and the costs are clearly prohibitive only in the special case.

Case studies in the determination of rights

The process of rights definition and determination is so pervasive in a modern society that a comprehensive examination of the activities and results is impossible. But it may be instructive to provide a look at three illustrative cases, though each is examined only superficially. A complete analysis of any of them would require another book.

The right to collective bargaining

Do sellers of labor have the right to contract among themselves to act as a single unit in negotiating the labor contract with an employer? Must each person reach a contract in isolation from other workers? The answers to those questions are very fluid. They depend upon the time and the context. They involve socially defined rights. Let me break into history at some of the points where the determination of those rights reflects the actions taken by people who would ultimately be affected.

Following the American Civil War, there was a period of centralization of production. The period of the "trusts" was at its height and a political determination had to be made as to the rights of business to combine and act in concert. Changes in legislatively defined rights to general incorporation made much of this change in the structure of the economy possible.[22] Following the election of 1888 when both parties ran on platforms stressing a need to control the excesses of

---

[21] Samuels, "Interrelations," p. 448.
[22] James Willard Hurst, *The Legitimacy of the Business Corporation*, University of Virginia Press, Charlottesville, Va., 1970.

combinations of capital, Congress began work on legislation designed to implement that mandate. It is clear from both the historical context and the record in Congress that it was those combinations that were the basis of the Sherman Antitrust Act of 1890.

Very brief in its language and very broad in its implications, the Sherman Act had only two substantive sections. The first stated that, "every contract, combination in the form of a trust or otherwise, or conspiracy, in restraint of trade or commerce among the several States, or with foreign nations, is declared to be illegal."[23] The purpose of the statute seemed clear, but the actual impact on rights required court determination. What really was the Sherman Act to mean?

In the spring of 1894 workers at the Pullman Palace Car Company went on strike in protest over wage cuts. Members of the new and powerful American Railroad Union quickly refused to move Pullman cars anywhere on the national railroad system and railroad traffic came to a virtual halt. The union was attempting to redefine rights. The final determination involved broader social institutions.[24]

The railroads sought to have the union power eliminated. They turned to the attorney general of the United States, Richard Olney. His appeal to President Cleveland for federal troops to break the strike was rebuffed because, in Cleveland's view, no federal law had been broken. Olney then appointed a railroad lawyer as special counsel to the federal attorney in Chicago and they in turn sought an injunction from a federal judge, based on the theory that the union was "a combination in restraint of trade or commerce" and thus in violation of the Sherman Act. The judge was willing to act on this basis, and the refusal of the union to abide by the injunction provided the violation of federal law necessary to justify the introduction of troops to break the strike and ultimately the union.

What was the right to act collectively? That depended upon a social process. A federal court, acting at the request of officials with strong ties to railroads, using a vague statute in a manner unanticipated by Congress, and relying on the oath of the president altered the rights of the parties. The rights did not simply emerge or evolve. They were actively and purposefully changed.

The story, of course, does not end there. Rights determination is an ongoing process. For decades thereafter the use of injunctions to restrict the rights of labor to act collectively was an element in the

---

[23] Sherman Antitrust Act, 26 statutes 209, Section 1.

[24] A more complete accounting of these events can be found in Joseph G. Raybeck, *A History of American Labor*, Free Press, New York, 1966, pp. 200–207.

conflict between employers and employees. Changes in the political climate and in the composition of Congress, coupled of course with changes in the patterns of produced political influence, caused the rights of the parties to ebb and flow.[25]

It was two decades before the legacy of the Pullman Strike was addressed by Congress. In 1914 it gave more guidance to the courts in their antitrust function with the Clayton Act. This statute was longer and contained more specific detail than the Sherman Act. Section 20 explicitly restricts the use of injunctions in disputes between employers and employees. Yet for another twenty years, judges largely ignored the seemingly obvious purpose of Section 20 and continued to issue injunctions against labor unions. Not until the Great Depression of the 1930s, the assumption of office by Roosevelt, and a Democratic capture of Congress was there another attempt at redefining the rights of labor.

Here was a major conflict between groups in society as to the terms of a significant set of contracts. The conflict could not be resolved, the contracts could not be formed, until it was clear what were the relative rights of the two parties. No market could resolve those issues; no market could function without a resolution. Initially the power of the parties involved was such that employers were able to use the institutions of society to define and enforce the rights most favorable to their position. Over the course of the next forty years the power over social institutions shifted in favor of labor. By the time of Norris–LaGuardia, labor had an inherent right to bargain and act collectively and employers an affirmative duty to bargain in good faith with collective units. The rights had shifted in response to the intentional production of political pressure.

The rights did not simply evolve or emerge. Those are terms that imply a passive process unguided by the strategic decisions of interested, rational, maximizing actors. Indeed, given the potential for affecting rights via action within social institutions, a decision to stand apart from the process would be irrational indeed. The rights did not emerge. They were molded. They were acted upon. They were vigorously fought over. They were consciously shaped. Once shaped they granted power to the possessors. The process of shaping was itself a process of power.

---

[25] A useful summary of the development of law in this area and era, including excerpted cases, may be found in Harold J. Berman and Williams R. Greiner, *The Nature and Functions of Law*, 3rd ed., Foundation Press, Mineola, New York, 1972, pp. 677–826.

Asbestos exposure and worker rights

Another example of economic actors affecting rights redefinition involves exposure to asbestos in the workplace. One of the key corporate employers involved with asbestos over the years was Johns-Manville, which reorganized into a new entity, the Manville Corporation.[26] In 1982 this "new" actor, having reported $60.3 million in profits on $2.2 billion of sales, declared itself bankrupt.[27] This was an unprecedented use of the bankruptcy statutes in that it was based upon the potential for future liabilities rather than the presence of certain, current ones. It was interestingly also based upon a statute, the Bankruptcy Reform Act of 1978, that the U.S. Supreme Court had recently declared unconstitutional. The Court had, however, left a window in its invalidation until October 4 in order to permit Congress to redraft the law. Out that window Manville went.[28]

That exit substantially altered the rights of those who had been exposed to asbestos. It meant that all cases were removed from state and federal courts, where tort cases normally are tried, and then fell only under the jurisdiction of special federal bankruptcy courts. Within those courts there is no right to a trial by jury, and there is no provision for the granting of punitive damages. No new claims may be filed more than six months after the declaration of bankruptcy so that victims developing symptoms beyond that date had no legal recourse at all. Finally, any damage awards may only be paid after the claims of all secured creditors have first been met. Victims of asbestosis were suddenly moved to the very end of the line.

The story is clearly not over. There are legal issues to be resolved about the propriety of using bankruptcy proceedings in this fashion. There are political responses that may transfer liability from the stockholders and employees of Manville to taxpayers. Both sides to the controversy remain actively at work, attempting to affect the outcome of those social processes. That employment contract first made decades ago is still being reshaped in social processes of redefining rights. Manville has not, of course, controlled all of the rights redefinition. Neither have past employees. Each has sometimes been responding

[26] The reorganization was an initial attempt to escape liability for asbestos exposure. The argument was that Johns-Manville no longer existed (had, in effect, died) and that the new "person," the Manville Corporation, wasn't even "alive" when the wrongs were done. That approach met little success in the courts and the bankruptcy motion was the next strategy attempted. See Edward Greer, "Going Bankrupt to Flee the Public," *Nation*, Oct. 16, 1982.
[27] James Kelly, "Manville's Bold Maneuver," *Time*, Sept. 6, 1982, pp. 17–18.
[28] Greer, "Going Bankrupt."

to changes caused by other actors, but neither has been passive in the process. Much of the significant strategy of market actors has not involved direct negotiations over the pricing of product, levels of production, wage rates, conditions of employment, or rates of investment. Much of it has been social action aimed at redefining specific rights.

Unjust termination

Another area of case law just now being shaped involves the rights of employees fired for reasons unrelated to work performance. One such case involves an employee of IBM who was personally involved with an employee of a competing company. She was pressured to give up the relationship and ultimately felt compelled to give up her job. She sued for damages on the principle of unjust termination, arguing that she had a right to her job that could not be interfered with without cause directly related to unacceptable performance on the job. Courts have increasingly recognized such a right and have held employers liable for violating it.[29]

As this set of rights emerges from the courts, pressures are being brought on legislatures to reshape judicially determined rights. What Congress does in response will not depend upon abstract visions of justice or prescriptions for efficiency, but upon which parties to the controversy are able to mount the most effective pressures to accept or overturn the rights as established by courts.

I cannot resist a brief return to the Alchian and Demsetz argument noted in the last chapter. They claimed that an employer could in no special way punish an employee by ceasing to "buy" his labor. The relationship is the same as that between a consumer and a grocer. That vision implies that there is no differential in the rights in the two situations, and they can, if they chose, hypothesize about a mythical land where that is the case. Rights, however, are not determined by economic theorists but by endogenous social processes. Rights are whatever the relevant social institutions in the relevant society say they are. In the United States in the late twentieth century, employees do have rights to a job that a grocer does not have to a sale. Alchian and Demsetz may wish it were not so. They may actively engage in political action to make it not so. They may not, however, change the system of rights by pretending it is not so. Their model is interesting, but it is an invalid tool for drawing conclusions about the ability to punish

[29] Susan Dentzer et al., "You Can't Fire Me, I'll Sue," *Newsweek*, July 12, 1982, pp. 63.

when there is a right. Taking something to which there is a socially established right is doing harm.

Summary and conclusions

Societies are, in large part, systems of group-established rights determining who may do what, with what, to whom, when, and for what purpose. Markets simply cannot exist without particular forms of these socially established and defended rights. While a particular trade within a market may be free of power, the social process of defining those rights almost never is. Rights definition is not an exogenous process taking place outside of society, isolated from its members. Rational maximizers will participate in the rights-definition process in order to alter the outcome of subsequent trades whenever the costs of doing so are justified by the potential benefits.

This process of rights definition and redefinition is not a one-time historical event. In any dynamic society experiencing technological change, rights must be reexamined constantly. Thus one inescapable part of any market society is this social process, a process involving conflicts that are often resolvable only via the exercise of real, negative power. Power may be absent from any particular exchange. It cannot be absent from a system of market-based exchanges.

CHAPTER 9

Value power

> The content of a conscience, like the particular language that is
> learned, depends upon the society in which the individual grows up.
>
> Joan Robinson, *Economic Philosophy*

As dusk fell over the jungles of Midnapore, India, on the evening of
October 9, 1920, the Reverend J. A. L. Singh was waiting atop a hunting platform high in a tree. Rev. Singh had established an orphanage
for abandoned children and periodically traveled to remote villages
in search of children in need. On one such trip the residents of a
village begged his help in ridding the area of Manush-Baghas, ter-
rifying "man-ghosts." They believed the ghosts lived in a den within
an abandoned termite mound, and Rev. Singh was perched above
that spot, hoping to identify the cause of their fears.[1] From an opening
at the base of the mound came three adult wolves, followed by a pair
of cubs:

Close after the cubs came the ghost – a hideous-looking being – hand, foot,
and body like a human being; but the head was a big ball of something
covering the shoulders and upper portion of the bust, leaving only a sharp
contour of the face visible, and it was human. Close at its heels there came
another awful creature exactly like the first, but smaller in size. Their eyes
were bright and piercing, unlike human eyes. I at once came to the conclusion
that these were human beings.[2]

Unable to convince the villagers, he was thus unable to hire the
labor necessary to open the den and capture its occupants. No one
would risk disturbing the ghosts. Rev. Singh traveled until he was
beyond where knowledge of the phenomenon had spread and hired
some laborers to help in the capture. Without disclosing the nature
of the hunt, and carefully avoiding contact with the locals (a classic

---

[1] J. A. L. Singh, "The Diary of the Wolf Children of Midnapore (India)," reprinted
in J. A. L. Singh and Robert Zingg, *Wolf Children and Feral Man*, Archon, Hamden,
Conn., 1966, Chapter 1.
[2] Ibid., p. 5.

example of the blind-date principle in a labor market) he returned
some days later and dug open the den. The two captured "ghosts"
did indeed turn out to be human, at least in physical form. Shorn of
the matted hair that gave such an unnatural appearance to their heads,
they became but two young girls, one perhaps ten, the other less than
two.

Returning with them to his orphanage, Rev. Singh kept a journal
of the development of these two feral children. The younger took
sick and died within a year, but the older, named Kamala, remained
in his care for nine years. He recorded the impacts on Kamala of an
evolving interaction with human society, as well as the residual impacts
of living in a world devoid of humans.

Never before having observed upright walking, both girls moved
on all fours, their bodies so thoroughly adapting that they were unable
even to assume the normal posture we associate with humans.[3] With
no model to guide the use of hands, they used them only as a wolf
would use its forepaws. Food was consumed directly by the mouth
off of the ground.[4] Deprived of language exposure as a young child,
Kamala developed only a rudimentary ability to communicate, evolving a vocabulary of less than fifty words over the nine-year period of
her life among humans.[5] The girls would not eat cooked food but
would follow the smell of carrion and consume it with relish.[6] On one
occasion, Kamala was found outside the orphanage compound de-
lightedly eating the entrails of a dead fowl she had found.[7]

It seemed clear from the beginning that human society held no
appeal to Kamala. She much preferred and sought the company of
other animals, quickly forming a bond with a captured hyena, while
resisting contact or interaction with humans.[8]

Social relations and endogenous utility functions

Kamala and her "sister" are not the only cases of feral children, but
they are among the best documented. Something stronger would appear to be happening here than a simple alteration in the constraints
facing a preformed, rational maximizer. The severe isolation from
human society and its replacement with wolf society seems to have

---

[3] Ibid., p. 18, 25.
[4] Ibid., p. 27–28, 79
[5] Ibid., p. 103–104.
[6] Ibid., p. 29.
[7] Ibid., p. 24, 77.
[8] Ibid., p. 58, 79.

changed not only what they did. It changed what they were. Had they had "given" preference functions, the change in constraints resulting from their "rescue" should have been sufficient to extinguish past modes of behavior. Yet when the constraints around Kamala changed, her behavior did not become human. Her past experiences changed dramatically the utility she would forever be able to derive from various forms of Stuff. Throughout her life she preferred carrion taken from vultures to meals given by humans.

In Becker's terms, she had to learn the technology of "household production" *from other living creatures*. Once learned it became an inextricable part of her. She had to learn from watching how to move, what to eat, how to interact, and what to value. The utility she experienced depended upon the Stuff available to her, the physical environment around her, *and on the social contacts experienced*.

Perhaps another way of looking at Kamala is to say that the utility level she was able to attain at each moment depended on the Stuff available, the physical environment, and her own human capital. But that, in turn, depended upon the information to which she was exposed, and which she retained, over certain formative periods of her life. She may have been the same container into which differing globs of "putty" capital could be poured. Once there, however, it quickly hardened into fired clay. Her current technology of household production depended upon her past "investments" in information. That language is perhaps less foreign to economists (though it is pure jibberish to normal people), but it buys very little in terms of reattaining the purely powerless world. Unless one is willing to reassume that all information is a fixture of the natural world awaiting individual discovery and acquisition independent of the actions and awareness of other humans, potential power is still there. If human beings shape the content of the information that is made available to others, then those humans are altering the utility attainable; they are by definition exercising power. Culture, that set of behaviors and beliefs that separate Greeks from Callatiae and humans from wolves, is explicitly taught as part of all social interactions. Children are not simply exposed to random subsets of the totality of human-held information. They are taught culture. The institutions that teach that culture are thus instruments of human power. Those who learn culture, that is, all social humans, are then subject to a new form of power – power over values. The payoffs experienced at the end of each decision/chance pathway are, in part, socially determined. Kamala's delight in the raw entrails of a dead fowl differed from the payoff I would experience at such a juncture in a decision tree. More importantly, it differed from the payoff she herself would have felt had she never been socialized by wolves.

This possibility of social influences on human utility functions (or household production functions) expands the horizons of this inquiry to a wholly new scale. It opens the way for this entirely new form of power. At the same time it destroys the very measure of power, to say nothing of the basis of all welfare economics. If utility functions are actually endogenous, we are left making interpersonal utility comparisons about single individuals! As she was when found, Kamala seemed happier in the wolf den than in confinement at the orphanage. The Rev. Singh's well-intentioned actions may well have lowered her experienced utility for her remaining years. Had she just been taken to the wolf den, or been there only briefly, the "rescue" might well have been her salvation. How things and actions affected her utility depended upon who she really was, and that in turn depended upon the social interactions she had experienced.

Value power as a new qualitative form

In Chapter 1 different perceptions of power in market societies were partly attributable to differences in presumptions about the nature of human beings. Are they fully formed and independent of social influence? Do people merely change the options for others or do they really change other human beings? For Friedman, persons existed fully free of social influence. The only external forms of behavior control were a gun at the head or a dollar in the hand. Nothing else was admitted to consideration. For Dugger and Galbraith, humans were, by definition, constructed from human relationships. They were always made, never born. Thus influences over humans were an inevitable part of society. The gun and the dollar need appear only when other forms of social control fade.

That difference in presumptions is not, of course, the sole basis of differences in conclusions about power. I am only now explicitly facing the possibility of influences over values. All of the power explored in Chapters 5 through 8 has involved an ability to change the constraints that define "optimum" human behavior. All resulted from a relaxation of the conditions that defined the special case. None involved the exercise of value power. When information is imperfect, when it is unevenly owned, when persons are limited in their abilities to hold and process it, power can arise even between actors with fixed and inviolable preference functions. When transactions become expensive and contracting imperfect, when administrative organizations with layers of agents and principals form, power can arise among such actors. When the source of vision is expanded to recognize that rights themselves are endogenous, fully formed actors may participate in the process of rights definition and thus exercise power. Even religious adherence to the principle of given, identical, and immutable preference functions is insufficient to expunge power from the less restricted world outside of the special case. Power enters via Becker's methodology being "used relentlessly and unflinchingly."[9] It appears even if the disagreement about the nature of human values remains unresolved.

If the controversy itself is directly met and if the general utility function specified in (2.1) is openly admitted to consideration, then Kamala's experience suggests a generalizable hypothesis. Social interactions matter. None of us in an island. We are joined in ways that forever change what we are. Genetics may help to place limits on our potential. Our interactions with humans help to define our reality. That hypothesis is not the introduction of power. Liberation from the confines of the special case breached that threshold already. It merely extends the potential scope of power into new dimensions.

Internalized values and irrational behavior

Thomas Kuhn has argued that science progresses by resolving "anomalies," results that are unexpected and initially unexplained by the experience and theory of the observer. The work of scientists is to solve such puzzles, to resolve the paradoxes.[10] Consider an example of seemingly irrational behavior.

The excess-change paradox

Not long ago I was in store when the clerk, working quickly, gave back to a customer a $20 bill as change when $10 was the appropriate denomination. The clerk was not aware of the mistake. Neither were any of the other people in the store. Only the customer knew. Had she quietly left the store she would have had a gain of $10 and no apparent cost. Rational behavior would seem to dictate a hasty, but inconspicuous departure. Instead, the customer called the error to the attention of the clerk and returned the excess change.

---

[9] Gary Becker, *The Economic Approach to Human Behavior*, University of Chicago Press, Chicago, 1976, p. 5.

[10] Thomas Kuhn, *The Structure of Scientific Revolutions*, 2nd ed., University of Chicago Press, Chicago, 1970.

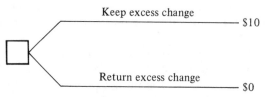

Figure 9.1. The excess-change paradox.

In terms of a decision tree the relevent choice would appear to follow that of Figure 9.1. The customer could return the excess change or could keep it. Any reasonable analysis of the payoffs would seem to indicate that the second option is $10 better than the first. There is really no chance of detection and no real penalty even if the clerk catches on. But that was not the path chosen. Hence the payoffs, as perceived by the customer, must have been affected by some other factors:

> When an apparently profitable opportunity to a firm, worker, or household is not exploited, the economic approach does not take refuge in assertions about irrationality, contentment with wealth already acquired, or convenient ad hoc shifts in values (i.e., preferences). Rather it postulates the existence of costs, monetary or psychic, of taking advantage of these opportunities that eliminate their profitability – costs that may not be easily "seen" by outside observers.[11]

There must, therefore, have been a cost associated with keeping that $10 that was apparent only to the customer, a psychic cost, a loss in her own utility, which would have resulted from a violation of *someone else's rights*. There is apparently empirical evidence of a conscience!

Rights and wrongs

Cohesive and stable social systems are based in large part on structures of socially determined rights. That was a conclusion defended at some length in the last chapter. They are also marked by systems of widely, though not necessarily universally, shared beliefs and values. These are related phenomena. What must be widely believed in a stable society is that these social rights are also morally right. Violation of the rights must be widely viewed as wrong.

When that shared perception adds internal utility payoffs to actions that affect the rights of other persons, the very utility function upon

[11] Becker, *The Economic Approach*, p. 7.

which human behavior is assumed based is itself altered by morality. It is those morally determined payoffs, then, that must account for our often observed failure to exploit apparently profitable opportunities. Most of us do not steal, commit murder, or engage in fraudulent transactions even when the chance of legal prosecution is virtually nil. Most of us can identify with the killer in Poe's "Tell-Tale Heart" whose conscience punished him even when the law did not. The law stands as a protection of the last resort. Our reliance on shared social values that morally affirm rights is the first resort.

Is morality then the path back to the pure, powerless world of the special case? Yes and no. If the world were found to be wholly free of all exercises of power even when conditions prevail (as described in Chapters 5 through 8) that would make such exercises appear profitable, the search for the hidden costs might lead to morally affected utility payoffs. Morality could, conceptually, cause the peculiar isoquant in Figure 4.4. If each individual were so fraught with guilt by the exercise of any form of power other than simple economic power that no apparent gains would ever be sufficient to justify the psychic pain, then the full costs of all other forms of power would everywhere be prohibitive.[12] That, however, would be only a potential answer to a fact-generated question. Given the general tenor of human history, I, for one, would be reluctant to conclude that morality has always clearly prevailed. There seems to be ample empirical evidence that at times a seeking of personal gain offers advantages of payoffs greater than any expected personal pyschic pain from guilt.

Even if perfect morality were observed, that would still not be sufficient to prove an absence of power. The acquisition of those moral payoffs would also have to be shown to have been powerless. That is a large issue that will be addressed shortly.

Morality as efficiency

The presence of internalized utility payoffs from respecting the rights of others not only permits the resolution of the excess-change paradox. It also holds the promise of vastly increased efficiency in the functioning of markets. Economists should take great delight. Morality is not only good, it is also efficient!

Markets cannot function well without (1) certain forms of exchange rights in property and (2) *social* enforcement of those rights. Without

---

[12] Charles Staelin, one of my colleagues at Smith, first brought this argument to my attention.

effective enforcement, there are no real rights, and the advantages of exchanging rights are largely lost. The Fifteenth Amendment to the Constitution of the United States guarantees to all citizens the right to vote regardless of race. That right has been nominally established for 120 years, but for only a small portion of that time has the right been effectively enforced. When not enforced, it was not really a right.

There must, therefore, be social mechanisms to enforce rights if the social fabric is to hold and if markets are to function efficiently. Rights could be enforced by overt police activity. In some cities of the world, a driver parking a car will pay one of the kids on the street to watch it while the driver is gone. It is then common practice to pay another kid to watch the watcher. The possibilities become endless. If a society were to be a perfect external enforcer of rights, each right would have to have a protector, and then, of course, others to protect against incursions by the protector.

The social advantages of having systems of well-defined rights come from the order they give to human interactions. It is in the exercise of rights, and in the case of markets from their free exchange, that social advantage is derived. Resources that must be devoted to defending rights are not in themselves productive. They add nothing. Any mechanism that would reduce the resources required for the defense of rights per se would increase the potential efficiency of the social system. Morality, I argue, does precisely that.

What an extraordinarily efficient mechanism for the enforcement of rights! In the excess-change paradox, no state resources were involved. No one other than the potential violator of the rights was involved. She monitored herself, weighed the potential cost she would have imposed upon herself, and protected the other person's rights all by herself. Once in place, there could hardly be a less costly process of rights enforcement than internalized, morally defined, utility payoffs.

Conclusions

These observations do not yet give rise to value power; they are but observations about individuals and societies. They set the stage, however. If social systems are indeed marked by *shared* social values, the question arises, "Why?" Where did the shared values come from? Why would constrained maximizers internalize similar morally based utility payoffs? Are they part of those genetically determined, immutable, basic preference functions of Gary Becker's? Are they in-

dependent, individual responses to impersonal environmental constraints? Are they instead the product of human social processes?
These are questions that need to be pursued. The pursuit may finally
bring us back to the wolf den in Midnapore.

Self-enforced rights – the powerless case

The excess-change paradox was solved only by postulating a prior
event that affixed those utility payoffs to the general utility function
of the customer. There had to be a prior act, process, or conscious
choice shaping the utility function itself with the appropriate moral
weights. If all power is to be expunged from the model, then that
prior act or process must itself have been wholly free of any exercises
of power such as those discussed in the last four chapters. If any other
human being in any way affected the content of the moral weights
chosen that human exercised value power. What would be necessary
to ensure that this power was wholly absent?

Genetic morality

I suppose moral weights could be an element of nature, sociobiolog-
ically controlled by immutable genes. They could precede all social
interaction. They could be beyond human control or individual
choice. There could be no free will or real personal responsibility.
Our responses to ethical problems arising out of conflicts with others'
socially determined rights could be no different from a bean plant's
response to light. DNA could be all.

Genetic material could have latent weights for newly established
rights. We could be programmed to define the "right" rights as technology evolves and then to internalize them as socially advantageous.
All of the ongoing social processes of rights definition and redefinition
outlined in the preceding chapter could be biological and beyond the
influence of any human. All of that could be, but there really seems
little evidence that it is.

If that is not so, if humans have some existential freedom to make
genuine choices about their behaviors, if they themselves may make
real moral decisions, then powerlessness must depend on social processes rather than impersonal, but all-powerful chains of nucleic acids.
If psychic weights do not come from nature, they must have human
origins.

The choice of moral weights

There must be a prior event in which the weights determining the response to the presentation of excess change are themselves chosen. That event could be independent or interdependent. An individual could, I suppose, freely and independently choose his own morality, that is, the set of psychic weights to be internalized into his preference function. In a power-free world, that prior act would have to be power free and an independent maximizing choice. Would that ever be rational for a single individual?

Self-enforcement of rights is a classic public good. If it exists, I reap the benefits whether I contribute or not. If others practice it, I may gain by not doing so. If others do not practice it, I only lose by doing so. No matter what the rest do, my optimal strategy is not to self-enforce others' rights.[13] For an individual to decide to self-enforce others' rights leads to no social gain. There is a critical mass of acceptance that must be attained. That critical mass could only be attained asocially if most individuals make irrational, independent decisions simultaneously. That is not a promising basis for an economically based theory of a power-free world.

Individuals could, of course, agree to choose moral weights as part of an interdependent process. That raises the likelihood of a coordinated outcome but still does not overcome the free-rider problem. It may raise, however, the likelihood of a power-affected outcome. If there is a *social* process of establishing culture, that whole process needs to be powerless if the system is to be so. Thus we need a perfectly powerless "social contract," unanimously and freely accepted, devoid of fraud or coercion, and bargained for in perfect honesty and good faith in which individuals agree to internalize a set of shared rights and values.

Hypothetical bargains such as these are not unknown in theories of state formation. John Locke, and much later Robert Nozick, examined the formation of a state as a conscious agreement among individuals choosing new arrangements as part of individual welfare-maximizing strategies.[14] James Buchanan and Gordon Tullock use a model of political states consciously created from pure anarchy, via a process of rational debate and persuasion. Unanimous agreement is reached on the rules of a government formed from nothing, if not

---

[13] Cf. Mancur Olson, Jr., *The Logic of Collective Action*, Schocken, New York, 1968, for the classic argument about group size and collective behavior.

[14] John Locke, *Two Treatises of Government*, 2nd ed., Cambridge University Press, 1967, and Robert Nozick, *Anarchy, State, and Utopia*, Basic, New York, 1974.

on its operation, because it is impossible to predict who will be benefited or harmed by the application of the rules.[15]

It is conceptually possible, I suppose, to use the idea of a social contract in considering the origins of cultures. After all, shared values and rights are as much a mark of social cohesion as shared citizenship. Shared citizenship without broader cultural bonds is very weak social glue indeed. Perhaps social values are initially adopted by a similar process. Individuals who are the purest of the economic species, caring only about their individual gains, gather in convention to discuss the personal payoffs associated with different systems of social rights and values. After careful debate each is convinced that altering his personal preference (or household production) function to include weights called for by social values is personally superior to the old system. People are persuaded of the wisdom of altering their values by explicit interaction with others. Cultural morality is just like a contract for a tomato crop. It is a product of overt negotiation aimed at controlling event power and promoting mutual gain. We will all choose our values together after collective debate, but no one can force another to adopt the values. One can only persuade (or perhaps influence with side payments). The persuasion must be based on logic and unbiased information. All points of view must have an equal hearing. Unanimous consent ensues and a cohesive social structure appears.

Internalized moral payoffs must be irrevocable

Internalized moral payoffs are still not real, and the potential social gains from them are lost, unless agreed internalized payoffs are irrevocable. Morality once adopted may not be abandoned via a second act of will. In embryology and child development there appear to be "windows" when certain things may occur. Once the specific opportunity is past, there is no going back. The acquisition of language seems to be such a phenomenon. If a child is not exposed to human language at a crucial stage, the ability to acquire it is lost.[16] Something like this must occur in self-shaped moral payoffs. Once self-imposed they may not be reconsidered as part of a later strategy, or they cease to have any meaning.

If the recipient of excess change once could select her values as an independent act of will, she should be able to reconsider them as well.

[15] James Buchanan and Gordon Tullock, *The Calculus of Consent*, University of Michigan Press, Ann Arbor, 1962.
[16] Susan Curtiss, "The Critical Period and Feral Children," 1980 (unpublished).

Only if some biological window has closed so that a selection of morality, once made, can never be undone can there really be powerlessly created and unseen psychic costs. Morality, which supplies the costs that resolve the paradox, can then be itself powerless only if one of two conditions holds. It is either genetically and immutably based or it is a system of weights willingly and irrevocably added to utility functions via a social process that itself contains no hint of power. Even that is not quite enough. There is one thing more.

The generation problem

People, unfortunately, are mortal. Even if all persons' wholly independent and irrevocable choices once matched, they must do so again for each new generation. Even if a social contract was once made among free and equal individuals, based upon shared and unbiased information, the contract needs to be renewed. No person can contract for another without an express principal–agent relationship, and there is no such contracted status between us and our progeny.

Either each new individual must reach a decision to adopt the dominant set of social values in an independent process, or each generation must gather for a repeat of the grand debate. If the choice of social values is to be powerless, then there must be no human-generated bias in the stock of information used by the new generation *and* no decision power over the selection. Unless the choice of social values is itself free of any exercise of power, later decisions made using payoffs based upon that value system are not powerless either.

Bounded rationality – a partial solution

The requirements for a powerless acquisition are made a bit less restrictive if actors are assumed to operate under bounded rationality. That at least permits a resolution of the excess-change paradox without having to postulate irrevocably chosen internalized payoffs. Perhaps her decision to return the excess change was not part of a rational decision tree at all. Perhaps the single choice in question is a reflection of a behavioral rule of thumb or standard operating procedure. What happens at the decision node in Figure 9.1 is not a rational calculation of the possible range of alternatives, possible consequences, and probabilities with which various outcomes may occur. It is certainly not an internal debate on the future course of Western civilization if a belief in the sanctity of private property is eroded by a widespread failure of self-enforced rights.

The decision is a two-stage process. In the first, the customer places the event into some artificial category of events for which she has historically developed behavioral responses, and then takes the "normal" path for decisions of that type. Unless shocked by repeated external events, the boundedly rational actor does what she has learned to do in the past. She does not search for and evaluate other options. She responds in a conditioned rather than a consciously strategic sense.

That still leaves the second level questions. How is the rule of thumb established? Who affects the standard operating procedure? If that process is clearly free of power, then her single choice may be said to be powerless. If power is part of the process, then its influence carries over to a variety of seemingly independent actions.

In a bounded-rationality model, there is what appears to the individual to be a chance event that determines the information, incentives, arguments, and world views to which the individual is exposed. She is then aware, not of all possible options and arguments, but of only some externally determined subset. Assuming that this culture in some sense works, she stops looking for alternate cultures and operates on the basis of the behavior rules.

The issue that becomes crucial is the nature of the "chance" event that determines which set of social values the individual will see and will ultimately adopt. Is it really chance or is it in the explicit control of other human beings? If there is to be no value power, there must be no human influence on the process of acquiring culture. There must be no bias, intentional or unintentional, in the information, values, and ideas to which each infant is exposed. We must not teach our children to be like ourselves. We must teach them about all cultures, with no hint of bias, and perhaps hope that they will see the clear superiority of our own. If we affect the things to which they are exposed, we are exercising value power.

Reductio ad absurdum

In logic there is a principle of proof (or disproof) based upon demonstrating that a hypothesis fully explored leads to wholly adsurd implications. The phrase is sometimes used in a pejorative sense, however, implying that the arguer has not dealt with the real proposition, but only a caricature of it. I have clearly arrived at a set of absurd propositions here. There is no evidence of cultures arising from nothing following a great debate taking place in a state of nature. There is no evidence of all individuals arriving in this world fully

formed, having been constrained in their information and understanding only by the impersonal forces of nature. There is no evidence
that the process of socializing new generations is one of providing an
impartial look at all cultures in order to promote uninfluenced choice.
All evidence is to the contrary.

These results do not, however, arise from some caricature of economics. They arise from a faithful adherence to two of its central
propositions, one methodological, the other ideological. The first is
that human behavior is to be understood as the result of the constrained maximizing of individuals. The second is that, if interactions
occur between those individuals in markets, only simple economic
power is a possibility. In order for that methodology to support that
conclusion, all of the absurd conditions just specified must hold. That
is not a dictate of my choosing. It is a result of logic. It in effect
demonstrates that logical analysis will simply not support the ideological proposition. The null hypothesis of wholly exogenous utility
(or household production) functions is not really tenable.

There is a simple way out. We could simply recognize that we are
all like Kamala, that social experiences in our past help to shape what
we are. Social influences determine what we will wish to do and what
we will be able to do. We could accept the hypothesis of socially
endogenous utility. That is a powerful admission, however, in every
sense of the word, for if other humans help to shape our values, then
they have, for better or worse, value power over us. If it is absurd to
suppose that they do not; it is sensible to consider the implications if
they do.

Value power as socialized internalization of rights

If each of us is socially shaped at least to some degree, then the set
of shared and socially determined rights displayed by members of a
social group are learned. They are also taught. If they are to be
effective and unchanging, they must not be subject to constant strategic adjustment solely at individuals' discretion. They must become
internalized and remain somewhat unexamined. The persons and
institutions, ranging from parents, schools, media, and organizations,
that help to shape what becomes internalized as psychic weights are
then exercising value power.

Acceptance of value power as rational behavior

Economists often imply that humans enter this world omniscient.
They may occasionally experience a slight shortage of information,

but they seem to acquire most of the world's information before they begin interacting with others. In fact, perfect ignorance would be a closer approximation. It takes some months before an infant begins to realize that the moving object in front of her eyes is, in fact, her own hand. It takes a good deal longer before she can begin to recognize variations in systems of social rights and their implications.

Humans cannot long function in a state of total ignorance. They cannot survive without the care of others who have already acquired some information and survival skills. In order to become independent, they need to acquire vast stores of data (or, in Becker's terms, they need to participate in a process of technology diffusion related to household production functions). Some of that information will be made available at very low cost. Some of it may even be hard to avoid. We punish our children if they fail to internalize the social weights we ourselves hold. For Kamala the cheap world view was the one offered to her by wolves. For most of the rest of us the cheapest world view comes from other humans.

It is, of course, also most efficient for older humans to share with younger ones the information that they already possess. It would be most expensive to share information that they do not. Unless the first generation was wholly omniscient and in possession of complete unbiased information, then each succeeding one, seeking information in order to survive, will be exposed to and acquire a systematically biased vision.[17] Only acculturating societies can be long maintained. People will largely, therefore, exist in acculturated societies. Anything else would be simply irrational.

Value power as unconscious power

When I was a child I had a book on the cover of which was a picture of a bear lying in bed reading a book. His book was also my book, and on the cover of his book was a picture of him, reading a book with a picture of him on the cover, and so on, and so on, and so on. I have no memory at all of the content of the story, but the problem of an infinite regression of bears and books has stayed with me to this day. Reliance on boundedly rational individuals to accept and enforce the cultural values and rights presented by the previous generation puts us into a dilemma much like my bear-book problem. Where does it end? The generation that is now shaping the values of children

---

[17] For a more detailed discussion see Randall Bartlett, *Economic Foundations of Political Power*, Free Press, New York, 1973, esp. Part IV.

were themselves shaped by the previous generation, who in turn were shaped by the generation before that, and so on, and so on.

The power exercised need not even be conscious on the part of the exercisers. They are merely teaching others about the world as they see it. As boundedly rational actors themselves, they will have no comprehensive awareness of the options about which they are not teaching. That implies that there is, and was, no careful consideration and selection of social values. The shared culture seems accidental. Each generation has power over the succeeding one but was subject to the power of the preceding one.

At the end of Chapter 4, I warned of the limits to the approach I developed in Part II. It is a method best suited to an examination of power in its most overt forms. It is a method that supports a functionalist view of social institutions, that is, a vision of them as consciously created and designed to fulfill some identified need. The formation of institutions, including cultural values, would seem to be just one more example of rational, maximizing behavior.

Yet the value power under discussion here involves a major qualitative shift. It is much more subtle. It is not part of a conscious strategy. Culture, social values, and shared behaviors, like bears on book covers, are seen now as self-perpetuating in a seemingly endless regression of influence. There was no clear act of design or intention. There seems to be only an ongoing process beyond any specific, human intent, rather than singular, controlled events.

As a result, the tools to analyze such phenomena are less developed than those familar techniques for defining static equilibria. There are economic pioneers exploring that frontier, but they have barely established wilderness forts, let alone intellectual schools. Andrew Schotter's analysis of institutions via game theory speaks of rules and conventions that evolve from the repeated play of games, rather than explicit negotiations. These behaviors may then be passed on to later generations of players with no clear concept of reasons, only tradition-based expectations.[18] Richard Nelson and Sidney Winter's creative adaptation of evolutionary principles to economic change opens the door to more of a process orientation.[19]

Richard Langlois attempts to draw some of these efforts together in a recent edited volume and provides a useful synthesis of several

---

[18] Andrew Schotter, *The Economic Theory of Social Institutions*, Cambridge University Press, 1981.

[19] Richard Nelson and Sidney Winter, *An Evolutionary Theory of Economic Change*, Harvard University Press, Cambridge, Mass., 1982.

common themes.[20] Timur Kuran provides an analysis of value power as process rather than strategy, explaining how even the lowest castes in India may come to accept the system that subjugates them.[21] Despite these attempts, explicit economic analysis of this complex exercise of social power is in its infancy.

Researchers in other disciplines have offered more systematic attempts at explanation. B. F. Skinner is but one example.[22] Organisms, according to Skinner, engage in random behaviors but may come to associate subsequent events causally. A rat who presses a lever and then finds food pellets appearing may become conditioned to press the lever in an attempt to cause the desired result. A baby trying random sounds may find that certain ones cause her parents to clap and laugh. The sound is repeated in expectation of recreating the response. Humans may engage in random behaviors and find, by accident, that certain ones tend to generate better results. Trial and error, not strategic planning, dominate human experimentation. Thus in Skinner's argument, favorable consequences of random behaviors will teach humans to repeat the action. (This fits more closely boundedly, rather than globally, rational behavior. Skinner does not argue that humans will keep trying new behaviors until they find the very best. When they chance upon something effective, they stick with whatever works.)

Culture then becomes the teaching of the "discovered" behaviors to succeeding generations. As with genetically based adaptive selection, changes in the environment may alter the consequences of specific behaviors, and random activity may lead to discovery of a superior behavior. Culture may then become modified to reflect the new conditioned behavior.

Social values are largely arrived at by chance, but if they are effective, a society based upon them will flourish. Societies based upon less effective social values will fail. The initial determination of values, rights, and culture is not part of a process of the careful design of human institutions in response to well-understood constraints. It is a process of random behaviors generating different responses from an imperfectly understood environment. People do not create cultures for Skinner. Environments select cultures that in turn create people.

[20] Richard Langlois, ed., *Economics as a Process*, Cambridge University Press, 1986, esp. Chapters 1 and 10.
[21] Timur Kuran, "Preference Falsification, Policy Continuity and Collective Conservatism," *Economic Journal*, Vol. 97, September 1987, pp. 642–645.
[22] B. F. Skinner, *Beyond Freedom and Dignity*, Knopf, New York, 1971.

Value power as invisible power

It is perhaps not surprising that this value power is so hard for economists to see. Their tools are ill suited to seeing it. Moreover, of all the forms of power discussed so far, it is the one least likely to be noticed by either exercisers or subjects. When it is effective, it makes the rights of the status quo seem to be natural and right. If the rights appear relative, or worse manipulative, value power ceases to provide the efficiency and stability of widespread, self-enforcement of those rights.

It is perhaps easier to see the contextual social nature of values in others than in ourselves. It is astonishing to twentieth-century observers that people of other times should hold value positions that seem so untenable. Kneeling before the headsman on Tower Green, both of Henry VIII's soon to be beheaded wives made brief statements. They did not, however, condemn the injustice of a system that required them to die to meet the whims of a tyrannical monarch. They did not call for an uprising to forestall such abuse of human rights in the future. Each, instead, extolled the virtues of the king and the justness of the sentence and asked those remaining to be good and obedient subjects of the king.[23] Given the situation, it would be hard to argue that there was much to be gained from such statements in a personal strategic sense. After their heads, what more of significance did they have to lose?

In the case of Katherine Howard, her crime had been infidelity. It seems never to have occured to her, or others of her generation, that extramarital relations should not be a capital offense for the queen, even though the king could engage in such activity with impunity. It seemed not to occur to them that the king could, and should, be able to order such punishment, when lesser husbands could not. One can only imagine the final speech of a modern feminist in such circumstances.

To be sure there were different political consequences then and now. An unfaithful queen put into jeopardy the principles of succession of the Crown since the paternity of potential heirs became suspect. However, that merely moves the shared social values to another level. In the sixteenth century, the wisdom of hereditary monarchy was seldom questioned. Not only was it a fact. It was an accepted social

---

[23] Jasper Ridley, *Henry VIII: The Politics of Tyranny*, Viking/Penguin, New York, 1985, p. 270, 362.

value. It is today viewed as a rather silly anachronism, and proponents of a return to such a system of government are viewed as crackpots.

Henry, of course, did not create those values himself, nor was he necessarily conscious of them as relative. The entire cultural background of each of the actors, from the king to the headsman to the queens, prepared each to perceive the events and the rights that they reflected as correct and natural. Each was subject to the human influences of the age. None was independent of social context.

The shared social values of a society are often so very basic that they are not even recognized as values by those subject to them. They are viewed as absolutes rather than as historical and situational relatives. They are virtually never perceived as social conventions based simply upon expediency or efficiency, though others, looking from outside the shared social perspective, may be able to interpret them as such.

Eugene Genovese's study of slavery in the United States offers much anecdotal evidence of the forces that shaped a shared belief, not only in the efficiency of slavery, but in its moral righteousness.[24] Law, religion, culture, and education all adapted to help promote a system of self-enforcement of the rights of slavery. When he quotes the president of Planters College in Mississippi, the words seem transparently absurd to us. They clearly did not to either the president or his audience. They shared a set of values foreign to us:

Slavery is the duty and obligation of the slave to labor for the mutual benefit of both master and slave, under a warrant to the slave to protection, and a comfortable subsistence, under all circumstances.... The master, as head of the system, has a right to the obedience and labor of the slave, but the slave has also his mutual rights in the master; the right of protection, the right of counsel and guidance, the right of subsistence, the right of care and attention in sickness and old age. He has also a right in his master as the sole arbiter in all his wrongs and difficulties, and as a merciful judge and dispenser of law to award the penalty of his misdeeds.[25]

The tone of this language is clear. The author is speaking not just of rights in the legalistic sense. He is speaking of rights in the moral sense. The social obligations of each side of this "exchange" compel certain types of behavior, and it is "good" and "just" that it is so. There is no discussion and probably no conscious awareness of the future efficiency implications of individual incentives. It may be that the

[24] Eugene Genovese, *Roll, Jordan, Roll: The World the Slaves Made*, Pantheon, New York, 1974.
[25] Ibid., p. 76.

discussion is truly disingenuous, that the author believes none of it to be true and is merely trying to convince us of false beliefs for personal gain. It may be that he shares these beliefs, and the fact that they result in personal gain is purely secondary to the true moral wisdom they contain.

It is probably not, however, purely coincidental that persons who have held those views are predominantly from cultures with slaves. Without the social reality there is little use for the internalized social values. It is not hard for any of us to reach the conclusion that what is good for us is also good absolutely. Few of us ever perceive ourselves as evil. For all armies it seems, even when fighting each other, "God is on *our* side."

Value power as strategy

In normal times, the process of socializing values is so subtle as to appear powerless. Rights do change, however, and the internalized payoffs necessary to support the new rights must also change. Sometimes, then, actors may set out to change, consciously, the shared set of social values. In order to do that they invariably must revert to abnormal methods, for they must overcome the old values while imposing the new. Henry VIII decided for personal and political reasons that a break with the Catholic church would be to his advantage. (It is interesting that it was apparently very difficult for him to accept the necessity of that break because it violated his own accepted prior values as well. A pure maximizer would have adopted the strategy much sooner and less reluctantly.)

In order to reeducate the populace to his new religion he had to impose strict licensing provisions on all preachers, requiring that only those willing to accept his position speak. He required an oath from all residents of the realm to accept him as head of the church. Failure to comply was high treason punishable by being hanged, drawn, and quartered. It was illegal to possess any book or bible that espoused different views. The penalty again was death.[26]

Two interesting observations arise. First, it must have been difficult to change social values if all of those measures were required, though it must have been possible else England would be Catholic today. Second, given the personal benefits and costs, it is astonishing that many people chose to accept torture and death rather than sign the oath. It is important, however, that their early embracing of the Cath-

---

[26] Ridley, *Henry VIII*.

olic church was not itself independent of the actions of other persons.[27] The productivity of the old household production function must have been very firmly internalized indeed!

The grand dilemma

The excess-change paradox has been resolved, but this analysis has created a much grander one. Powerless societies cannot be efficient. Efficient societies cannot be powerless. Not only is powerlessness most unlikely, its attainment would also reduce efficiency! Globally rational actors, it appears, would never internalize social value weights into their preference functions. Constantly reevaluating the personal wisdom of strategies, they would quickly negate any values they might appear to have adopted coming out of some mythical state of nature. Yet without the widespread presence of those social value weights, rights can be defended only by externally generated forces. There must then be external protectors of all rights – and guardians for all protectors. It is never truly rational, in a strategic sense of self-interested individuals, to be moral. Social cohesion would be limited to personal gain. Actors would be free of all power but at the expense of being part of an inefficient society.

Boundedly rational actors, who do not regularly challenge rules of behavior once adopted, have the efficiency advantages of self-enforced social rights, but only if they are subject to value power in the adoption process. Acculturation is a human phenomenon. It is humans affecting the self-perceptions of other humans. Individuals may not choose who they are to be. Society does it for them. Marx seems to be right after all. "Social being determines consciousness," and human institutions determine social being.[28]

[27] The extraordinary costs willingly born in defense of religious doctrine by socialized humans should be, perhaps, contrasted with the intensity of feelings displayed by nonsocialized persons. Anselm Von Feuerbach published an account of such a person in 1833 under a title scarcely shorter than the manuscript itself. *Casper Hauser: An Account of an Individual Kept in a Dungeon, Separated From All Communications with the World, From Early Childhood to About the Age of Seventeen*, originally published by Simpkin and Marshall, London, and reprinted in Singh and Zingg, *Wolf Children*. Feuerbach notes the fervor of religious feeling in Hauser: "Not a spark of religion, not the smallest particle of any dogmatic system was to be found in his soul; how great soever the ill-timed pains be which, immediately or in the first week after his arrival, were taken by several clergymen to seek for and to awaken them. Indeed no animal could have shown itself more unable to comprehend, or to form any conception of what they meant by all their questions, discourses and sermons, than Casper" (p. 299 in Singh and Zingg).

[28] Karl Marx, "Preface to *A Contribution to the Critique of Political Economy*," reprinted in Robert Tucker, ed. *The Marx–Engels Reader*, 2nd ed., Norton, New York, 1978, p. 4.

No wonder debate about such propositions is avoided, at least by neoclassical economists. It would appear that, in order for the world to be fully efficient, there must be value power. In order to be without value power, the world must accept substantial inefficiency. When the model that is the basis of belief has two basic precepts, (1) that individuals are free and independent and (2) that such individuals can achieve total efficiency in perfect markets, this grand dilemma is cutting at the very foundation. Rather than being separable issues, efficiency and power have at last become part of the same thing!

Value power in the choice of goods

It seems a bit mundane, having explored some of the social functions of culture and society, to turn to a set of values that may remain purely personal. It is important for all (most?) members of a social group to accept the rights established. It does not matter if they agree on a brand of soda pop. Yet it would be a bit peculiar if people could be externally influenced to prefer being Swedish, Catholic, socialist, or part of a primitive kinship obligation group but come to this world with an inviolable preference for Pepsi over Coke.

There is a literature on the function of external information, specifically advertising, in affecting demand.[29] Institutional analysis has long postulated the potential for others to act to change consciously the tastes and preferences of others. In Galbraith's revised sequence, corporations use marketing techniques to create wants for the kinds of products they are able to produce and sell. Advertising is thus supposed to do more than provide information. It is a mechanism to change the utility associated with particular commodities.[30]

Issues of value power at this level are more amenable to analysis using the model of strategic decision making that has been the primary method of this study. They are important issues, but they are less central to a truly comprehensive analysis of power in all its social significance.

---

[29] Cf., for example, Philip Nelson, "Advertising as Information," *Journal of Political Economy*, July/August 1974, pp. 729–754, or Nelson, "Information and Consumer Behavior," *Journal of Political Economy*, March/April 1970, pp. 311–329, or Lester Telser, "Advertising and Competition," *Journal of Political Economy*, December 1964, pp. 537–562.

[30] John Kenneth Galbraith, *The New Industrial State*, 2nd ed., Houghton Mifflin, Boston, 1971.

Evaluating value power

Humans are social creatures. They live in well-defined groups with social roles and social rights. They receive and pass on visions of the world that define the morality of those rights and appropriate behaviors toward other humans. Biologic humans who are cut off from the acculturation of human society are different creatures indeed. Kamala did not just face a different sequence of momentary constraints. She became a different creature. If we too become what we are from our interactions with others, then these influences may also be viewed as forms of power. Unless all true preferences are contained in DNA coding and are invariant over time and among persons, or unless extraordinary social conditions hold, culture is a real form of power. It is the ultimate blind date.

Is this value power positive or negative? The question itself has lost its normal welfare-economics meaning in this context. Would the individuals who became cremating Greeks have had a higher lifetime utility if they had become (been acculturated as) cannabalistic Callatiae? The question makes no sense. Once preferences (values? household production functions?) have been established, we can speak of maximizing them. Is creating and fulfilling a preference an improvement over not fulfilling a not-yet-created preference? In order to use the welfare prescriptions of traditional economics there must be an absolute standard against which to compare different states of the world, different allocations of scarce resources. If both allocations and the utility payoffs of specific allocations may vary, there is no absolute at all. This power-inclusive world has become muddled indeed. First, value power becomes necessary if efficiency is to be attainable, and now when value power is present, efficiency is undefinable! It is perhaps no small wonder that a profession so enamored of well-defined tangencies and general equilibria should have avoided exploring such a world for so long.

PART IV

Power analysis in economics

CHAPTER 10

Power and economics

Economics is about the quality of human lives. That quality is surely affected by the Stuff available to humans. It is just as surely affected by the nature of the relations between persons that arise in the processes of creating and distributing the Stuff. It is relevant to economic inquiry, then, to ask about the character of those relationships surrounding the social institutions known as markets. Economists of all persuasions, rooted in all paradigms, have borne witness to their conflicting faiths over the years. They have been less religious in their devotion to proof. The purpose of this book has been to develop the tools necessary to undertake such an inquiry and to provide some tentative answers. Many different aspects of social interactions have been considered economically. The arguments and conclusions of the preceding chapters are not, however, separable. Together they constitute a vision of human society with implications for the way in which economic theory proceeds, for the content of policy, and for understanding of the world.

The argument as a whole

Modern economic history is a tale of accelerating technological change. Evolving technology also increases the stock of information relevant to market exchange. When that expanding knowledge of complex products, processes, and environments is unevenly owned and unequally interpretable, the old adage that "knowledge is power" takes on a wholly new meaning. Whether this is known as the blind-date principle or "opportunism coupled with information impactedness,"[1] the result is the same. Some actors in markets, if they are self-interested and rational, will be able to exploit the situation to their advantage, and *perhaps to the detriment of their trading partners*. The scope of the problem changes as the scope and distribution of information

---

[1] That language is from Oliver Williamson's analysis. See, for example, his *Markets and Hierarchies*, Free Press, New York, 1975.

change. Markets are no longer a perfect defense against such power (Chapter 5).

Rational actors, fearing the costs of being subject to market-generated power, will sometimes expend scarce resources and energy in attempts to contain it. Political and legal channels may be exploited to develop constraints on the exercise of this power. Thus external intervention in markets will not always be the introduction of power. Without external controls there *can* be power in markets. With external controls there *is* power in markets. The social choice is not power or powerlessness. It is which forms of power (Chapters 5 and 8).

The response to market-generated power may not be limited to political activity. Rational actors will sometimes choose to substitute administrative organization for the market in an attempt to reduce the impacts of market-generated power. When they do, they are introducing still different manifestations of power. When market trades do occur, they will be undertaken by agents, whose very existence is compelling evidence that those trades are under imperfect control by principals. Agency is a new form of power introduced into markets (Chapter 6).

In some organizations there is no real principal. Aggregations of individuals who are a collective principal may have conflicts over relative priorities. It may then be simply impossible to combine their individual preferences into a clear objective function for the organization. The principal then has neither the means to control agents nor a clear standard against which to judge their acts (Chapter 6).

Most of the agents who find themselves within these complex organizations are then part of a widespread system of employment contracts. While in the perfect world of the special case the purchase of labor is simply another spot transaction, in the imperfect, but institutionally rich, world outside the special case, employment involves other forms of human power (Chapter 7).

Finally, the forms of organization that arise alter the effectiveness of external controls on market-generated power. In a corporate form of organization, it is difficult to structure external penalties for the exercise of power within markets. Who, within the layers of agents and principals, is in a position to prevent the unwanted exercise and is justly able to bear the legally imposed costs? Even the forms of organizations that predominate are not exogenous. They are partially a result of private decisions and partially a product of political influence in legislative and judicial processes. Power in one arena helps to define power in another (Chapters 6 and 8).

Society has become a complex tapestry with threads of power running in all directions. Power in one set of institutions calls forth power in others. Attempts to void the negative impacts of one set of institutions requires exercising power via others. The harsh conditions of a dynamic, but imperfect, world inevitably introduce the possibilities for some persons to harm others. Those subject to potential harm must act to minimize the damage whenever it is economic to do so. Their optimal strategy is to control power in one form by its development and exercise in another.

Even that is not all. Markets are not the beginning of human activity. They cannot be. Without a prior social interaction that defines rights, and contemporaneous actions that defend them, market exchanges become a weak means of social coordination. Markets may be driven by an invisible hand, but the hand is attached to an arm of socially defined rights. The physiology of the hand is well understood, but its movements are unpredictable until there is equal attention paid to the physiology of the arm. Rights are themselves endogenous. In a society of self-interested maximizers no one would sit passively observing others reshaping her rights if it is economic to respond. The processes of rights formation are an inseparable and ongoing element of economic activity in a dynamic society. The negative power implicit in rights formation is thus part of all dynamic, market economies (Chapter 8).

Rational maximizers, *even if they enter this world with identical, immutable, and invariable preference functions*, will thus find themselves in a complex system of power relationships. Markets per se are not enough to prevent this. Only markets in the ridiculous world of the special case are. When the implicit basis of the assumption of given preferences is then made explicit, it becomes so absurd that the concept of power must clearly be made broader still. It is then rational for individuals to exercise influence over the culture, world view, and values of others. It is rational for individuals to submit to that power. It is even socially efficient for them to do so (Chapter 9).

A society, then, is a system of power. If the only question to be asked concerns expected movements in the price of bread when there is a drought in Kansas, that can be reasonably ignored. If, however, questions are asked about the nature of human relationships; about alterations in the quality of human lives as institutions vary; about the future implications of technological change, political structures, and cultural precepts; it cannot be ignored. It is the very basis of all plausible and perceptive answers.

There is then no such thing as a market system. There are multiple market systems embedded in, and rigorously linked with, cultures, laws, politics, technologies, and systems of rights. Changes in any of these areas ripple through all others. As products become more complex, the systems of power change. As the technology of information distribution changes, the systems of power change. In short, it should be clear that each real-world system is in a sense unique. Each needs to be considered holistically. Each needs to be examined in terms of complex interrelations among forms of institutions. Each system needs to be explored for circular feedbacks as impacts in any area work outward and then return.[2]

In fact, what this entire exercise shows is that institutionalists have been right all along. It also shows why. It is not an assertion by a Commons, a Veblen, a Galbraith, or a Myrdal that makes it so. It is the method of Gary Becker applied broadly and consistently. It is not the firmly held, but ill-defined, intuition of a theorist that supports the breadth of vision. It is the construction of a logical model built on a long-accepted, neoclassical foundation. It thus becomes a conclusion derived rather than a catechism delivered. It is a systematic examination of the behavior of rational maximizers operating under constraints that makes it so.

When I was in graduate school years ago I suffered, as did many of my colleagues, an attack of the trivias. As a senior in college I had been asked my opinions of major world events. I had debated the policy issues of the day. My first year of graduate school was spent on a desert island with Robinson Crusoe. There we carefully derived various mathematical forms of production functions. It was a wholly uncritical guided tour through a set of technical conditions. I could not find the quality of life issues.

In a moment of frustration I wrote a small parable about an economist transported in time to ancient Crete. There he was cast into the mythical labyrinth to face the horrible Minotaur. I told of his dilemma in facing a problem too complex to master and of his solution of assuming away all of the unpleasant ambiguities and difficulties. Needless to say, he met a tragic fate as a result. I still remember the smugness with which I wrote down the final line. "Micro theory has become the modern Minotaur in our economic maze – bearing a few recognizable human characteristics, but for the most part a lot of bull."

I have since come to the conclusion that I was wrong. The heart of

---

[2] These are "coincidentally" the exact characteristics which Gunnar Myrdal claims to be the distinguishing features of institutional economics in his article "Institutional Economics," *Journal of Economic Issues*, December 1978, pp. 771–783.

the economic method, as Becker has clearly spelled out, is not the questions we choose to ask, but the approach taken. That approach examines human behavior in terms of reactions to the constraints surrounding individuals. People respond to incentives. There is great power in that approach. It is not economics, but economists who have inhibited the full development of that power. As soon as those individuals are taken from the sterile environment of that isolated desert island where they are free of social interaction, its real power becomes apparent. It is economists, not economics, who have locked us into conceptual cocoons, effectively isolated from each other. It is economists, not economics, who permit us only to transact, never to interact.

Economics widely applied allows us to see much more. Humans, subject to constraints and living in a world of limited information unevenly held, hold power over trading partners. They thus create formal organizations with complex relationships. In a world where humans do not precede the physical environment and where knowledge and technology evolve, they act to shape socially defined rights. They do so not once but over and over in ongoing processes. In a world where all values and preferences are not contained in invariant DNA chains – chains that violate all known principles of genetics – they act to develop and promulgate cultures and values in others. They are rescued from the sterile environment of the special case. They are no longer feral children or dei economici. They become human. They enter a rich realm with complex human interactions. All of that follows not from an abandonment of Becker's economic method. It follows from his prescription to apply it "relentlessly and unflinchingly." It leads to a world where markets are but one element in larger and more complete systems of power.

Power and economic theory

This expansion of economic theory clearly makes the world seem more complex. It also has the potential to make it more comprehensible in at least two ways. First, intellectual conflicts that appeared to be based solely on faith can now be structured in terms that permit logical and factual resolution. Second, it argues for a reconsideration of theoretical tactics in economics. Greater understanding may require an occasional substitution of truly rigorous analysis for purely mathematical manipulation. Both points deserve elaboration.

Power analysis as a bridge across paradigms

This is a subversive book. I have tried to answer questions normally asked by institutionalists and Marxists using the tools of neoclassical economics. That eclectic approach permits serious, nonideological analysis of the conflicting positions taken by economists who are firmly embedded in competing paradigms. Consider an example.

In Chapter 1, I reviewed the arguments about power made by William Dugger and Milton Friedman.[3] They held diametrically opposed positions. For Dugger, power was pervasive and ubiquitous. It was at its very weakest when overt acts of coercion were seen. For Friedman, the absence of overt coercion was proof of the absence of all power. As they expressed their positions, the conclusions were articles of faith. They spoke different languages and simultaneous translation was impossible. They could not converse intelligently because neither provided a comprehensible concept to the other. The absence of threatened or actual violence became evidence for both pervasive power and perfect freedom.

The framework developed here allows their positions to be restated in a common language. They can then be compared and tested. Friedman implicitly defines power as only decision power. If there is no coercion apparent at explicit decision nodes, there is no power in the system. Dugger asserts that other forms of power are in fact more common and perhaps more important. He specifically postulates value power as the key aspect of social relations. That he defines as its truly "strong" form. Only when value power is becoming ineffective is "weaker," coercive decision power required.

This then becomes a controversy that can be treated logically and factually. It is possible to seek power in the full context of market transactions and to determine if, in any given situation, decision power is the only form of power present. It is possible to gather hard evidence of social influences on individual values. Social psychologists have been doing so for years. If evidence is found, it is conceptually possible to study differences between periods of stable and shared social values and periods of unstable and conflicting ones. Those seeking a true answer are in a position to attain one empirically. No matter which paradigm one begins in, answers methodologically defensible in both are possible. If it is understanding rather than validation that is sought, the path is now clearer.

---

[3] William Dugger, "Power: An Institutional Framework of Analysis," *Journal of Economic Issues*, December 1980, pp. 897–907. Milton Friedman, *Capitalism and Freedom*, University of Chicago Press, Chicago, 1962, esp. Chapter 1.

Power and rigor

Power analysis permits systematic inquiry into the broadest reaches of the relations between persons. The full value of its potential will not be realized, however, without a simultaneous consideration of what makes for "good" economic analysis. Economics has long been proud of its scientific tradition. No characteristic is more significant in achieving professional glory than an undying commitment to rigorous thinking. But think rigorously, for a moment, about rigor. Rigor requires a willingness to think hard, critically, and carefully about variable relationships. It demands sequential movement via lockstep logic from initial propositions to carefully derived conclusions. It forbids idle speculation and logically indefensible leaps of faith. It demands that evidence not be ignored for the sake of simple convenience. It requires that we not shy away from the hard questions. It insists that we meet them head on, clarifying via logic rather than obfuscating via assertion. Economists have come to equate mathematical modeling with intellectual rigor. That is a mistake. Mathematics is often a disciplining force promoting careful thought. Sometimes, however, a rigid devotion to tight models is, instead, the route to sloppy thought.

When I once discussed Oliver Williamson's analysis of organizations with a respected colleague and friend, the conversation reached an abrupt end.[4] My colleague, while admitting that there were many interesting and fertile ideas within the work, nevertheless dismissed it as second-rate economics because it could not be completely and rigorously modeled.

Models must meet certain rules. So, of course, must crossword puzzles. The rules of both permit solutions within the confines of those limits. They do not assure the significance of the result in a world wider than those rules. If the discipline of meeting the conditions requires ignoring, rather than meeting, significant aspects of a problem, the discipline loses much of its value. Elegantly stated nonsense is still, unfortunately, nonsense. Inelegant wisdom may, at times, be superior. For a model to be determinate, there can be no more variables than there are equations. When there seem to be too many variables, the modeler's solution is to *assume* some to be exogenous. That closes the system. It may also obscure the reality.

How easy it is to derive definitive answers when all market actors are assumed to be automatons devoid of social relationships and in-

---

[4] We were specifically discussing his arguments in the work cited in Note 1.

dependent of all other actors. How easy it is when their perceptions of the world are not in any way subject to the strategic manipulation of information by others. How simple it is when they are not part of complex organizations with varying positional authority. How easy it is when social structures and interactions play no role in determining rights, property, and endowments. How trivial it is when there is no social morality. Values, like hair color, are genetically given.

How hard it is to build a closed model when some of the actors are multilayered agency organizations for which there is no defined principal and no method for aggregating individual objectives. How difficult it is if the preference functions are partially endogenous and reflect, via complex lag structures with multiple feedbacks, strategic behaviors of other actors, past and present. How complex it becomes if the preferences, factor endowments, and content of knowledge for each actor become part of the solution. With current techniques, no complete model of that world is possible.

But which is the truly rigorous analysis, the one that simply refuses even to examine those factors, or the one that willingly, but imperfectly, grapples with them? The former buys a closed mathematical model only by willfully turning away from close, logical thinking about the implications of its assumptions. It reaches its tight answers by assuming things wholly inconsistent with evidence and experience. It maintains its respectability by adopting positions implicitly that would be too embarrassing to express explicitly. The special case sounds so strange only when it is fully spelled out and its implications are logically pursued. When it is stated briefly as the axiomatic definition of a formal model, it slips by without triggering any such concerns. It makes all of its leaps of faith before it goes public. It cannot leap far enough to escape the effects, however. It rests on very sloppy, rather than rigorous, thinking.

The latter analysis is, of course, also incomplete. The world becomes too complex to model carefully. It is, therefore, in constant danger that leaps of faith will occur within the sequence of logical steps that form the analysis. On the other hand, there the slips should be open to view for they will be made explicitly. In the strict mathematical approach, the failures of logic take place in obscurity. Debate is focused on technique while the nonrigorous thought takes place away from the scrutiny of others. The hard questions are avoided.

This charge is not a belated assault on Friedman's methodological assertions regarding the importance of the realism of assumptions.[5]

---

[5] Milton Friedman, *Essays in Positive Economics*, University of Chicago Press, Chicago, 1953, pp. 3–43.

Closed models have long proven their worth in predicting changes in resource allocations. If, however, I wish to predict how changes in the structure of organizations with their layers of principals, agents, and subagents will affect the welfare of those within and those who will ultimately contract with the organization, then those models provide no answers at all. It is not a matter of good or bad predictions. It is a matter of no predictions. When I assume that all producers are entrepreneurs with given preference functions who hire labor like pig iron and are devoid of specific institutional structures, it is the question, not the answer, that makes no sense in the context of formal models.

If I wish to predict how changes in technological processes and the location of information within institutional structures will affect the ability of some persons to harm others, existing rigorous models are of little help. If I wish to predict whether altered technologies of communication will affect the efficiency of shared, internalized values in promoting the exchange of socially defined rights, those models offer no help. They are very good at some predictions. They are not good at others. The only way to salvage the incontestable worth of those models for *all* economic questions is to define as valid only those questions for which such models can yield useful predictions. Ask only about Stuff, never about persons.

Power analysis and welfare economics

When is the quality of a human life improved? That is a troublesome, yet inescapable, question for economists. The utilitarian foundation of economics lets us avoid the issue at one level by transferring the question from the analyst to the person analyzed. When is a life improved? It is when the person living it feels it to be better. I, the analyst, then do not make value judgments. I merely validate yours.

I will here pass over the obvious fact that my defining the quality of your life via your perceived utility is, of course, a value judgment. That has often been noted before. Here I will even accept the broad philosophical position. My purpose is to show that, unfortunately, power analysis renders it largely inoperable.

Pareto optimality, revealed preferences, and power

The only welfare proposition arising from that utilitarian foundation that has been able to stand over time is the relatively weak principle of Pareto optimality. Markets are good because they improve the welfare of all participants. How do we know? Individuals would not participate if they were not made better off. In markets they reveal their preferences and thus permit us to judge changes in the quality of their lives. Markets make all lives better!

That, however, should now be seen as a proposition valid only for markets in the special case. In the complex world of power analysis we need more. The simple fact of participation in a market trade is no longer sufficient to support a conclusion that the overall welfare of the trader has been improved. By knowing more, we know less.

Even if a particular trade did empirically turn out to have been free of negative power in all its manifestations, it could still end up lowering the lifetime welfare of the trader. If the current value of an event changes over time because of the impact of time preference (on both past and future), when does the economist judge whether the quality of a life is improved? The moment of exchange is clearly appropriate for predicting behavior. It is not clearly so for evaluating it. If the person living a life of consequences can change his mind from one moment to the next, must not we? We are left with a very fluid standard. The standard used in power analysis, that is, lifetime utility as contemporaneously experienced relative to the next best path through life, is less fluid. It is also impossible to apply. The individual himself cannot judge what life would have been like on another path. He cannot reveal what he cannot know. Economists cannot, then, apply even the simple, objective standard to a single individual.

Endogenous utility and welfare

The search for objective rules of welfare has always been stopped short when more than a single person is involved. I can perhaps judge if I am happier than I was. I cannot judge whether I am happier than you are. There are no objective units like pounds or inches with which to measure the welfare of two separate persons. When the point of interpersonal utility comparisons is reached, the economist is compelled to sit down. Her normative standards can take her no farther.

When the complete world of power analysis is opened to exploration, value power enters. What a human being is becomes partially subject to social influence. If I had become one person with one set of values, I would experience some level of utility. If I had become another, with another, I would experience different utility *but not clearly more or less – just different.* If I am two or more potential persons, then judging my welfare across those states involves making interpersonal utility comparisons for the *same individual.* There is no way to evaluate the utility of a person if she herself is partially endogenous.

Not only has equity become an ambiguous and relative concept, so also has even efficiency. The weakest standards of welfare economics cannot be applied just to market exchange. A prior, complete power analysis is a prerequisite to applying even that. If the power analysis reveals any value power, it cannot be applied at all. The world has become a muddled place indeed.

Candide, economics, and existential angst

This does not mean that economists cannot, and should not, make choices about social situations and systems. Quite the contrary, it means that we cannot avoid political judgments, that is, we are *compelled* to make real *choices*. It means that we cannot escape those choices by reference to seemingly objective standards. We must grapple with the human reality of subjective choice.

The humans that Gary Becker postulates permit a simple, closed model. They live in a world where the quality of life can be externally and objectively judged. Uncertainties and ambiguities are cleared away. Humans enter this world with genetically given, invariant, and immutable preferences. They are compelled by nature to maximize those preference functions subject to the constraints imposed by an external world. These are people about whom positive predictions can be made. They are also people liberated from the anxiety of ever making real choices. Nature provides the DNA. The external world provides the constraints. The optimal path is determined by mindless comparison of the two. Free will is banished. We are programmed at conception. We do as we must, not as we may.

In 1759, Voltaire published his scathing satire, *Candide*. Candide was but an innocent given over for instruction in life to the sage philosopher Dr. Pangloss, whose philosophy was that "all is for the best in this, the best of all possible worlds." As Candide suffered horror after tragedy after disaster, often at the hands of his fellow humans, the sentiments of Dr. Pangloss were reasserted. "All is for the best in this, the best of all possible worlds." There can be nothing better. There is no call for human action to take sides in complex controversies. The impersonal forces of nature will assure the best of all possible outcomes. We are free of moral choice and personal responsibility.

Were Pangloss alive today he would undoubtedly be a neoclassical economist. That theory has sought to absolve us of responsibility, leaving outcomes always to the wise guidance of an invisible hand. It starts from two basic assertions about the world. First, it is a world of scarcity. There is not now, and never will be, enough to go around. Second, that world is populated by wholly selfish individuals, each of whom wants for himself what will thereby be denied to others. That is a harsh world populated by morally bankrupt persons with directly conflicting interests. It would seem to be a world where sides must sometimes be taken, where complex moral issues arise, where relatives replace absolutes, yet for economists it is not. We have found ways to escape the seeming conflict. We are free to believe and, like Pangloss, to proselytize that, if markets but exist, all is for the best in this, the best of all possible worlds.

Starting with Adam Smith, economists for 150 years refined the concept of markets as social mechanisms that would turn moral imperfection into a force for social good. Perfect markets took conflicts and turned them into mutuality. By the early part of this century the model was well formed, but also under attack. The real world was not exactly that of the perfect model. Imperfect competition was recognized as a factor in theory and in markets.[6] The presence of externalities and public goods meant that markets alone would fall short.[7] A market system, it appeared, might not be sufficient to assure stability for the economy as a whole.[8]

The immediate response to the failure of markets was to look for a solution to reattain that best of all possible worlds. That was found in, of all places, government. Theorists then spent years and careers developing the exact prescriptions to give to government in order to correct perfectly for the failures of the market. When real markets fail, good government should act.[9] That seemed an escape until the basic, logical flaw was highlighted. If other actors could not be relied upon to do as they should, why assume politicians to be different? When political behavior was analyzed as economic, it quickly became apparent that policies optimal for economists were not optimal for politicians.[10] Markets will fail and government will fail to be a perfect corrective. All was not for the best after all.

---

[6] Cf. the classics, Joan Robinson, *The Economics of Imperfect Competition*, Macmillan Press, London, 1933, and Edward Chamberlin, *The Theory of Monopolistic Competition*, Harvard University Press, Cambridge, Mass., 1933.

[7] See, for example, E. Lindahl, "Just Taxation: A Positive Solution," reprinted in R. A. Musgrave and A. T. Peacock, eds., *Classics in the Theory of Public Finance*, Macmillan Press, London, or Paul Samuelson, "The Pure Theory of Public Expenditures," *Review of Economics and Statistics*, Vol. 36, 1954, pp. 387–389.

[8] Obviously see J. M. Keynes, *The General Theory of Employment, Interest, and Money*, Harcourt Brace & World, New York, 1936.

[9] Richard Musgrave, *The Theory of Public Finance*, McGraw-Hill, New York, 1959.

[10] Cf. Anthony Downs, *An Economic Theory of Democracy*, Harper & Row, New York,

Markets, per se, then underwent rehabilitation in many ways. For Nozick and others, bothersome income-distribution problems arising from a market need not be problems after all. The objective definition of justice in an income distribution is that it is market generated. If it arises from markets, it is just. That problem is eliminated.[11] For many modern macroeconomists, aggregated markets are not unstable. The observed cycles in aggregate activity result not from markets but from external intervention in markets.[12] Eliminate policy discretion, and that problem is also eliminated. Markets provide the best of all possible worlds.

Even the allocation problems of market failure can be eliminated by impersonal forces. They are problems only because they are not really part of markets. If clear property rights are established to everything, then markets can handle externalities after all.[13] Not even allocation choices need be made by economists. Impersonal forces will do all. We will have the best of all possible worlds. If the law and lawyers will but apply economic thinking, appropriate market incentives will be established. Given a chance, markets can do virtually all.[14]

There remain some nagging problems with internal operations of markets. Difficulties with transactions costs and imperfect contracting seem to nibble away at the best of all possible worlds. Institutional adjustments may serve to minimize those flaws. The world will not be perfect, but it will automatically become the best of all *possible* worlds if we stand back and leave it all to markets.[15]

Power analysis upsets that comfortable vision. It challenges the most basic precepts of market theory upon which these objective conclusions are based. The outcomes of market exchange may, in their full complexity, yield winners and losers, not just winners. Power analysis thus does not provide a final answer to the economist's search for an impersonal, objective rule for assuring the best of all possible worlds. It instead points to the absurdity of the question. In a world that has too little to go around and is populated by selfish individuals subject to ignorance, social influence, group determined rights, and inevitable

1957, or R. Bartlett, *Economic Foundations of Political Power*, Free Press, New York, 1973.

[11] Robert Nozick, *Anarchy, State, and Utopia*, Basic, New York, 1974, esp. Chapter 7.

[12] Cf., for example, Robert Barro, *Macroeconomics*, Wiley, New York, 1984.

[13] Ronald Coase, "The Problem of Social Cost," *Journal of Law and Economics*, October 1960, pp. 1–44.

[14] Richard Posner, *Economic Analysis of the Law*, 2nd ed., Little, Brown, Boston, 1977.

[15] That is the implicit conclusion that Williamson reaches about the power which he isolates but does not really discover in his *Markets and Hierarchies*.

conflict, there is no objective best. There is no assurance of systematically approaching that undefined solution.

Ours is never a choice between the perfect markets of the special case and an imperfect, flawed government. Ours is never a choice between optimal government policies and the complex, ambiguous world of power-affected markets. Whenever flawed government intervenes in complex markets, the outcome is imperfect. Whenever flawed government does not, the outcome is imperfect. Personal and social choices are never avoidable by reference to abstract perfections. They are always situational. They are thus always choices.

This is not an argument that economic analysis *should* be political. It is an argument that it inevitably *is* political. In the best traditions this has been a positive rather than a normative analysis. I am now willing to make an explicit value judgment, however. The political judgments implicit in theory should be made explicit. They should be spelled out as such for all to see. The analysis is really political, not when it does that, but when it promotes relative positions as if they were absolute, objective ones. When it seeks unexamined support for a particular solution to social dilemmas, it is being dishonest. That is a bad trait to display in a pursuit of truth.

Power analysis is thus a danger to the comforts of our theoretical world. It implies a world of relatives. It denies absolutes. It requires actors and analysts to recognize that human interactions, with or without markets, may involve winners and losers. Economists must make real choices about a world permanently short of the best one. They must grapple with defining and achieving a better one. Dr. Pangloss is dead at last. Existential angst is an inevitable part of the economic, indeed of the human, experience. When power is introduced in economic analysis, economic analysis gains real power.

Index